IMAGES
of America

KENMORE
NEW YORK

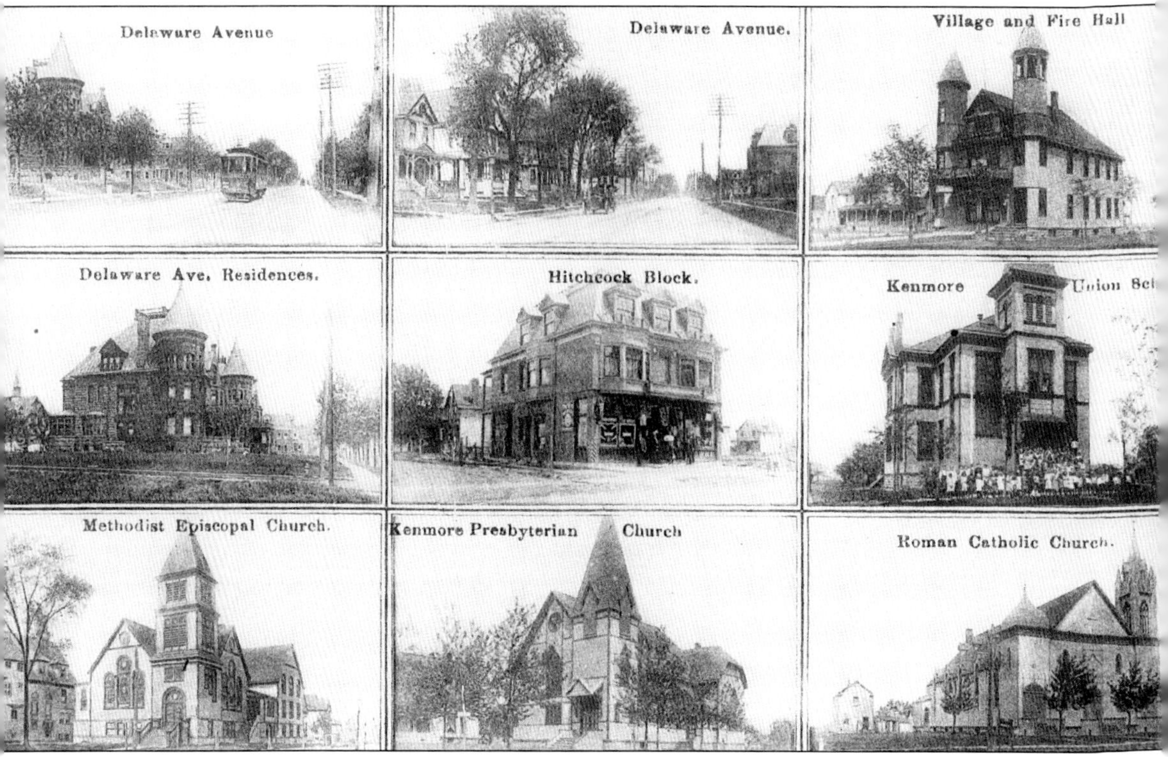

A c. 1905 COLLAGE OF POSTCARDS SHOWING THE YOUNG VILLAGE OF KENMORE. Almost a century of change has left only two of these buildings still standing. Which buildings they are and what became of the others forms but part of this history.

IMAGES
of America

KENMORE
NEW YORK

John Percy
and Graham Millar

ARCADIA
PUBLISHING

ISBN 978-0-7385-8785-1

Published by Arcadia Publishing
Charleston, South Carolina

Printed in the United States of America

Library of Congress Catalog Card Number: 98-89445

For all general information contact Arcadia Publishing at:
Telephone 843-853-2070
Fax 843-853-0044
E-mail sales@arcadiapublishing.com
For customer service and orders:
Toll-Free 1-888-313-2665

Visit us on the Internet at www.arcadiapublishing.com

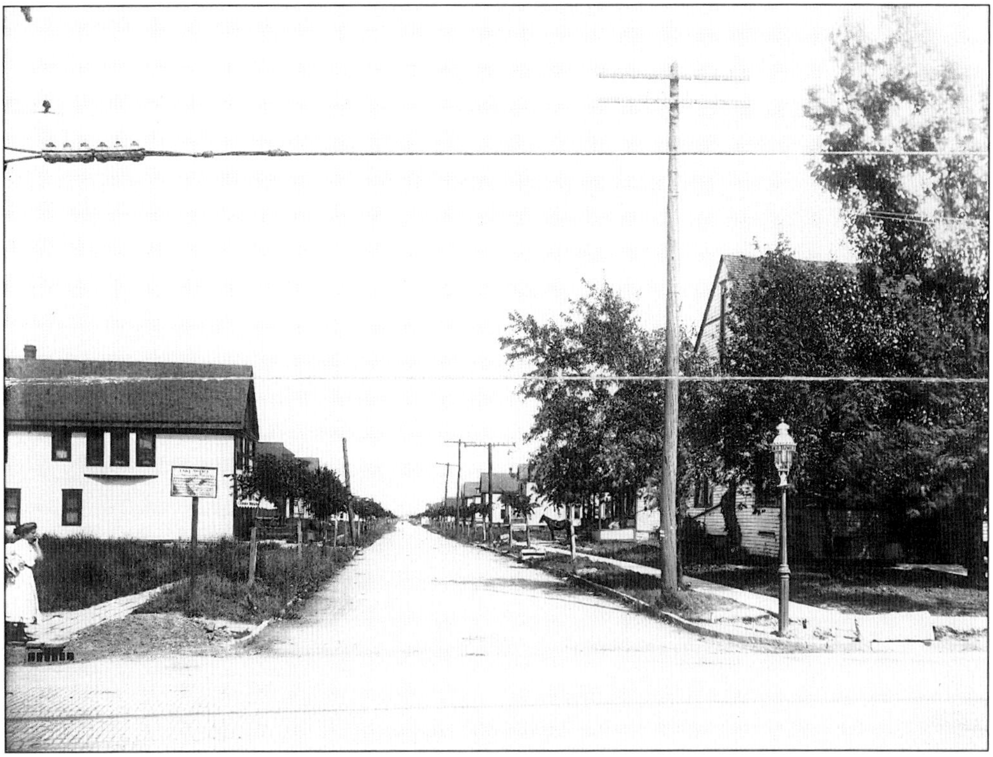

PARKWOOD, LOOKING EAST FROM DELAWARE AVENUE. Myron Phelps was the village president when this photograph was taken, prior to 1910. The "Take Notice" sign warns of the consequences of violating the village speed limit. Kenmore's wooden sidewalks and unpaved side streets are very evident. A horse and wagon appear just beyond the second house on the right. The meat market on the left belonged to Charles Stephens.

Contents

went for $250 apiece. To solve the problem of getting to and from the Belt Line, Frank Stillwell was engaged to operate a free, horse-drawn omnibus to carry residents between the trains and the town line. By 1899, natural gas was being supplied from a local well, and the settlement had grown to number some 300 residents.

When it came to naming the new suburb, Eberhardt rejected notions of calling it after himself. He believed that to do so would identify it as a German enclave, discouraging other potential buyers among Buffalo's diverse ethnic populations. What he sought was a name in keeping with the prime residential real estate he and fellow realtors were selling. On hearing that the Erie Railroad was considering the name "Kenmore" for a new station it was about to open in the city, L.P.A. decided that he liked the name, and appropriated it. Thus, Kenmore it became, and Kenmore it remains.

By 1891, Kenmore had its own post office, and two churches had been organized. In 1892 a school was opened on what would become the "village green," and by 1893 trolley service was extended along Military Road, Kenmore Avenue, and along Delaware Avenue. Belt Line commuters could now disembark from their trains at the Military Road station and ride the streetcar to near their Kenmore homes. Soon, another line was extended from Hertel Avenue in Buffalo and along Kenmore Avenue. By then Delaware Avenue was illuminated and paved with brick. The trolley company, which wanted a straight line for its tracks, did not utilize the section that eventually became Delaware Road; it remained a dirt roadway, as did most of Kenmore's streets. The few sidewalks that did exist were wooden planks laid in the mud.

Public delivery of the amenities that Kenmore residents desired, including paved streets, sidewalks, and dependable water and sewer systems, was unlikely to occur as long as it remained an unincorporated hamlet. In the first place, Tonawanda's rural residents would hardly agree to pay higher taxes for the benefit of the few suburbanites in the southern part of their town. Also, New York State law, on the assumption that towns were essentially rural areas, limited what services their governments could provide. Kenmore, it seemed, had two choices: annexation to the City of Buffalo or incorporation as a village within the town. Eventually the latter choice was adopted, and on September 18, 1899, the Village of Kenmore was incorporated. Buffalo's "pioneer suburb," its first planned bedroom community, now had its own government.

A century has passed since incorporation brought about many changes in and to Kenmore. When the former Village of Tonawanda chose to separate as a city in 1903, Kenmore became the population and political center of the now somewhat smaller town. Between 1920 and 1930, Kenmore grew fivefold. By 1927, there were enough residents to qualify as a first-class village, and it remained the population center until the 1950s, when it was overtaken by suburban developments outside its square mile and a half. The municipal building in the center of the village is still the political hub of both the village and the town, containing the legislative chambers of both, the village's administrative offices, and many of the town's offices, including those of the supervisor and clerk. Delaware Avenue, envisioned by L.P.A. Eberhardt as a grand residential thoroughfare, evolved largely into a street of businesses—a process that continues today. Although heavy industry never appeared, Elmwood Avenue and Military Road took on mainly commercial aspects. The once sparsely settled streets off Delaware became filled with homes, most characteristically those of single families, but multiple dwellings also were built. In the 1970s and later, high rises appeared, giving parts of the village a more urban appearance.

L.P.A. Eberhardt's mansion was demolished in 1978 and his brother's adjoining home is now an office building, but even though L.P.A. might hardly recognize it, the village of his dream continues to retain its own identity. Efforts to merge its government into that of the town, or to annex both to Buffalo, have been thoroughly rejected. The community has adopted the slogan "Ken-Ton, A First Rate Community Where Community Counts!" As Kenmore begins it second century, it looks forward to one as challenging and as interesting as its first.

One

The Infant Settlement

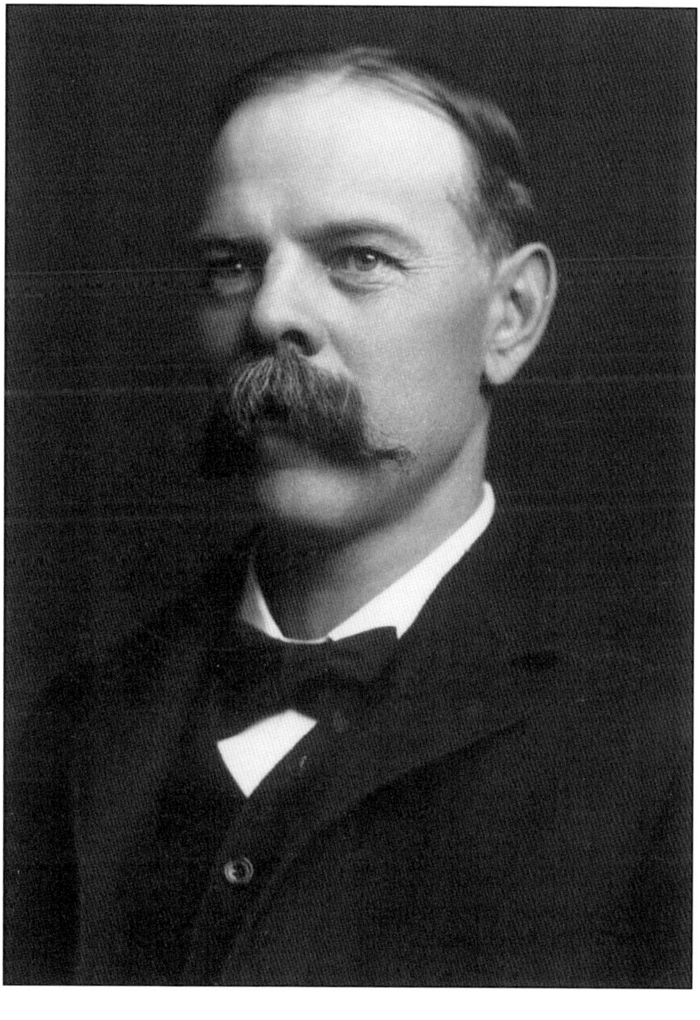

Louis Phillip Adolph Eberhardt (1860–1939). The "Daddy" of Kenmore is shown here early in the 20th century. He conceived the idea of an ideal bedroom community located away from the bustling city but connected to it by public transit, allowing residents to commute to their urban jobs while enjoying healthful semi-rural residences. He developed that idea into the Village of Kenmore, the first true suburb in Western New York and one of the earliest in the nation.

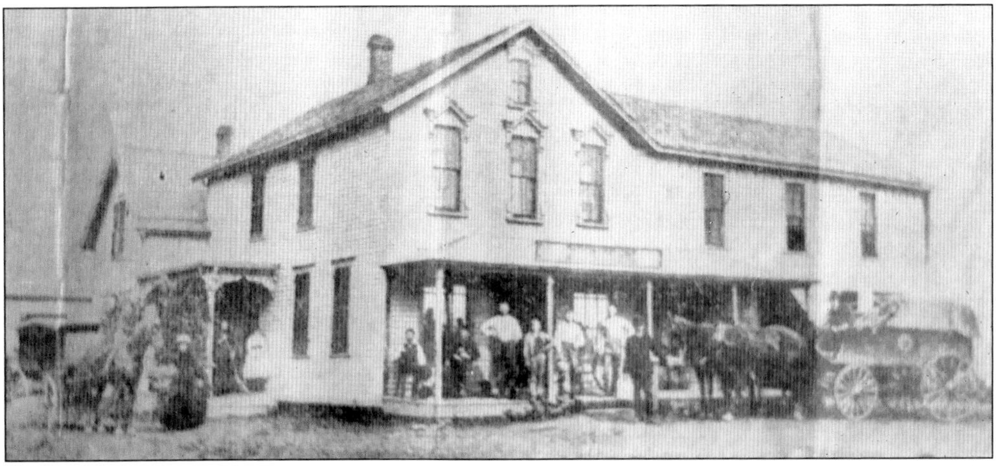

An early Kenmore landmark, the Winfield Mang store and saloon, c. 1880s. The proprietor and customers pose on the front porch with one of the many freight wagons that traveled Delaware Road on the way to and from Buffalo. Note the "Mang" sign over the porch. Kenmore's founders bought the building and turned it into a pharmacy and residence for Kenmore's first physician, Dr. J.J. Drake. The building was divided and moved in 1893 to make way for the Eberhardt mansions. The portion at 12 Warren Avenue was demolished in 1998. The remaining portion serves as part of the Saratoga Restaurant at Delaware and Ramsdell Avenues in Buffalo.

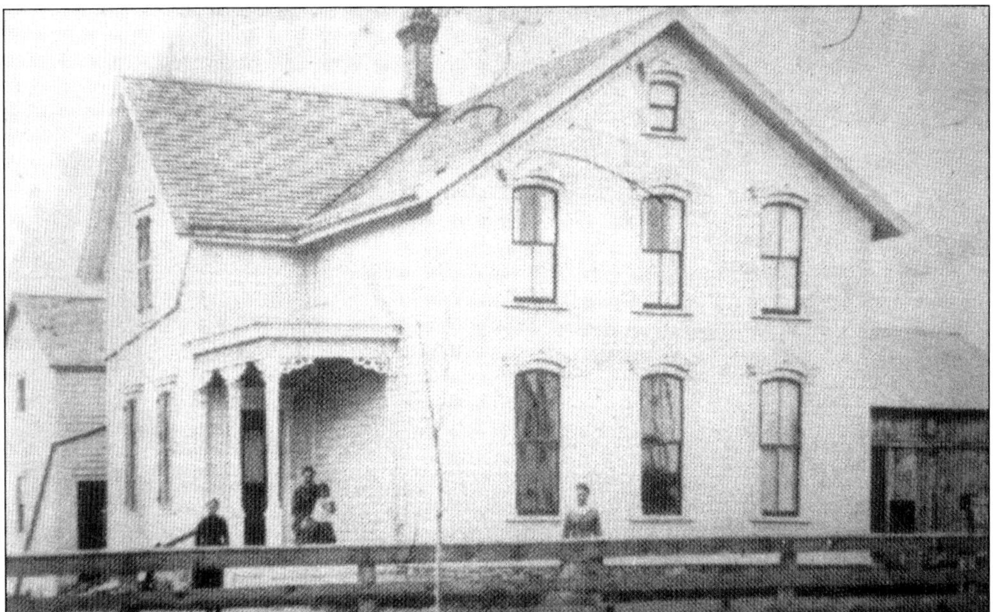

The Frank Mang farmhouse, located where Key Bank is today at Mang and Delaware. This 19th-century photo shows two of the barns that were an important part of the farm, which at one time extended throughout most of Kenmore's west side. Corn, wheat, and vegetables were grown here, and in 1890 the farm was contracted to grow hay for Buffalo's zoo. Frank and Elizabeth Mang originally lived on the property in a log house built shortly before the Civil War. The farmhouse was divided in two and moved in 1924 to make way for the present bank building.

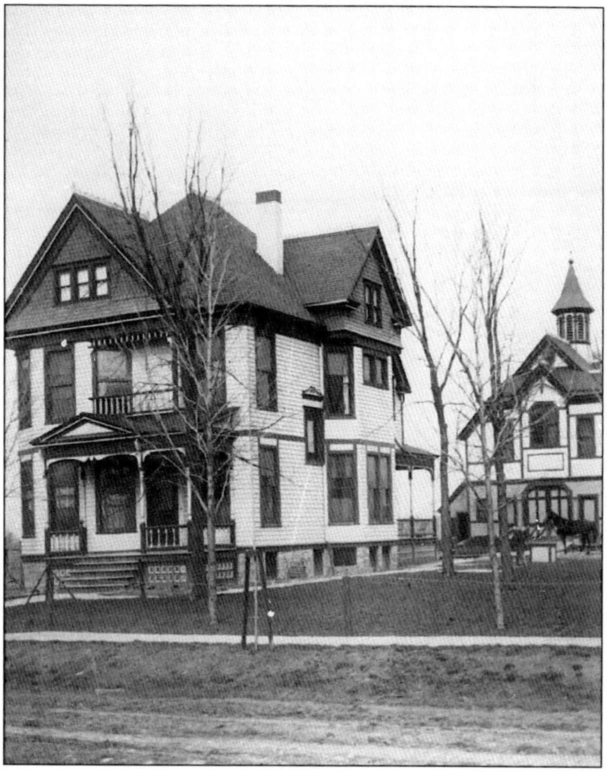

L.P.A. Eberhardt's first Kenmore home, built at 2749 Delaware Avenue in 1888–89. The Mang home was lost to fire in 1894 because Kenmore had no adequate fire protection. After the home burned, the elegant carriage house at the rear was moved across Delaware Avenue. It stood behind Eberhardt's new mansion at 2756 Delaware until the home and carriage house were demolished in 1977–78.

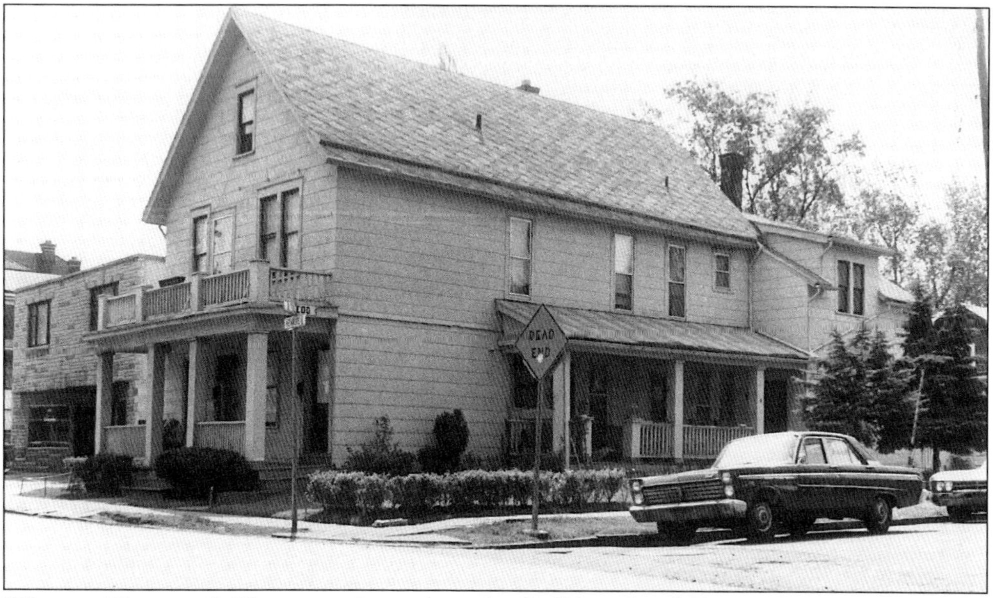

"Yankee Notions." This store, located on the Buffalo side of Kenmore Avenue at Toledo Place, was the first to sell groceries and notions to the residents of the newly developed community of Kenmore, which at the time had no retail establishments. Eventually stores were opened in what became the village, and shoppers could buy without crossing the city line. The building still stands, though somewhat altered from its original appearance. (Larry H. Oskin photo, TKHS collection.)

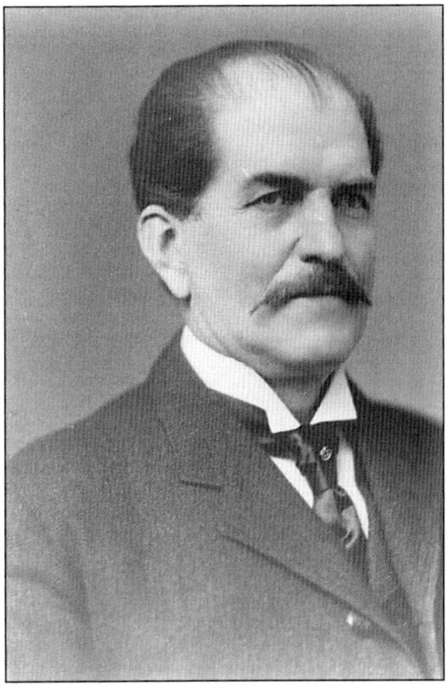

Myron A. Phelps, the first village president (from 1899 to 1901). The first village election was held soon after incorporation of the Village of Kenmore in September 1899. On October 3, a total of 30 votes were cast for village president. Myron Phelps received 29 of those votes. He presided over the first village board meeting, which was held the next day at his home. During the two decades before his death in 1910, Mr. Phelps was active in both real estate and home construction in the young village as well as several other business ventures. He was sergeant-at-arms in the state capitol building in Albany for the last seven years of his life, and is buried in Elmlawn Cemetery.

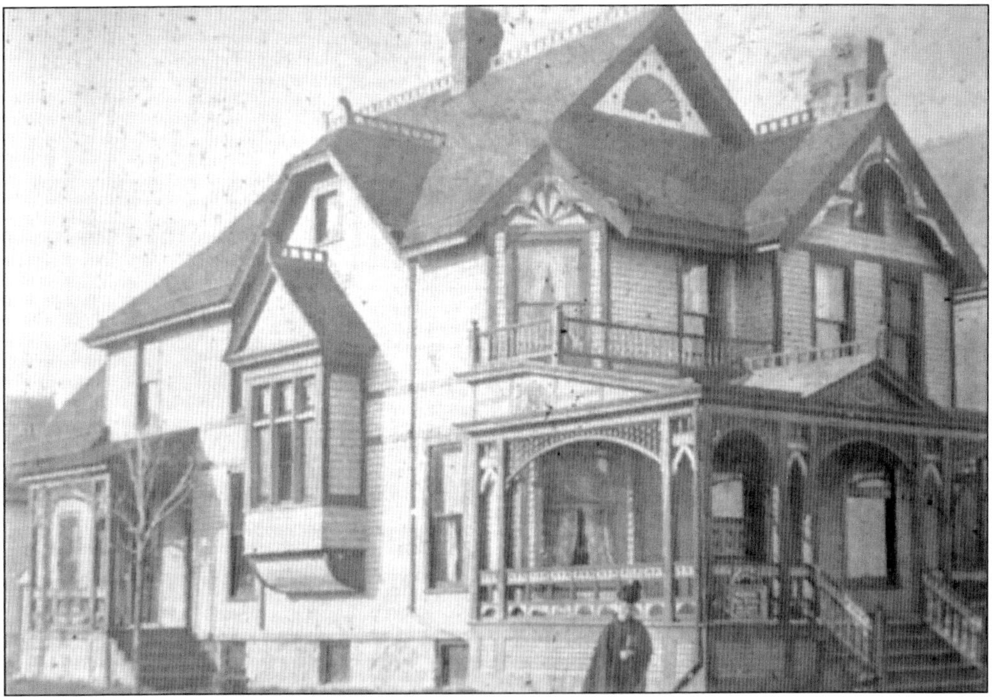

The Myron Phelps home, c. 1890. This was Kenmore's second suburban home, erected in 1889 at a cost of $4,500 on a plot of land subdivided from the Nicholas Mang farm. Tremaine Avenue was cut through the property on the south side. Mr. and Mrs. Phelps helped to organize Kenmore's Methodists from this home in 1891. After Myron Phelp's death in 1910, a store front was added to the Delaware side. Over the ensuing years the old home operated as a funeral home, furniture store, dance studio, the "House of Life," and the Village Antiques store. It was demolished just short of its centennial to make way for an automobile sales lot.

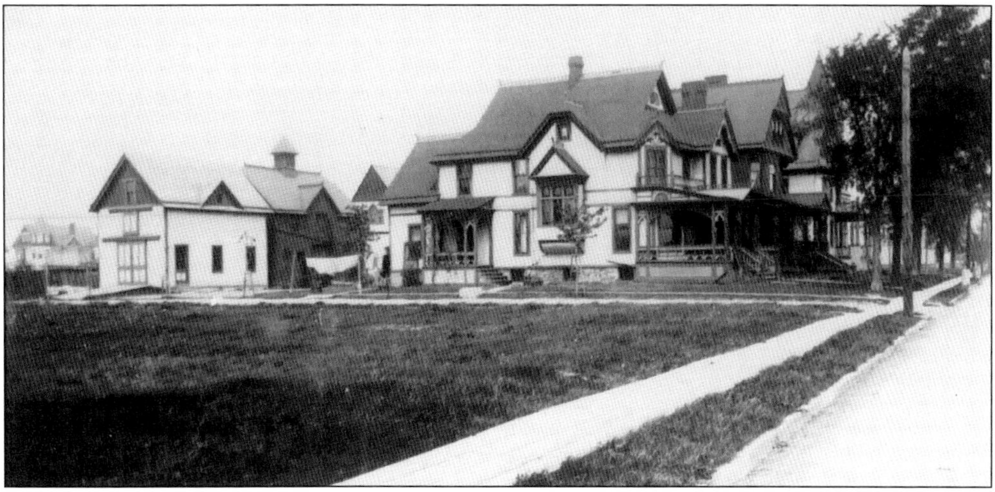

Myron Phelps' home and barn on Delaware Avenue at Tremaine, a decade later. Note the wooden sidewalks that served many years before being replaced by concrete walks. In the spring children used to spread mud on the boards, then run and slide on the slick walks. Adults who had to use the walks to avoid the muddy streets were not amused.

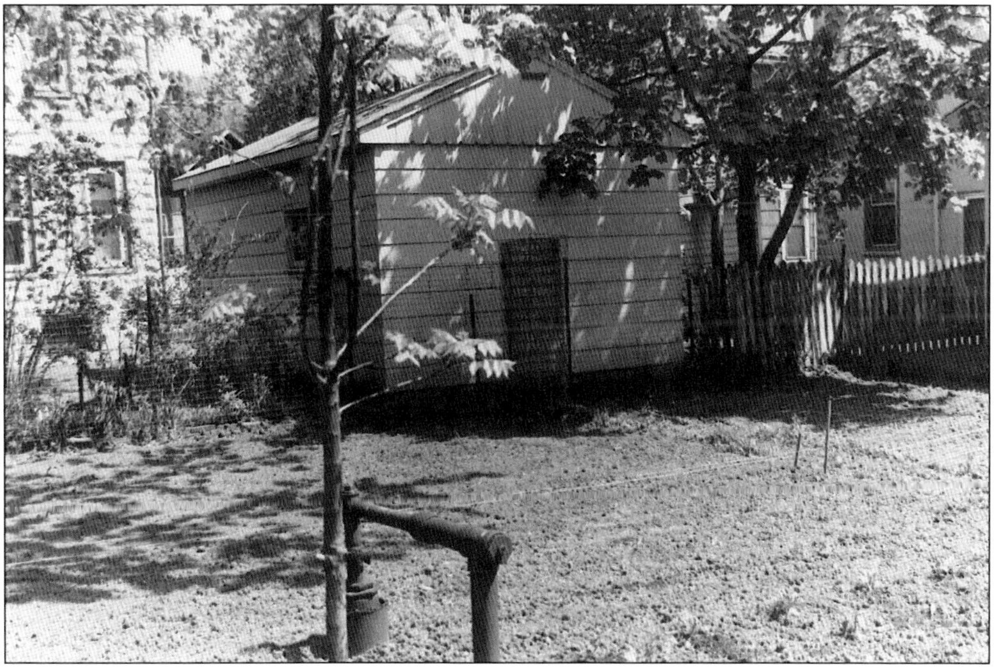

One of Kenmore's many natural gas wells, as photographed at 1303 Kenmore Avenue in 1971. Natural gas, which lies under much of the town of Tonawanda, was first tapped in 1890 by the "Kenmore Oil, Natural Gas, and Fuel Company, Limited." The president of this enterprise was Myron Phelps, and the treasurer was L.P.A. Eberhardt. This was the test well they drilled near Myron Avenue. Gas was struck at 736 feet and the 500-pound pressure of escaping gas could be heard a mile away. Unfortunately, the finishing procedure, a "shot" of nitroglycerin, was overdone and the flow greatly subsided thereafter. Nevertheless, the well supplied fuel to several Kenmore homes for many years. (Larry H. Askin photo, TKHS collection.)

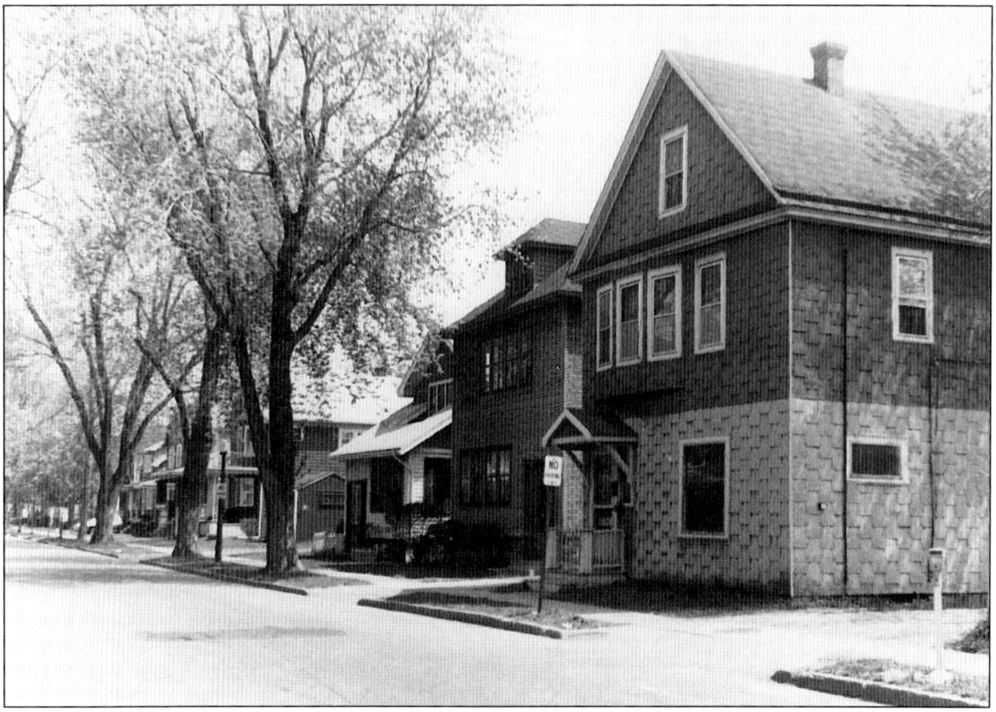

The two-family residence at 17 East Hazeltine Avenue in 1971. In the earliest days of Kenmore, this building was a hostelry known as the White House. It stood at the corner of Kenmore and Delaware Avenues until that land was developed for other business uses, at which time the building was moved to its current site at 17 East Hazeltine Avenue. (Larry H. Oskin photo, TKHS collection.)

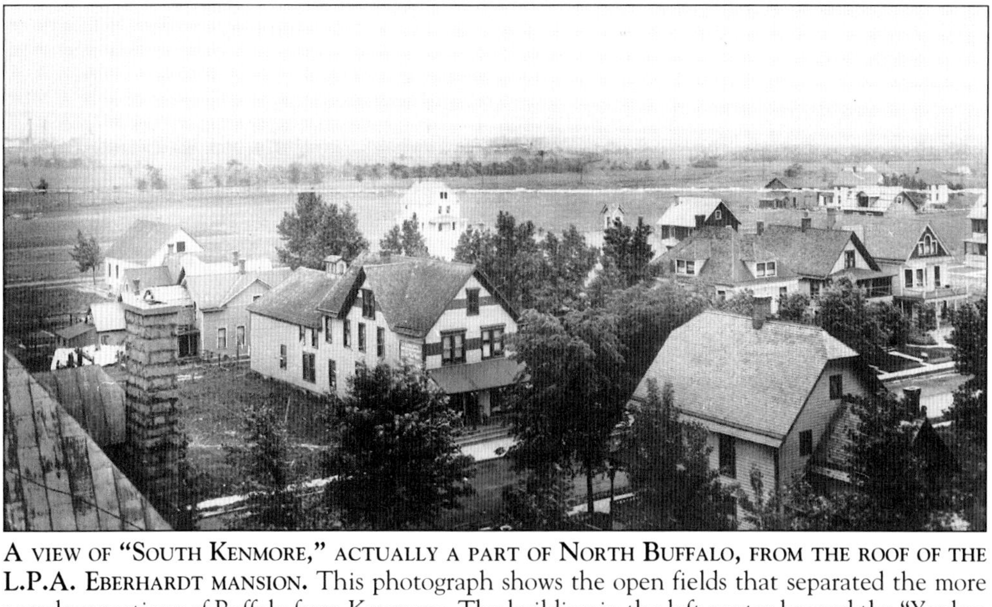

A view of "South Kenmore," actually a part of North Buffalo, from the roof of the L.P.A. Eberhardt mansion. This photograph shows the open fields that separated the more populous sections of Buffalo from Kenmore. The building in the left center housed the "Yankee Notions" store (now a multi-family residence) on Kenmore Avenue. The clump of trees to its right obscures the area that eventually became Toledo Place.

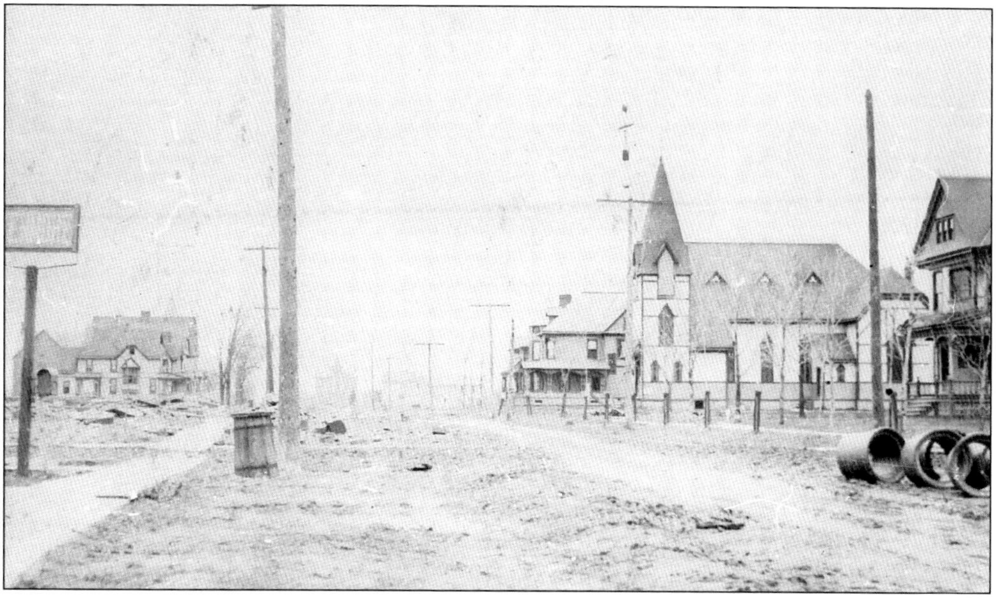

Kenmore's first sewer being installed on Delaware Avenue in 1893, six years before the village was incorporated. Wooden sidewalks, a "Kenmore" sign, and the Myron Phelps house can be seen on the left. On the right stands L.P.A. Eberhardt's first house, which was built in 1888 and burned to the ground the year after this photo was taken. Beyond it, across East Hazeltine, is the Presbyterian church, and next to that the home of Dr. Gideon Smith. The Union School can be seen faintly in the center background.

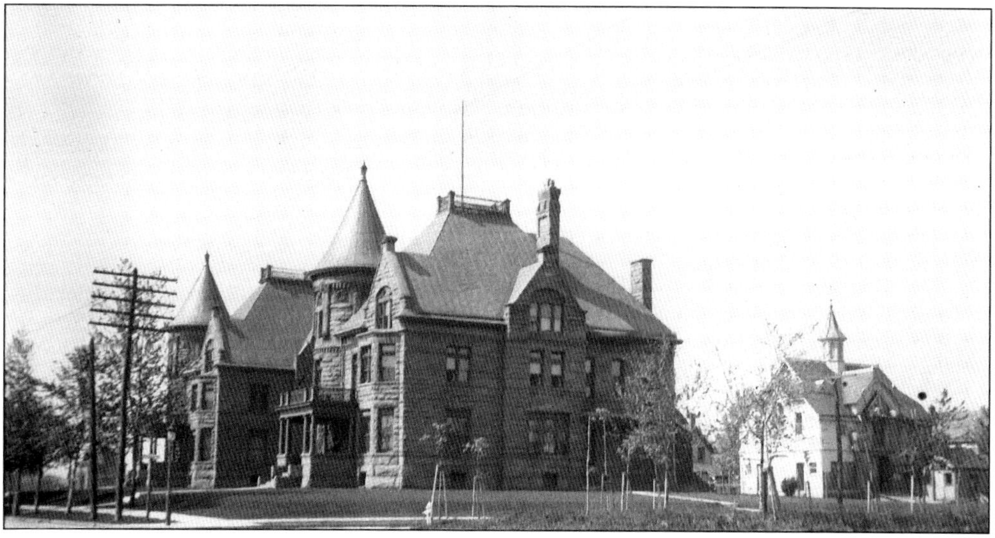

Kenmore's "Twin Sentinels" on Delaware between Kenmore Avenue and West Hazeltine early in the 20th century. L.P.A. Eberhardt's 1893 mansion is at center, with the mansion of his brother Fred at left. Each cost $15,000 to build. L.P.A.'s carriage house at right was moved from across Delaware after his first Kenmore home burned in 1894. Note the men on ladders repainting the front of it. Fred's home was sold to the Wheel Chair Home in 1916. Today it is the Jack Hunt Coin Mansion. L.P.A.'s home was sold to the YWCA in 1918. The home and its carriage house were demolished in 1978 after the Wheel Chair Home purchased the property. Today it is a lawn and parking lot.

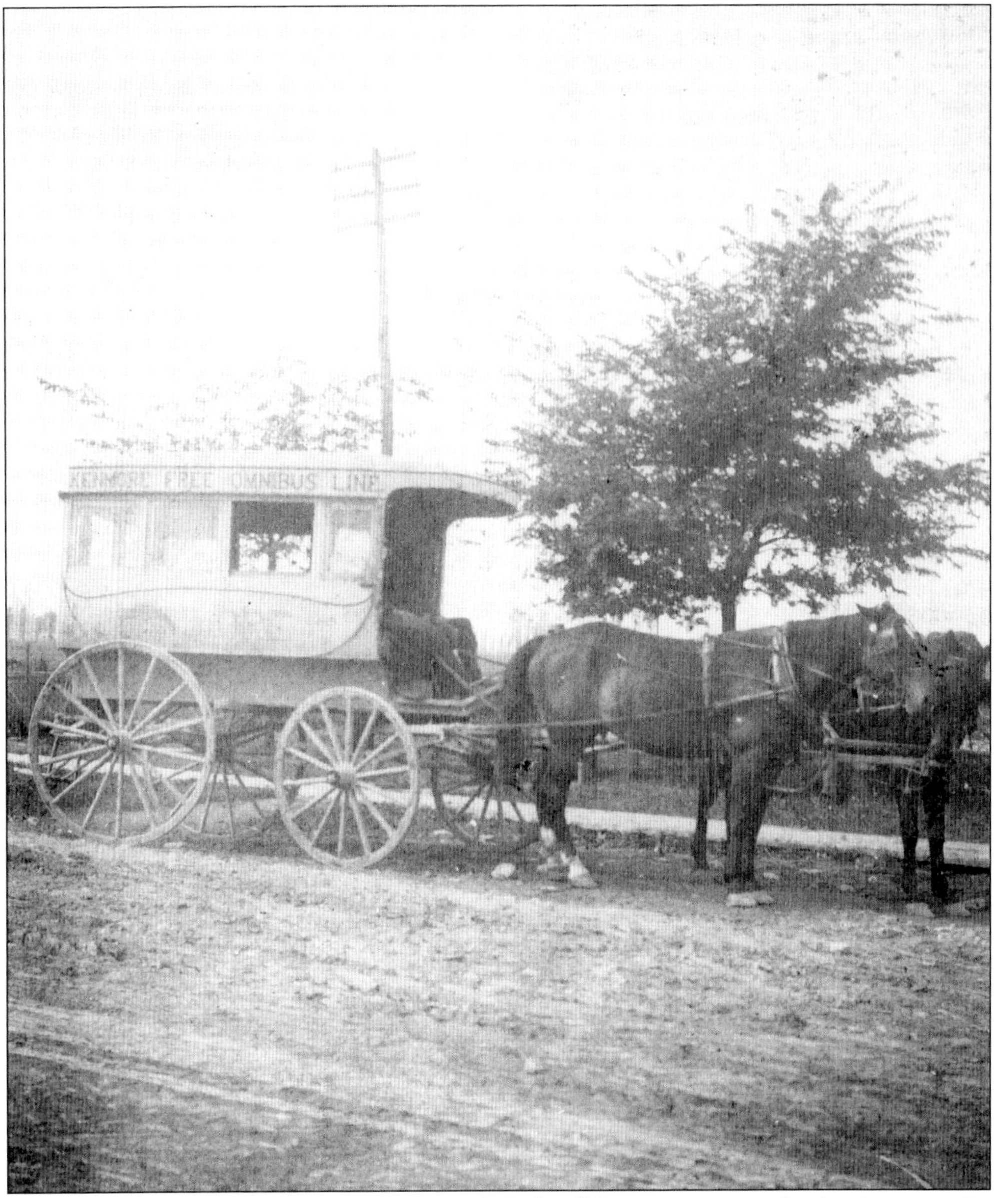

The Kenmore Free Omnibus, c. 1890. Frank Stillwell began operating this bus between the little hamlet of Kenmore and the New York Central Belt Line station at Delaware and Linden in December 1889. The bus line was subsidized by Kenmore realtors to get Buffalonians to the pioneer suburb to look at building lots. The free rides continued into 1894, when the Kenmore-Tonawanda street car line was opened. Stillwell Avenue was named to honor the operator of the village's first public transportation.

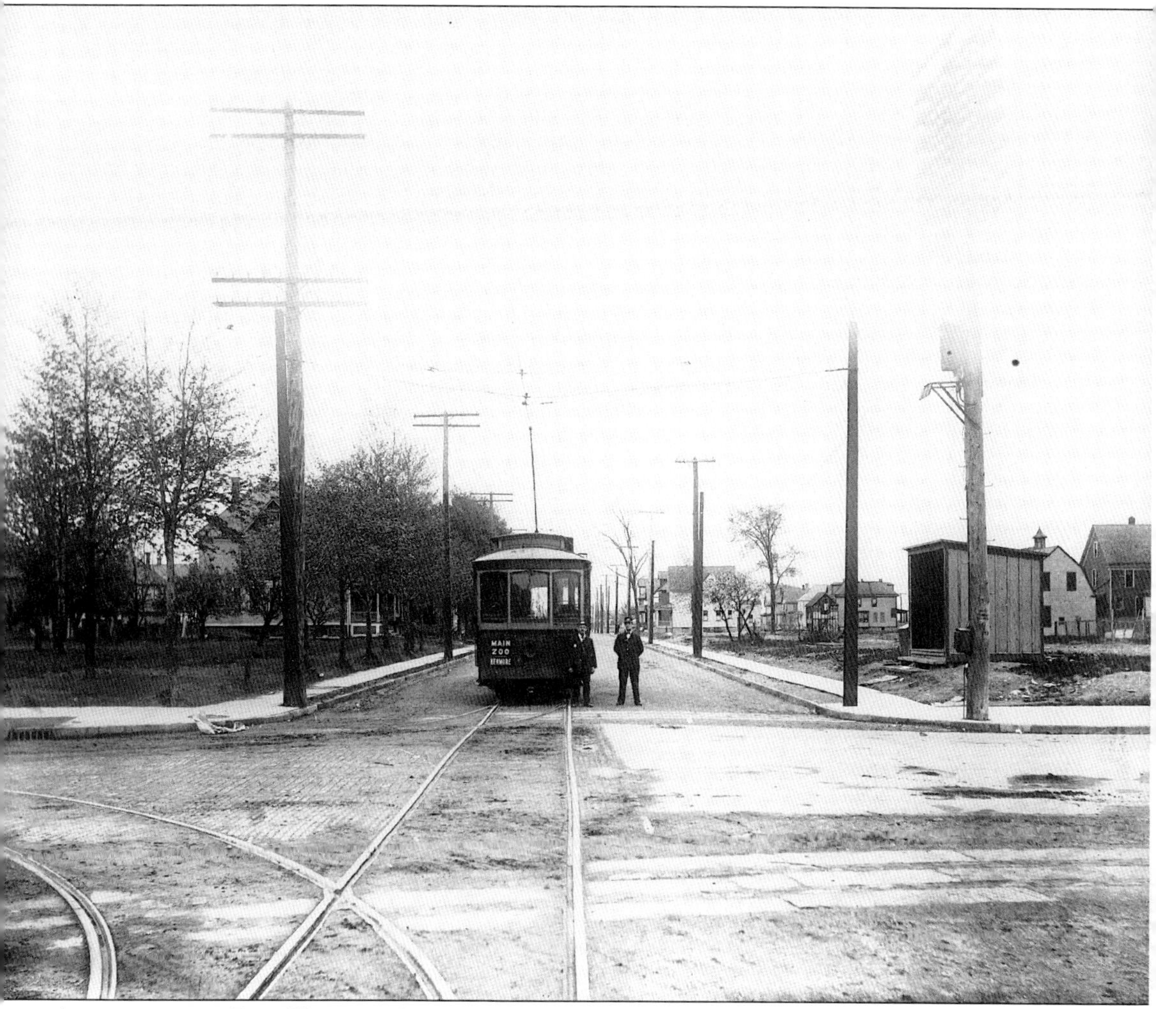

A STREETCAR ON EAST KENMORE AVENUE AT DELAWARE, C. 1900. The motorman who operated the electric car and the conductor who collected the 5¢ fares pose with their Brill "trolley car" on an autumn day. A shelter for waiting inbound passengers is at right. The trolley ran east on Kenmore Avenue to Virgil, then went to Hertel, and then followed Parkside past the zoo. After a jog across Florence Avenue the line followed Main Street to the waterfront. An earlier line followed West Kenmore Avenue to Military Road and Grant Street. The Y intersection at Kenmore Avenue allowed trolleys from Tonawanda to follow either route as traffic demanded. Early Kenmore residents used the well, called the "Village Pump," at the Ackerman farm at left. The farmhouse was the one referred to as the "White House."

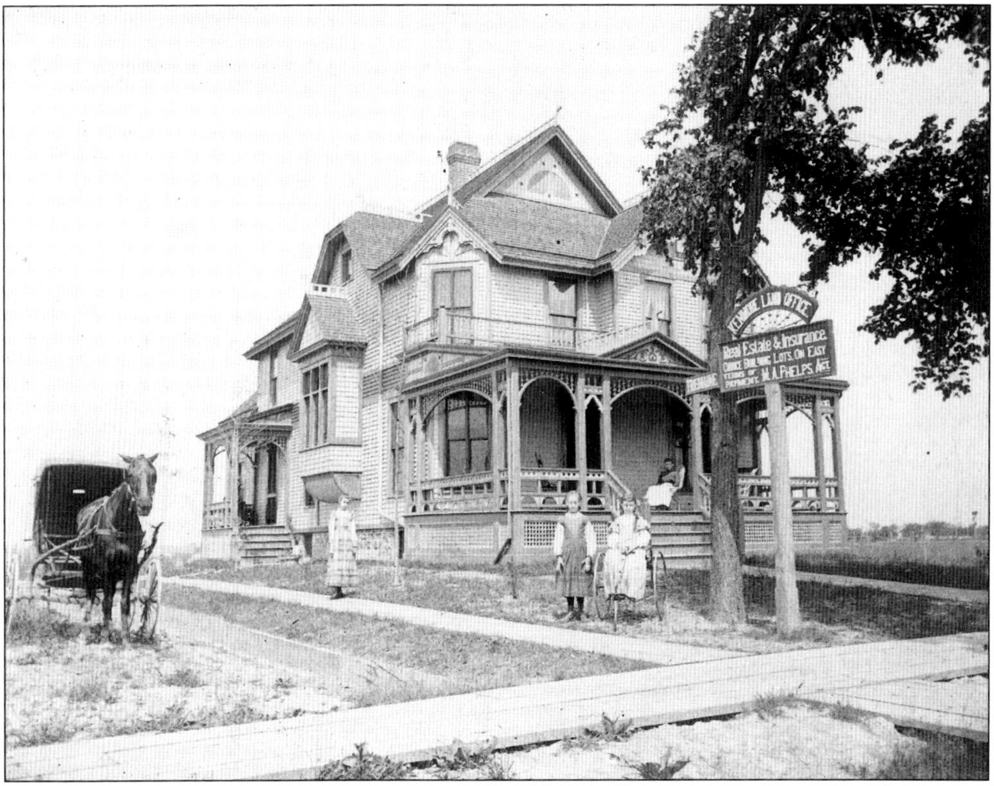

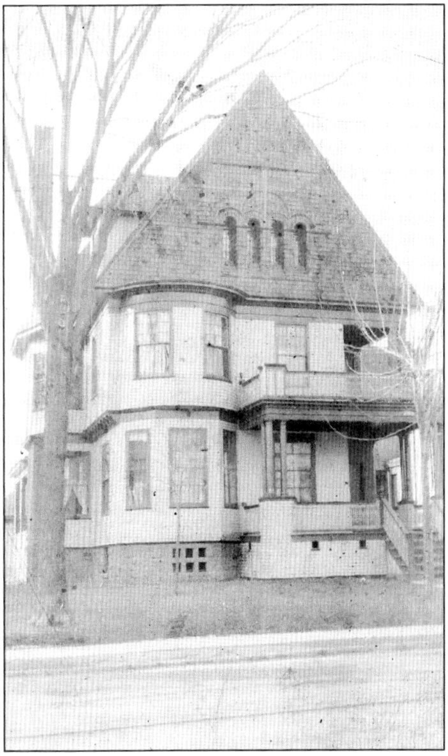

THE MYRON PHELPS HOME, C. 1890. This view shows his real estate sign, which reads "Kenmore Land Office. Real Estate & Insurance. Choice Building Lots On Easy Terms of Payment. M.A. Phelps, Agt." There is a "Tremaine" sign nailed to the tree. The family's one-horsepower rig is parked where Tremaine Avenue would later cut through the property. Mrs. Dulcena Phelps is sitting on the verandah while her three girls pose alongside a wooden walkway. One is sitting on a "Queen Anne," a three-wheeled velocipede. (KUMC.)

THE HERBERT A. ZIMMERMAN HOUSE AT 2808 DELAWARE AVENUE, C. 1900. This home was built at a cost of $8,000 for James Byron Zimmerman, who served as town supervisor from 1888 to 1894. His cooperation with the founders of Kenmore made the pioneer suburb possible. He so believed in the concept of a suburb that he sold his rural home and moved into this new house, which he had built next to his church.

Two

The Young Village

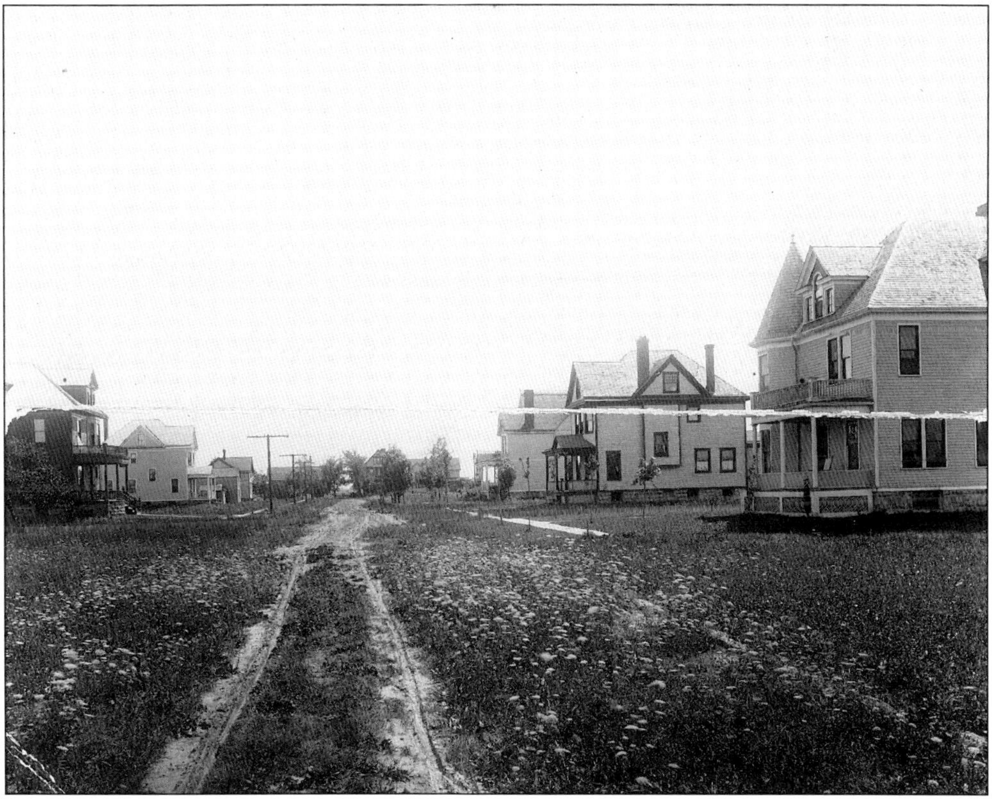

Mang Avenue between Eugene and Delaware. The roadway was little more than a pair of cart tracks through a field when this photo was taken. As befit the planned upscale suburb, the new homes here are spacious, and reflect fashionable designs of the time. Number 54, on the right, exhibits a modified Queen Anne style, coincidentally appropriate to the profusion of Queen Anne's lace in its surroundings.

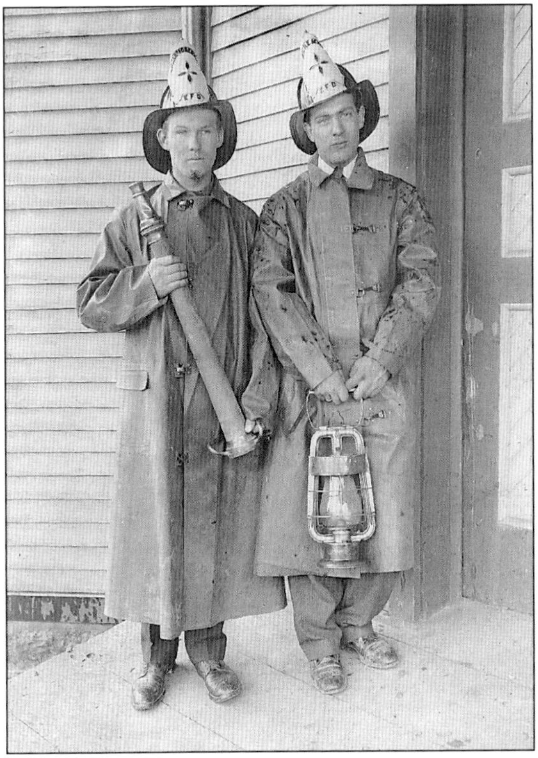

Assistant Foreman Edward Schmidt (holding the nozzle) and Foreman Henry Ebling (holding the lantern) on the ramp of the fire hall in 1909. The two are wearing their fire coats and hats—but in street shoes rather than boots. Ebling became the department chief in 1912; Schmidt assumed the position two years later. The nozzle was flexible, allowing firefighters to control the flow of water. In later years the titles of foreman and assistant foreman were changed to captain and lieutenant. (KVFD collection.)

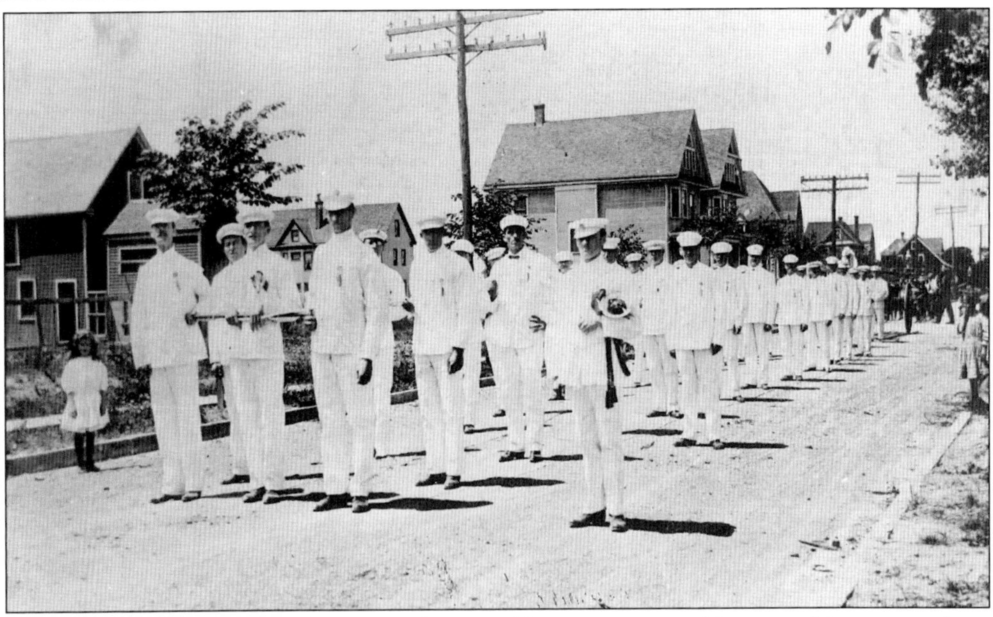

Members of the Kenmore Hook and Ladder Company of the Kenmore Volunteer Fire Department. The Kenmore Hook and Ladder Company was organized in April 1905, six years after the incorporation of the village. Its members, shown here in their white dress uniforms shortly after the company was organized, are ready for a parade. A very careful examination of the picture will reveal the parade hose reel behind the line of marchers. (KVFD collection.)

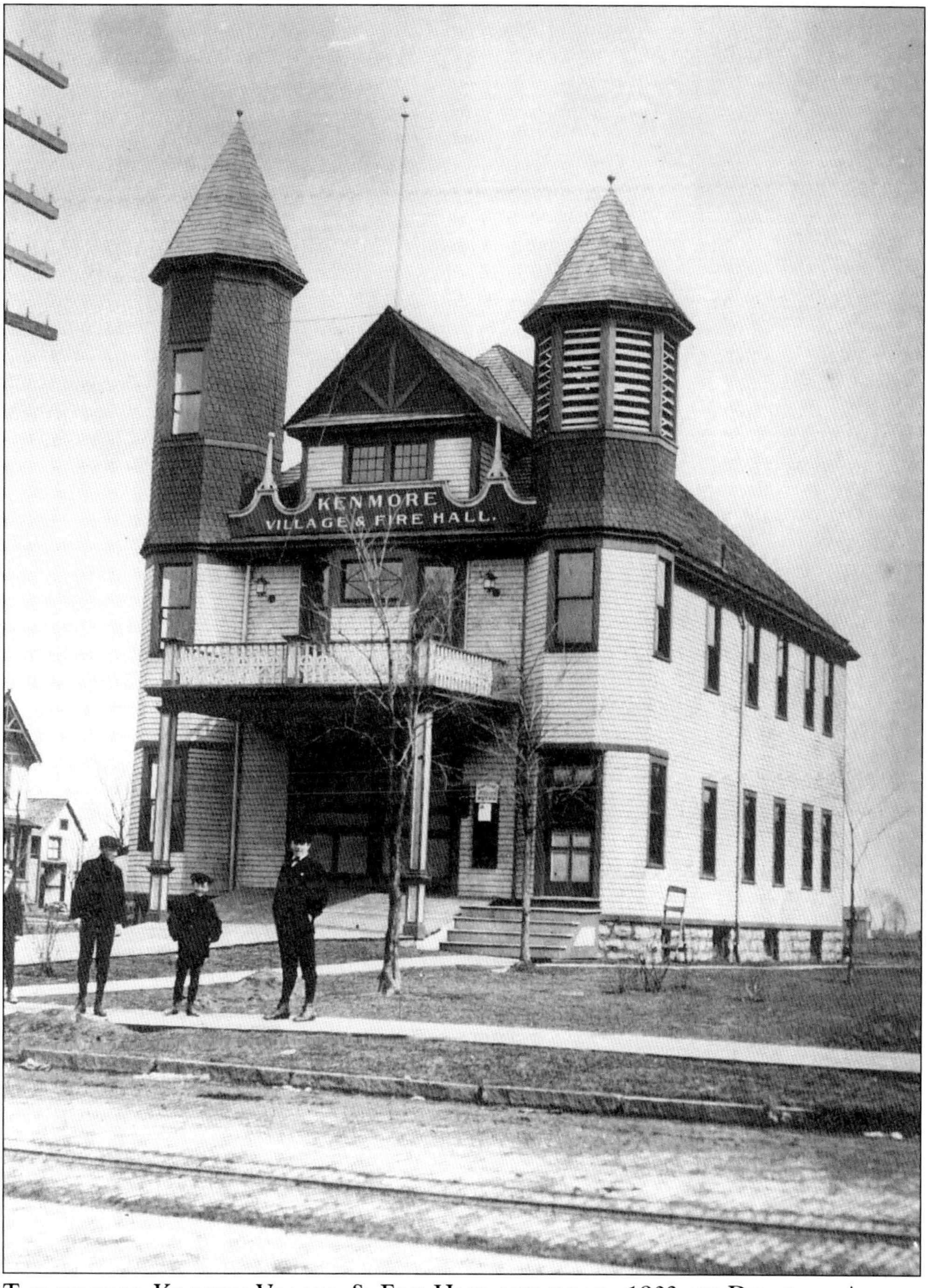

The original Kenmore Village & Fire Hall, erected in 1903 on Delaware Avenue between Warren and Euclid Avenues. The taller tower was for drying hoses, and the shorter tower held the fire bell, which is now on display in front of the 1929 Nash Road Fire Hall. Fire equipment was pulled by hand; no horse-drawn fire equipment was ever used in the village. Beginning in 1919 the fire hall housed Kenmore's early Atterbury fire engine. The building was demolished in 1929, when the present fire hall was opened.

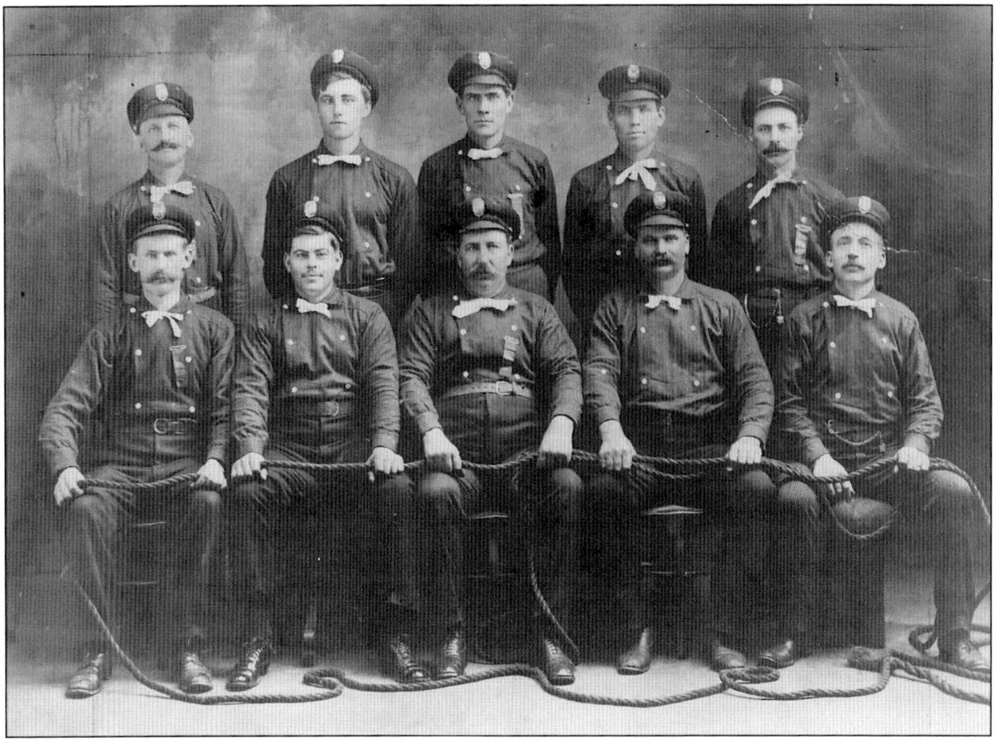

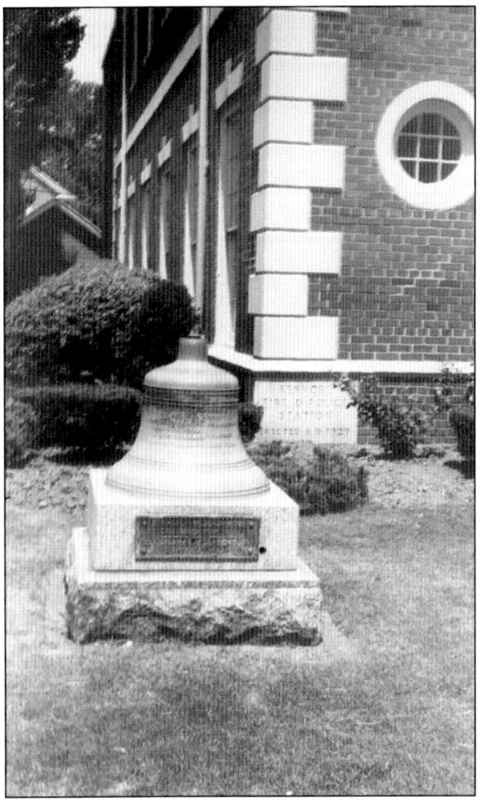

THE ALERT HOSE COMPANY'S TUG-OF-WAR TEAM DURING THE KENMORE FIRE DEPARTMENT'S FIRST ANNUAL FIELD DAY IN 1905. Shown here are, from left to right, as follows: (seated) Jacob Eva, Winfield Colvin, Philip Landel, John I. Keller, and Jacob Gall; (standing) Richard Failing, Ed Knab, Frank Zimmerman, Ed Zimmerman, and Ed Bleyle. (KVFD collection.)

KENMORE'S HISTORIC FIRE BELL, NOW DISPLAYED ON NASH ROAD. The village board authorized $235 for the purchase of this 500-pound bell in 1904. On the bell are inscribed the names of Chief Frank C. Stillwell and the members of the village board at that time. It was hung in the south tower of the 1903 fire hall and sounded fire alarms until 1917, when it was replaced by an electric siren. The village board planned to sell the bell but was persuaded by a petition from 100 village residents to retain it as a memorial to the work done by Kenmore's volunteer firemen. It was mounted in a suitable kiosk on the village green until re-dedicated at its present site in 1941.

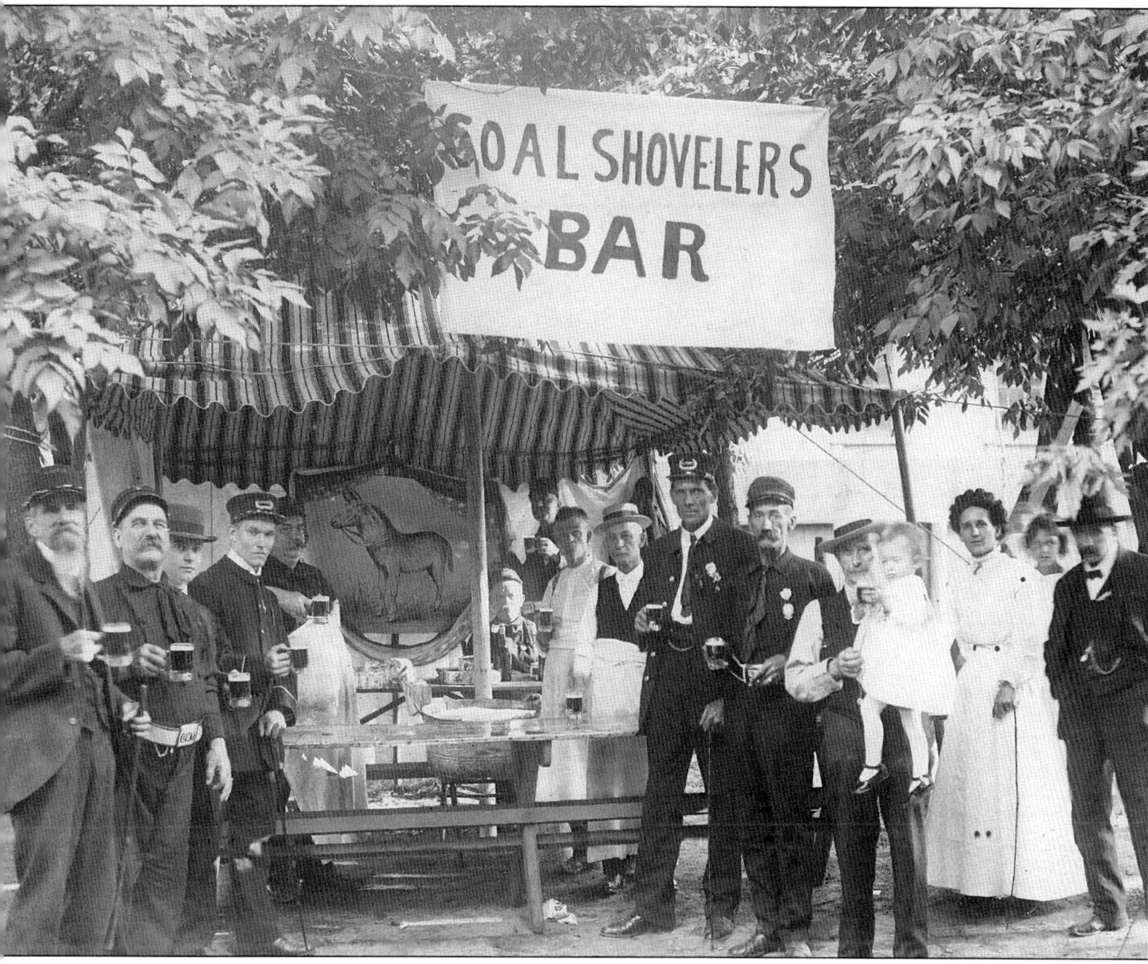

ONE OF THE ANNUAL FIELD DAYS HELD BEHIND THE COMBINATION VILLAGE HALL AND FIRE HALL ON DELAWARE AVENUE, SOUTH OF WARREN. Organized fire protection in Kenmore dates to 1893—the year before L.P.A. Eberhardt's first home in the village burned to the ground. No doubt with Mr. Eberhardt's support, if not at his behest, local businessmen helped form a fire-fighting unit. To quote the history of the Kenmore Volunteer Fire Department, "A company was organized that year . . . [but] No record can be found concerning the disposition of this organization or its activities." Nine years later, in 1902, a Kenmore Fire Association was approved by the village government, and a used hook and ladder apparatus, the village's first piece of fire fighting equipment, was purchased from the Village of Tonawanda for $350. The association was quickly superseded, and on May 25, 1903, the Kenmore Fire Department, now the Kenmore Volunteer Fire Department, was formally incorporated with 92 members. Myron Phelps, the treasurer of the 1893 company, was elected as the first president, and Frank Stillwell, the foreman of the original bucket brigade, became the new department's first chief. In the same year, a combination village hall and fire hall was constructed on Delaware Avenue, south of Warren. Future chief Edward Schmidt stands third from left; to his left is Frank Zimmerman. The others are unidentified, and the meaning of "Coal Shovelers Bar" is unknown. (KVFD collection.)

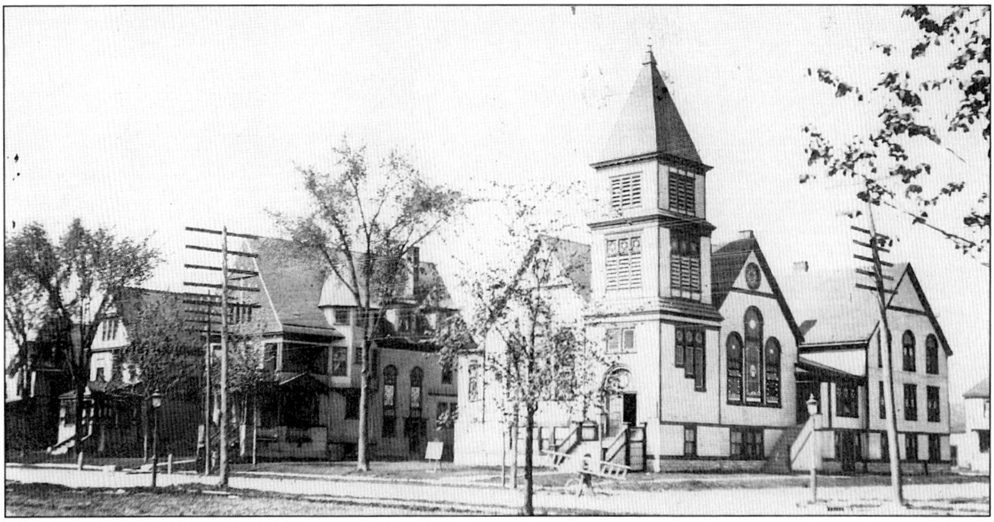

Kenmore Methodist-Episcopal Church, c. 1900. This frame building was dedicated in 1893 and served at Delaware Avenue and LaSalle until 1928, when the present Kenmore United Methodist Church building on Landers Road was erected. The large house next door was the home of James Byron Zimmerman. The home still stands, though with a store front. Note the boy carrying a ladder on his bicycle.

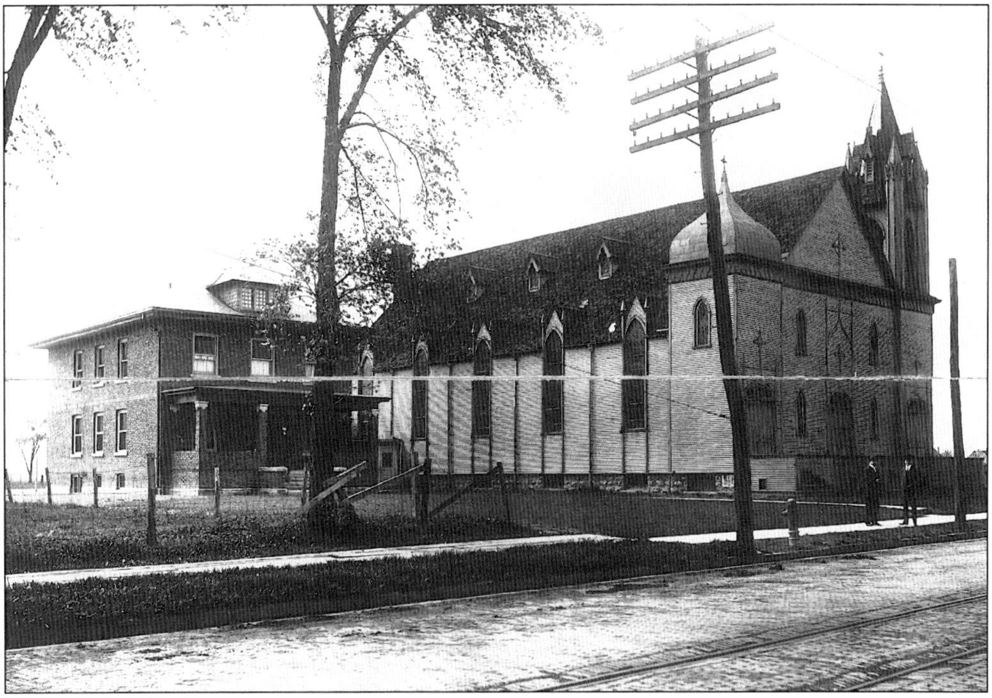

St. Paul's Roman Catholic Church. St. Paul's was founded in 1897 at the request of some 16 families, whose petition for a parish in Kenmore was approved by Bishop James Quigley. The Mang family donated 3 acres at the corner of Delaware and Victoria, and with loans (later forgiven) from the Mang and Keller families, a frame edifice was finished the next year. The original rectory, south of the church, was added in 1910. Both buildings have been replaced by the new present stone church, consecrated in 1954.

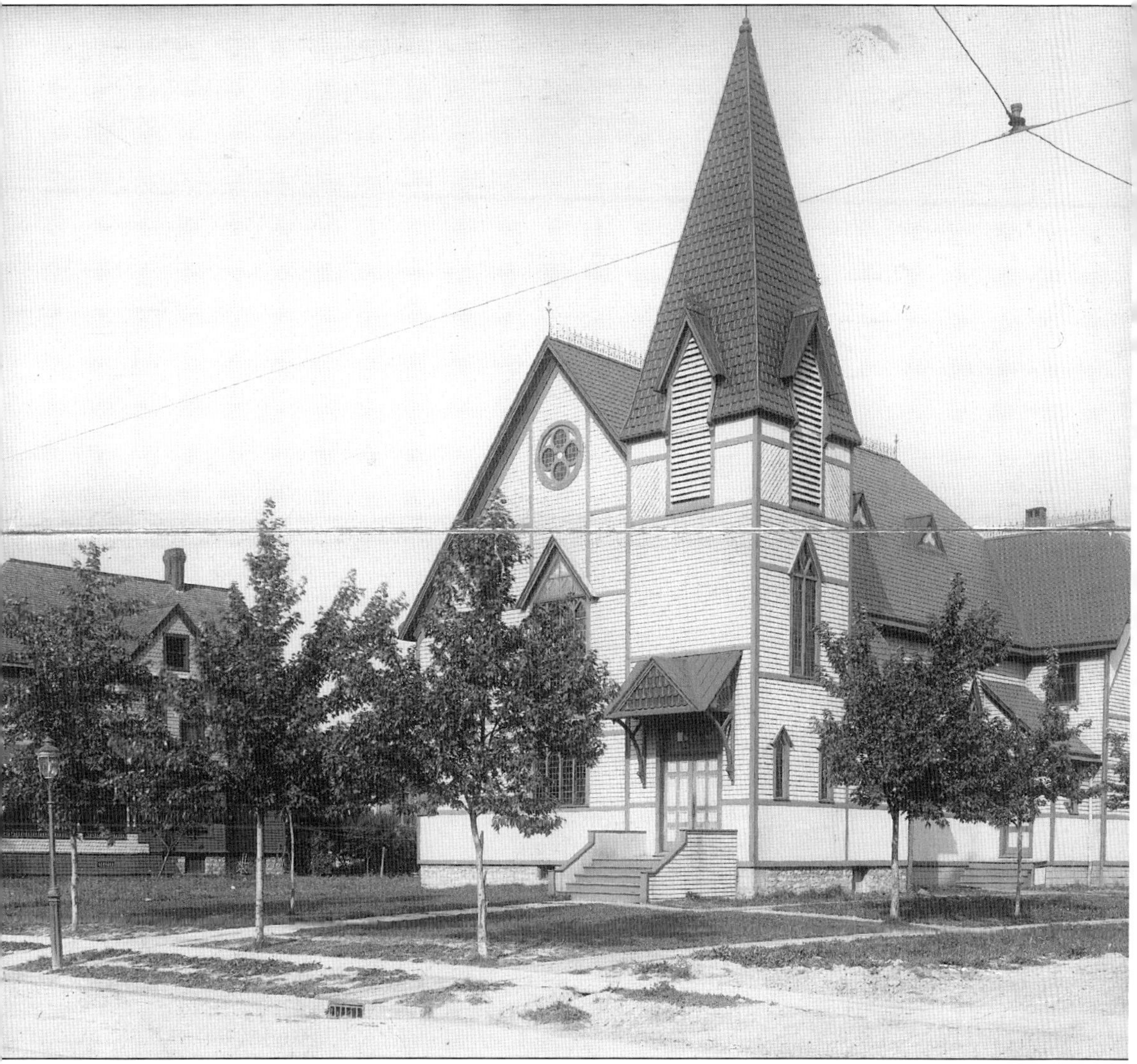

THE OLD KENMORE PRESBYTERIAN CHURCH, BUILT ON LAND DONATED IN 1891 BY L.P.A. EBERHARDT AT DELAWARE AND EAST HAZELTINE AVENUES. The church, originally a mission of Westminster Presbyterian Church in Buffalo, became an independent congregation in 1894, with 34 charter members. In 1908, a gymnasium, which for many years served the entire Kenmore community, was built adjacent on Hazeltine. In 1911 the church building was enlarged and raised on a higher foundation; it is shown here on its original lower foundation.

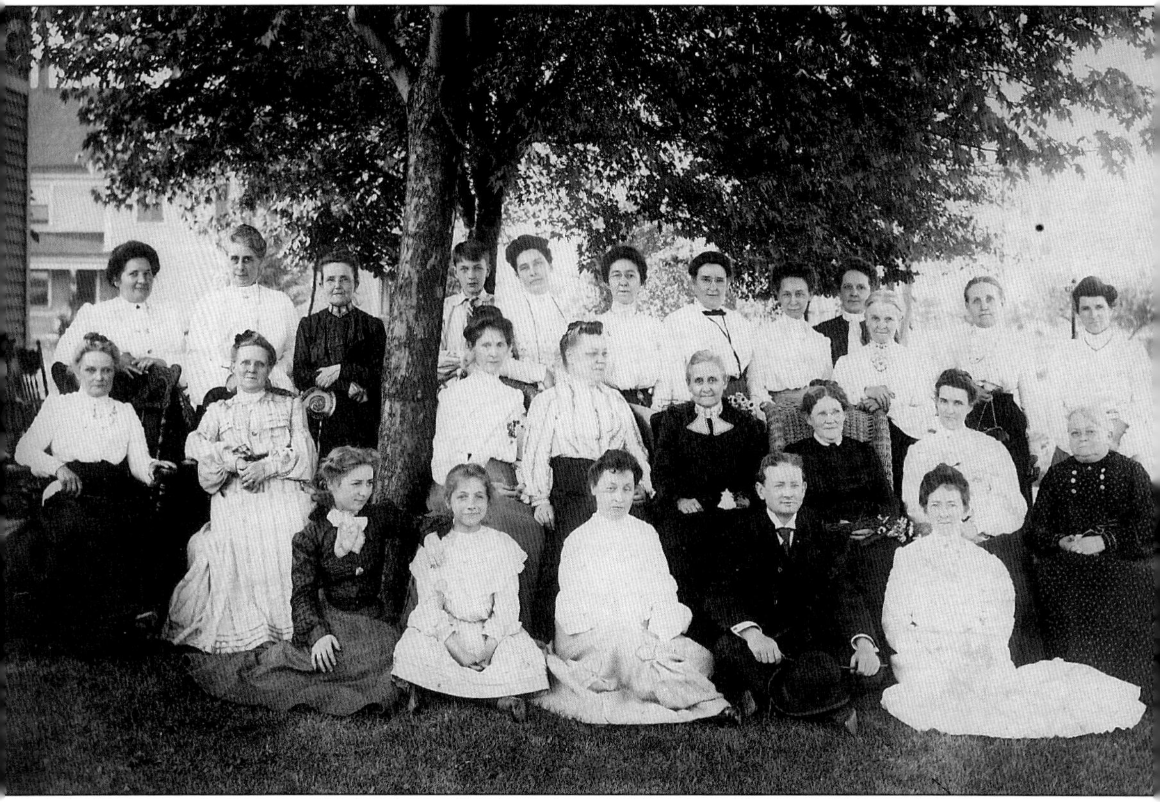

A c. 1900 group photograph of members of the Kenmore Presbyterian Church. A card attached to the back of this photo identifies the people shown here; most of the names can be read, but parts of some names, as indicated by ellipses, have been broken off. As far as can be discerned, they are, from left to right, as follows: (front row) Nellie Brown, Emma Lehman, "two unidentified ladies of Kenmore," and Rev. McDonald of Kenmore Church; (middle row) Mrs. Harry Brown, Mrs. W.M. Berry, Mrs. John Lehman, Mrs. U.U. (or U.V. or V.V.) Benedict, Mrs. Fred Harper, Mrs. Frank McPherson, and Mrs. Pheobe Buttlers; (back row) ...us Neilson, ? Albee, ...wly Eckert, ...ilgons son, ? Franklin, ? Clute, Fannie McKee, Anna Herman?, Mrs. Henry G. Phillips (who, it is noted, died in 1910), Mrs. Richard Osborn, Mrs. Richard Goodwin, and Mrs. Richard McKee. It is not known what the church organization was, why its members posed for this picture, and why a young boy and two young ladies are among the middle-aged-and-older group, but not knowing does not make this depiction of early village life any less interesting.

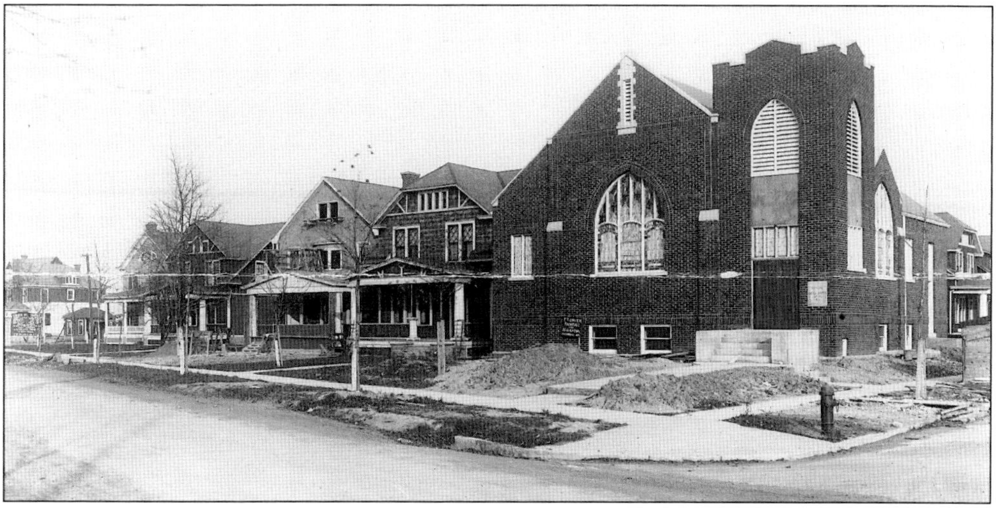

THE NEWLY CONSTRUCTED KENMORE BAPTIST CHURCH AT THE CORNER OF DELAWARE ROAD AND WARDMAN (FORMERLY CORNELL) IN 1916. The Baptist congregation, which was organized in 1911, first worshiped in locations in North Buffalo, and after five years erected the church shown here. The building was enlarged in 1924, and in 1961 a new sanctuary was added, along with rooms for the Sunday school and a new kitchen. The cost of the newest portion was 30 times that of the original structure.

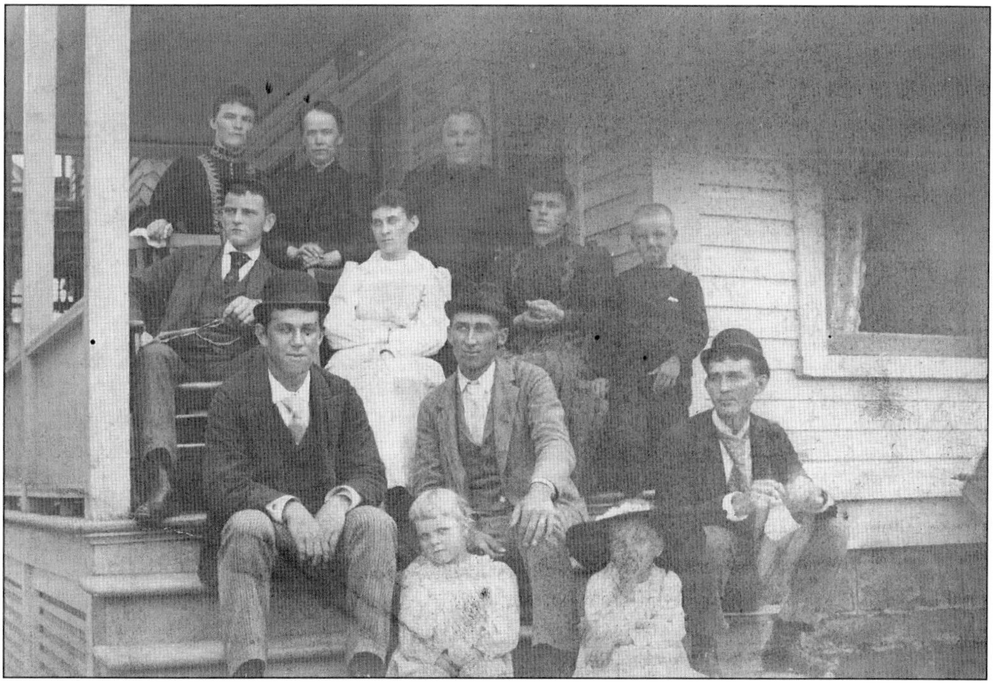

THE KENMORE COTTAGE AT CHAUTAUQUA. This undated photograph shows a group of Kenmore residents at the Eberhardt family cottage on the grounds of the Chautauqua Institution. As happened in many communities, a Chautauqua Literary and Scientific Circle, a "Little Chautauqua," was begun in the village around the turn of the 20th century. Less literary minded residents—"the profane," as Rev. Dr. Parkhurst called them—suggested that the initials CLSC stood for "come love, sit closer."

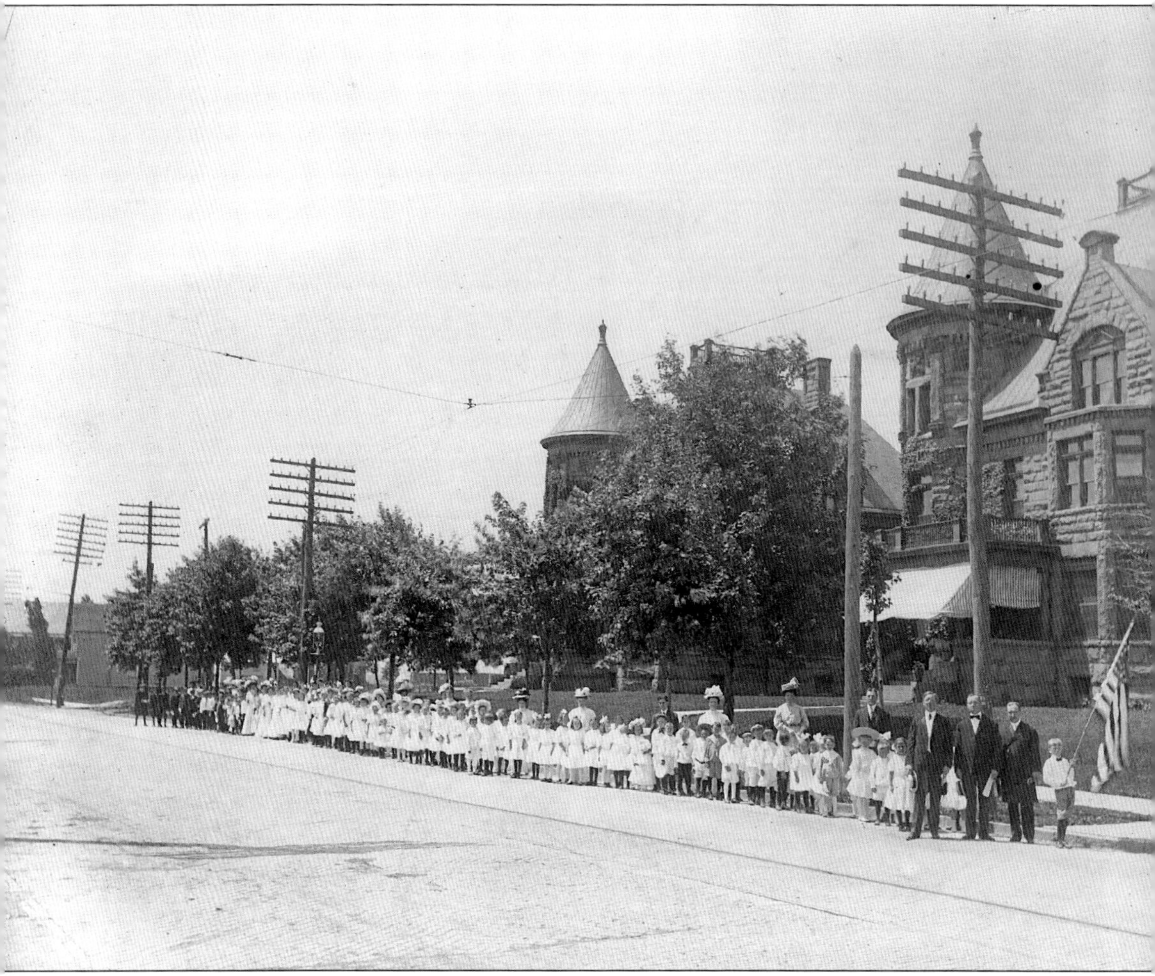

AN EARLY 1900S PHOTOGRAPH OF CHILDREN'S DAY. "On Parade" is the caption on the back of this photo. The children and adults are from the Sunday school of the Presbyterian church. Behind them on Delaware Avenue are the two Eberhardt mansions that stood for 80 years at the entrance to the village of Kenmore, symbolizing the founders' dreams of an ideal suburban residential community. L.P.A. Eberhardt's now demolished 1893 home is on the right, at the intersection of the avenue and West Hazeltine. The still existing home built for his brother Frederick is on the left, at the corner of Delaware and Town Line Road (long since renamed Kenmore Avenue). The connection between Louis Eberhardt and the church was a long and close one. It was he who donated the land diagonally across Delaware where the original church stood and the present church stands. He was an active member of the congregation for the rest of his life, and was memorialized at the church following his death at the age of 79 in April 1939.

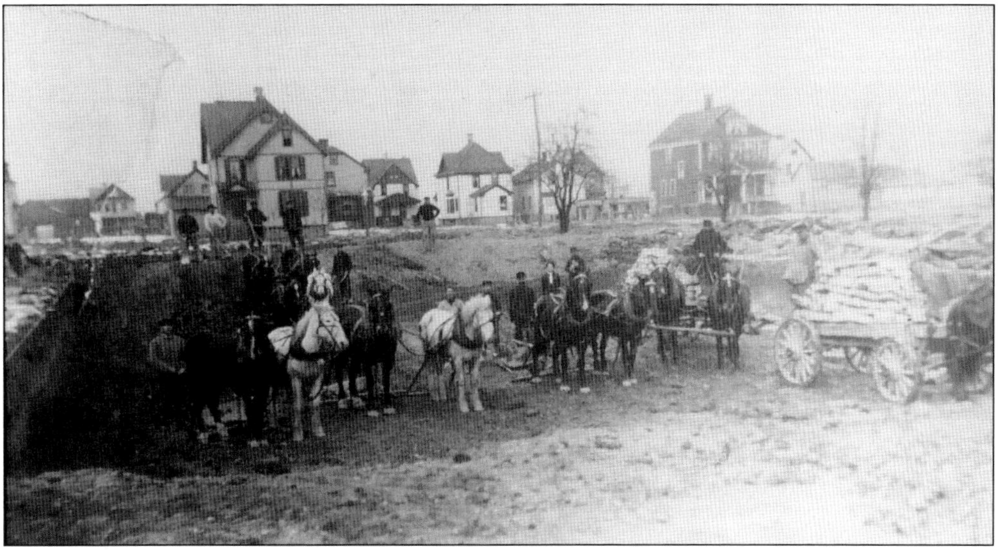

EXCAVATING THE BASEMENT FOR THE NEW GYMNASIUM, BUILT ON EAST HAZELTINE AVENUE IN 1907. Constructed just behind Kenmore Presbyterian Church, the building was a gift to the community and to his church by L.P.A. Eberhardt. Though steam shovels were common in 1907, this excavation was done largely with real horsepower.

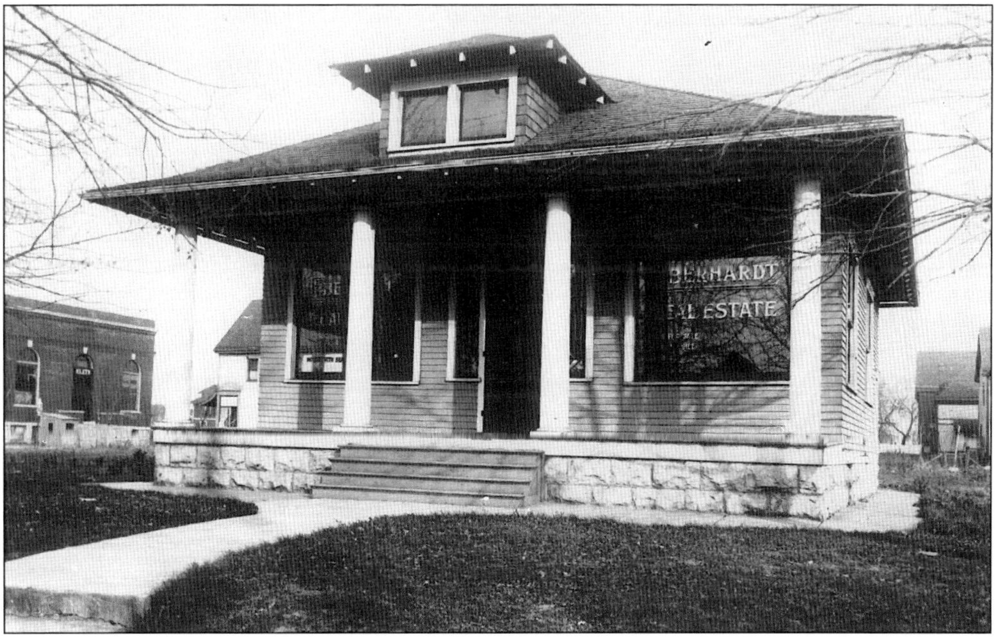

THE EBERHARDT REAL ESTATE OFFICE, ERECTED AT 2749 DELAWARE AVENUE IN 1912. This was where L.P.A. had built his first home, which burned in 1894. The office, located directly across the street from the twin mansions, is where Fred and L.P.A. conducted business. There is a sign in the left-hand window advertising "Notary with Seal," which meant that at least one of them was a notary public, a necessity in the land sales business. The building at left was erected in 1907 as a gift from L.P.A. to his church and community. Note the sign over the door, which reads "Elite," the name given to Kenmore's first theater building. A barber shop operated in the former office for many years before its demolition in 1978.

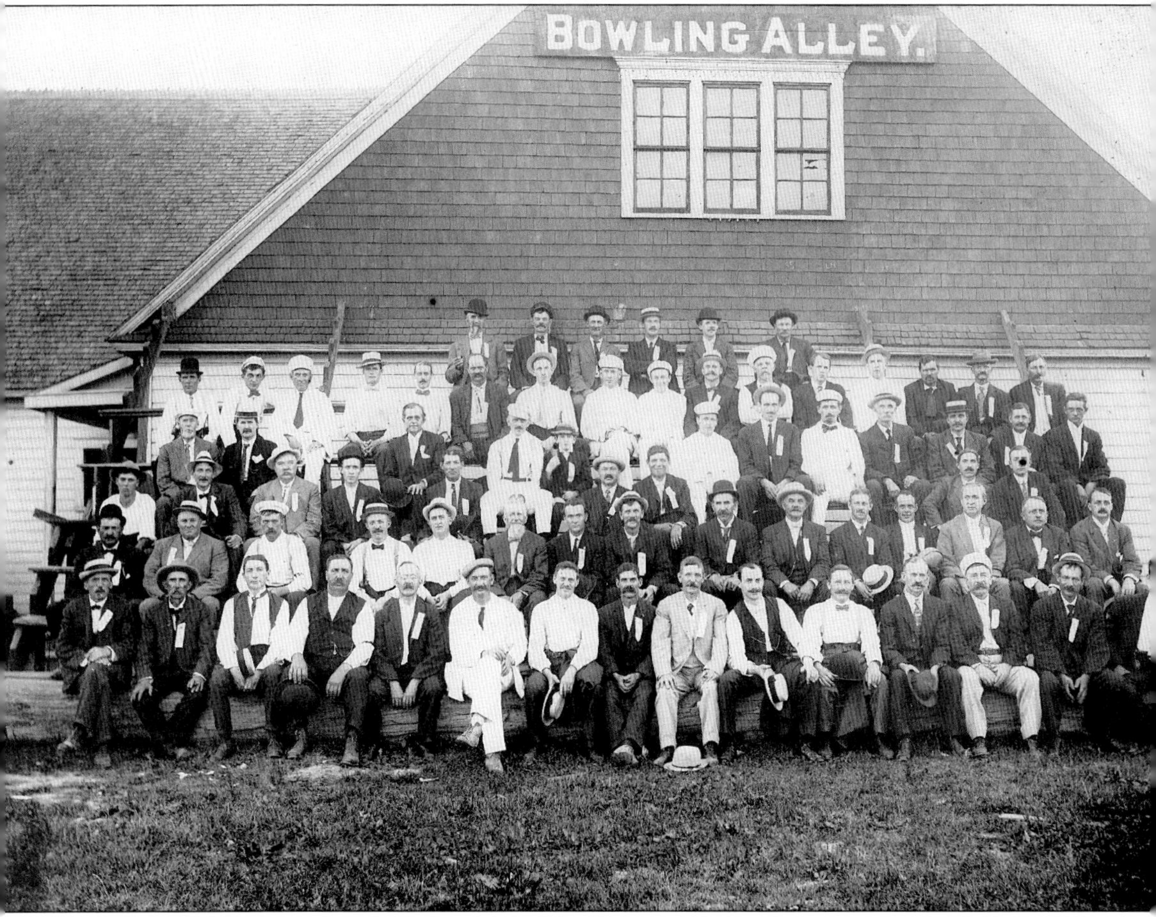

THE KENMORE CONVENTION HALL AT DELAWARE AND WABASH, c. 1910. Often called the "Wigwam," this hall served as a bowling alley, roller skating rink, and meeting place for political parties, gospel meetings, and temperance rallies. One fervent Prohibitionist was disturbed by the building's contrasting uses and was heard to exclaim "How the devil must be gnashing his teeth." Next door stood the Kenmore Tavern, which served those villagers unafraid of or unconcerned about the "demon." At times the village had to impose strict rules of conduct and regulate its hours. The building was torn down in 1914 to make way for a Nash automobile dealership.

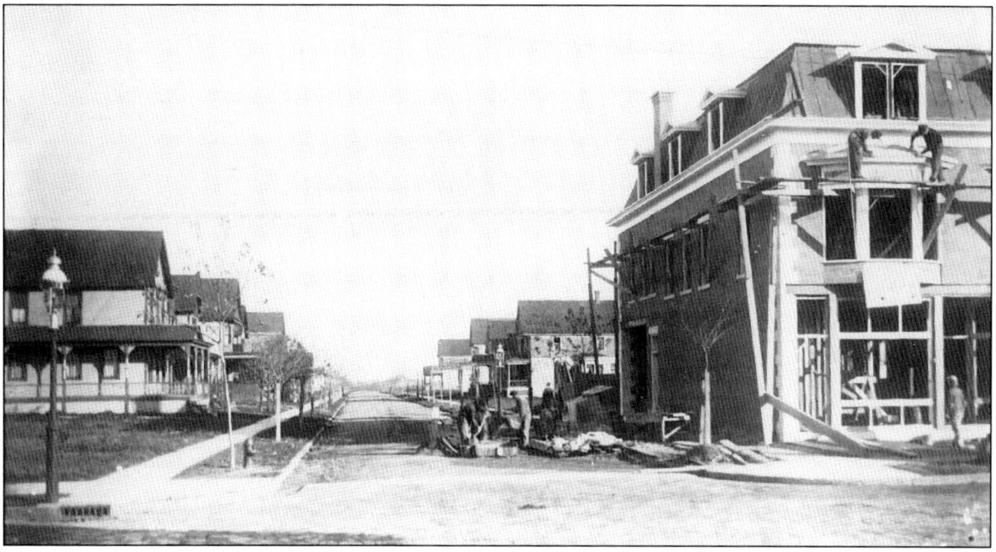

Warren and Delaware Avenues. Before the L.P.A. Eberhardt mansion could be built, the Mang Tavern, which already existed on the site, had to be divided and moved. One section, taken a block south into Buffalo, survives as a portion of the Saratoga Restaurant at Delaware and Ramsdell. The other was moved to 12 Warren Avenue, and appears on the immediate left in this picture, which also shows the construction of the business block at the corner of Warren and Delaware.

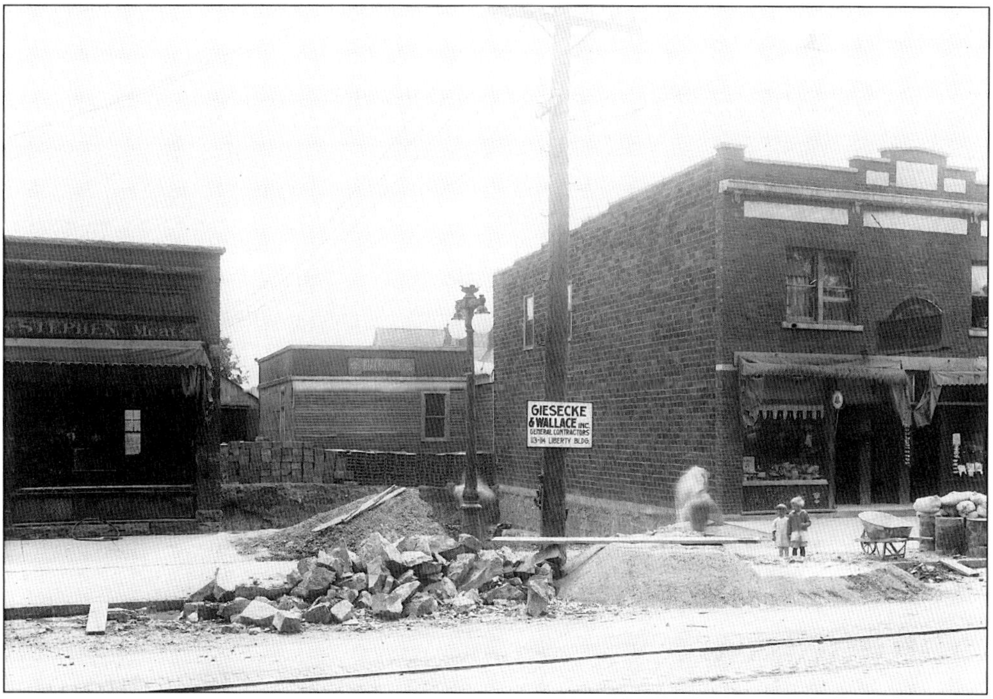

The east side of Delaware Avenue, between Parkwood and Euclid, early in the 20th century. Giesecke and Wallace of Buffalo were the contractors for the new commercial structure being built on the site. Two children watch as two men—working furiously, from their blurred images—go about their tasks. The building facades have since been much altered.

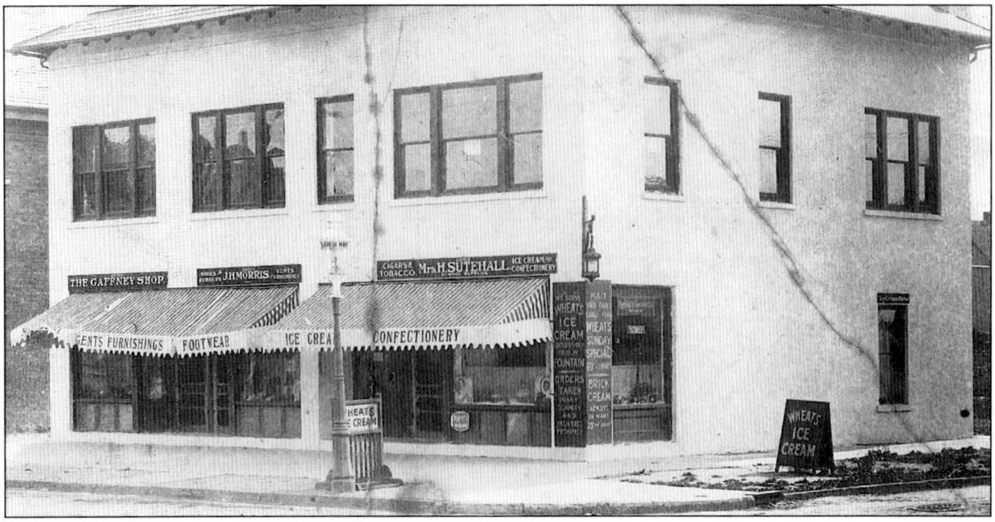

The commercial block at the southwest corner of Mang and Delaware. Of particular interest among the stores shown here is the confectionery of Mrs. Sarah Sutehall, who, with her husband, Henry, had emigrated from England. In 1910, their son Henry Jr., a violinist, left for what was planned to be an adventure, working his way around the world as a musician. Two years later young Henry booked passage home on the *Titanic*. He was the only Kenmore resident lost in its sinking. Woolworth's later occupied the site.

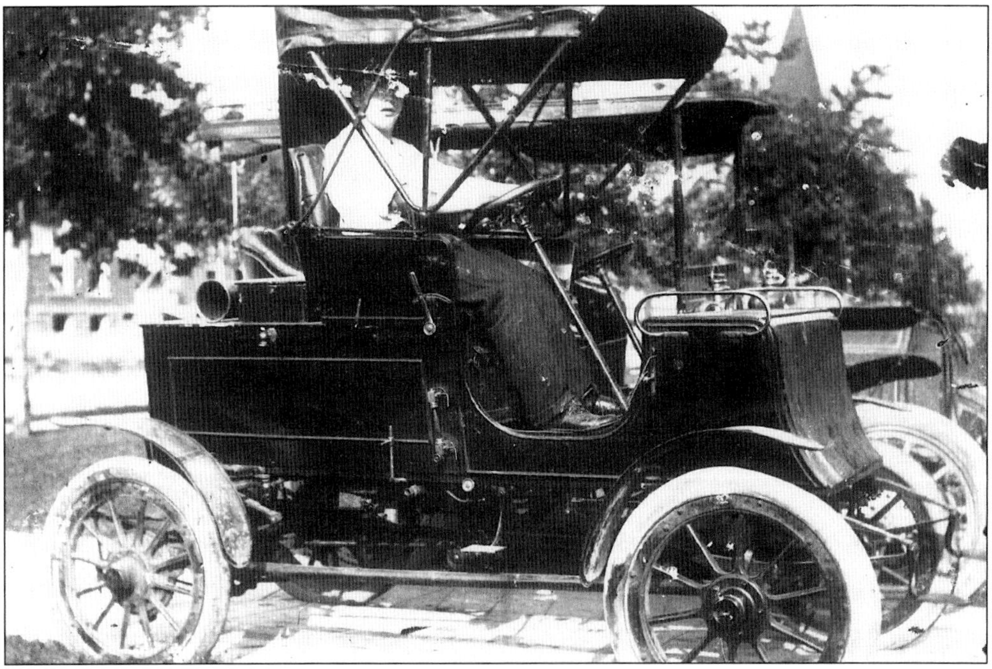

Louis K. Eberhardt in a stanhope, possibly the family's Stanley Steamer, in 1907. A stanhope had two additional seats that unfolded from the front of the car. Louis, one of L.P.A.'s sons, poses with the car at his father's home. There is a touring car parked alongside. In the background can be seen the steeple of Kenmore Presbyterian Church and the Elite Theater, which was under construction at the time. The print was made from a glass plate that was reversed in the process.

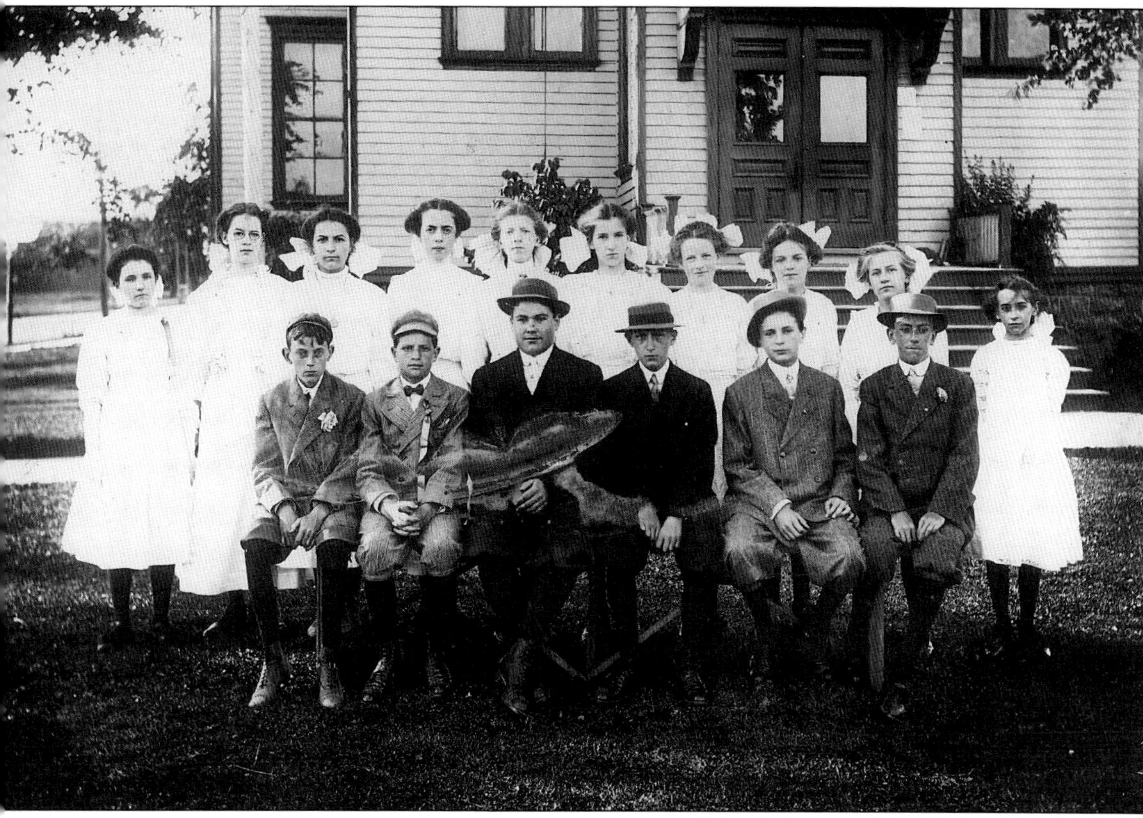

THE 1910 GRADUATING CLASS OF THE OLD GRAMMAR SCHOOL. Written by an unknown hand on the back of this old photograph is "Graduation Class of 1910 from the Old Grammer [sic] School which is now the Municipal Bldg at Delaware Ave. & Old Delaware Rd . . . This was the last class to graduate." The girls posing here are, from left to right (with their names reproduced as they appear on the back of the photo), Gladys Pratt, Annetta Peel, Ruth Blyde, Dorothy Carter, unknown, Martha Towns, Beatrice Morgan, Catherine Owens, unknown, and Catherine Lehr. The boys are, from left to right, Raymond Booth, Harry Rader, Irving Braunscheidle, Gorden Gilbert, Alfred Henry, and a determined-looking Frank C. Moore, a future leading figure in local and state Republican politics.

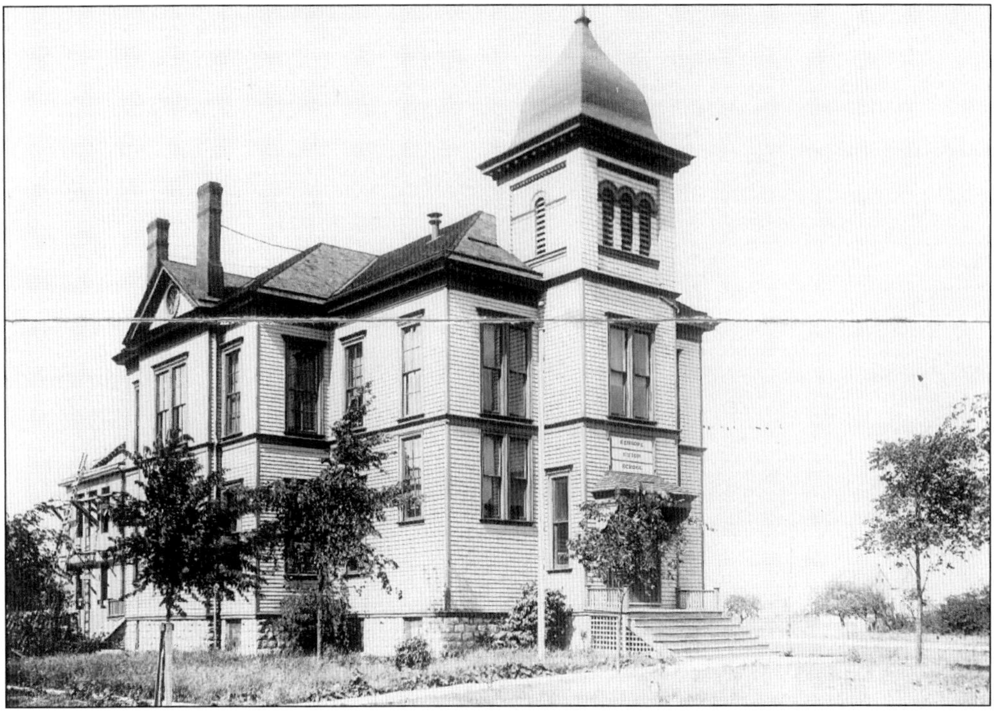

The Union Free School. This school was originally constructed at the intersection of the Delawares in 1892 as a grammar school for the children in the village (high school students had to go either to Tonawanda or Buffalo). In 1911, the overcrowded wooden school was replaced by the new high school building. The former school then became the village hall, and housed both Village of Kenmore and Town of Tonawanda offices until it was demolished and replaced by the present municipal building in 1936.

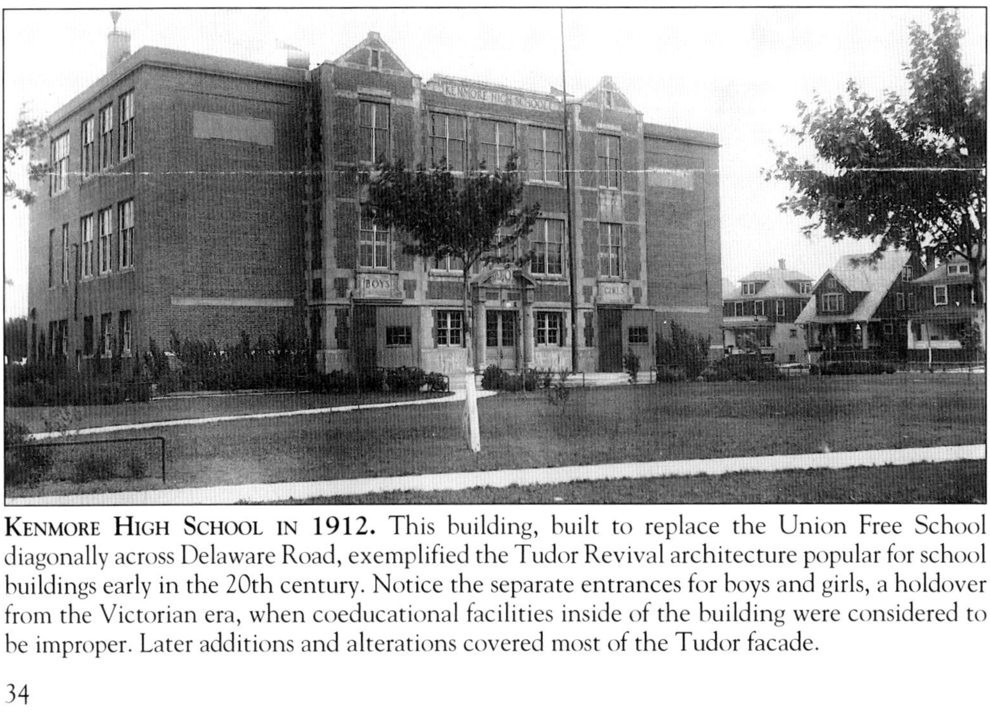

Kenmore High School in 1912. This building, built to replace the Union Free School diagonally across Delaware Road, exemplified the Tudor Revival architecture popular for school buildings early in the 20th century. Notice the separate entrances for boys and girls, a holdover from the Victorian era, when coeducational facilities inside of the building were considered to be improper. Later additions and alterations covered most of the Tudor facade.

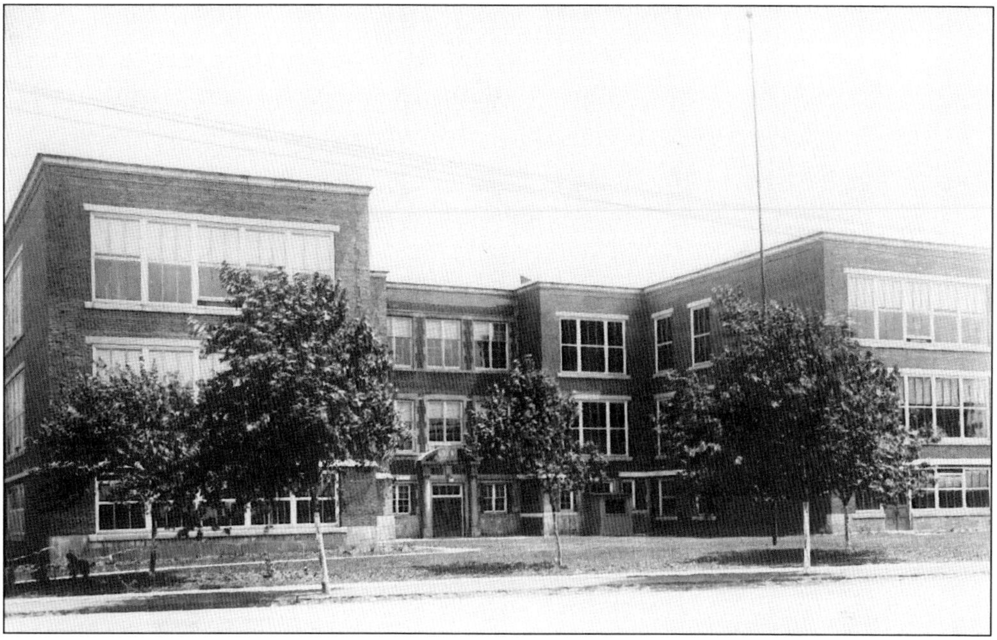

KENMORE HIGH SCHOOL, C. 1917. The two new wings significantly increased the capacity of the school, which continued to house all grades through senior high. Pupils graduating from eighth grade were given a diploma promoting them to the "high school department," housed in part of the same building.

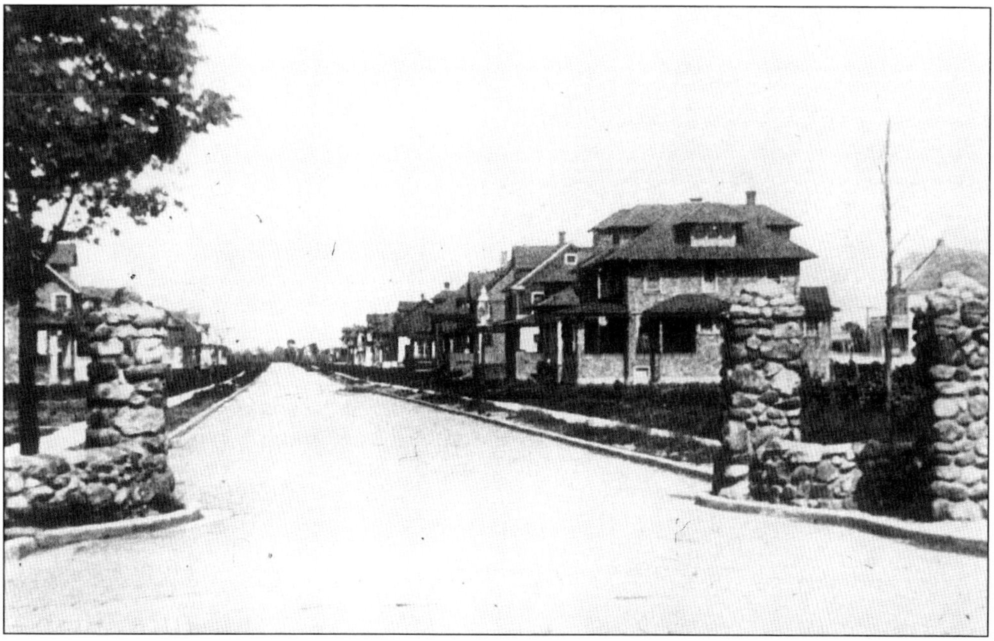

KNOWLTON AVENUE LOOKING EAST FROM DELAWARE, C. 1912. The unique fieldstone pillars at the entry to Knowlton gave the street a singular appearance, but they created a narrow passageway that proved to be inconvenient, if not hazardous, as automobile traffic increased in the 1920s. As a result, these pillars, like others throughout the village, were eventually removed.

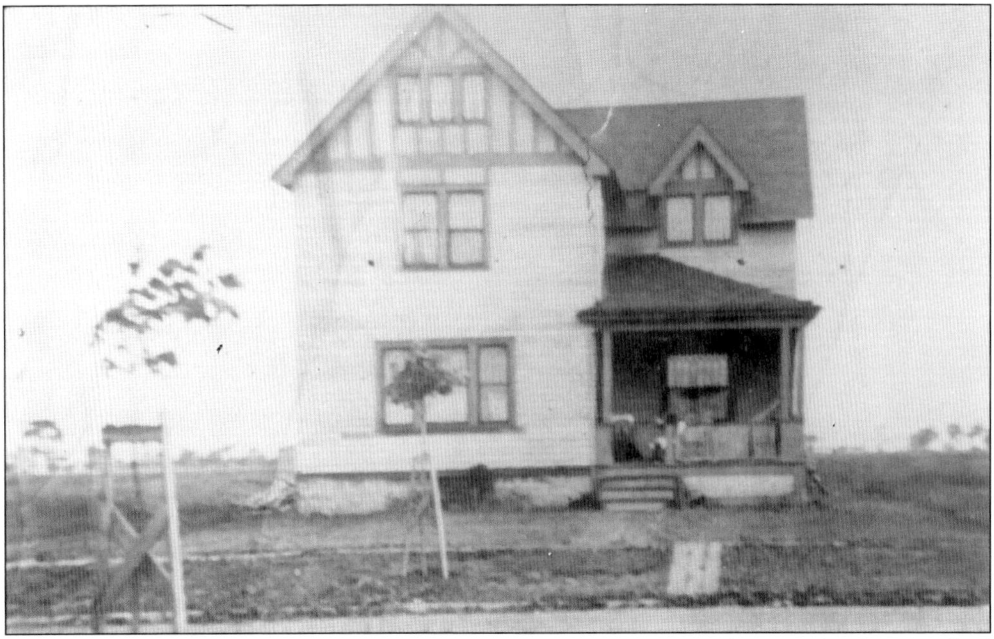

East Tremaine Avenue (now Parkwood Avenue), c. 1900. Residents in this home talked of watching from the porch as streetcars growled along Hertel Avenue. There was little development between Hertel Avenue and Kenmore until the 1920s. The wooden sidewalk allowed Kenmorites to cross muddy fields to get to Virgil Avenue and save the extra nickel fare charged to ride the trolley into Buffalo from the village.

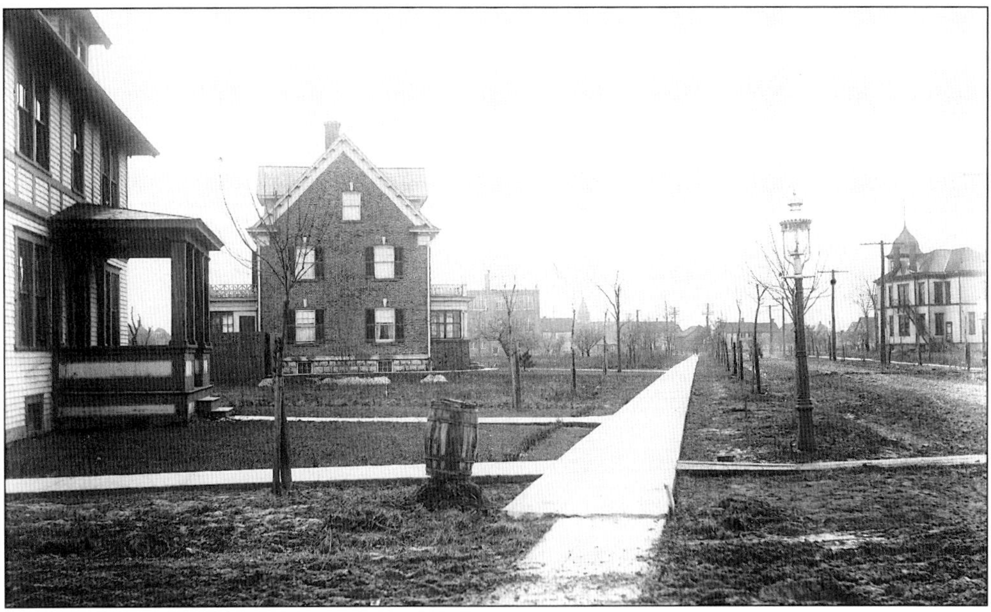

A post-1911 photograph of Delaware Road. The road sports gas street lights and new trees, but no pavement. Wooden sidewalks still ran for at least part of its length. The old Union School, which had become the village hall, and its educational replacement, the "new" high school, can both be seen here. The brick home at left center at one time belonged to R.D.C. Rudhard, who twice served as the village president and was the postmaster for several years.

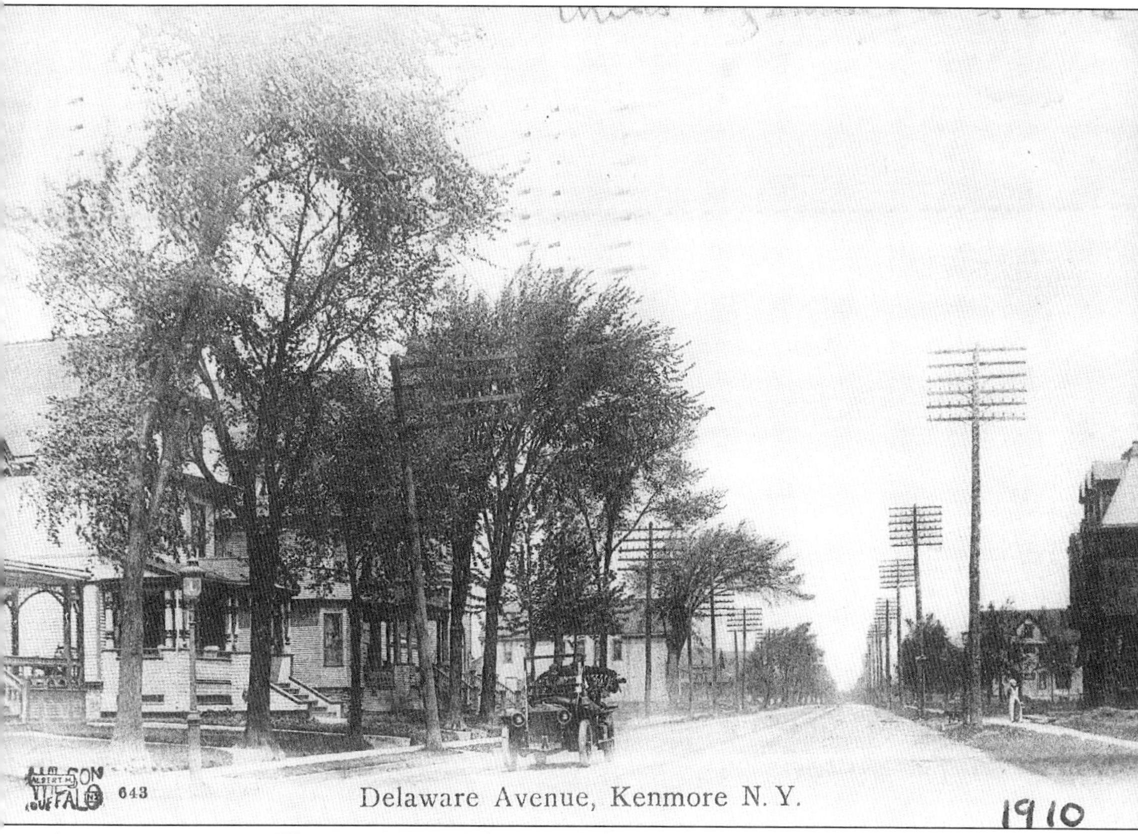

A POSTCARD VIEW OF KENMORE, 1910. This image shows the kind of quiet residential village that Louis Eberhardt envisioned as Buffalo's premier suburb. Substantial houses line both sides of Delaware Avenue just north of the intersections of what are now Parkwood and Tremaine. The only commercial building shown on the avenue is the Hitchcock Block, which from this angle might almost be mistaken for a large home. Only one automobile's engine breaks the almost rural silence; a lone pedestrian walks along on the other side. The trolley tracks are in evidence, proof that the village was accessible from other places, but no clanging streetcars can be seen. The only urban intrusions are the utility poles, and the producer of the card has taken the trouble to obliterate the wires that hung between them. (KVFD collection.)

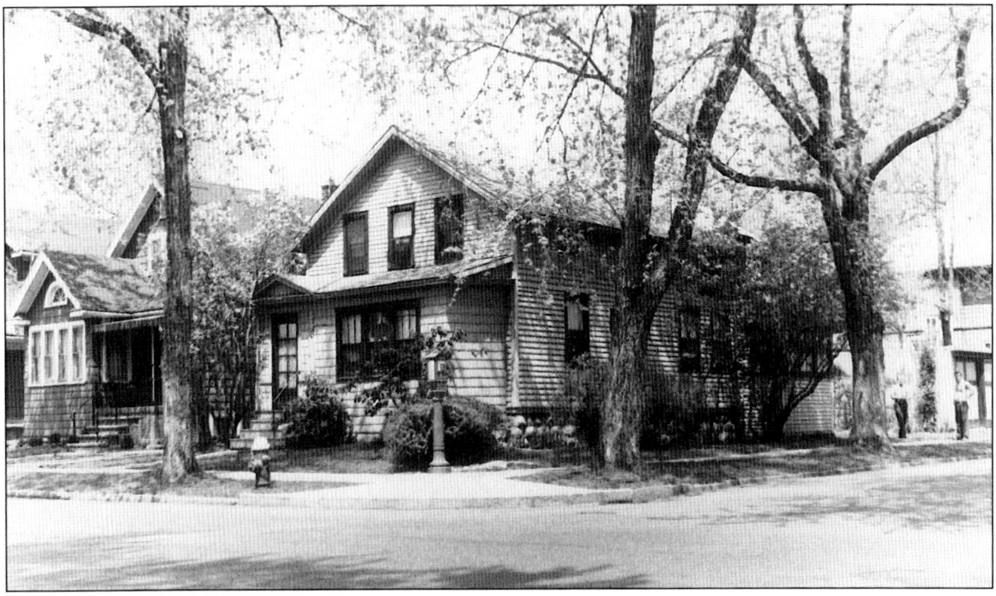

The home at the northwest corner of Myron and East Hazeltine Avenues, believed to be one of the oldest in the village. Piping in the basement of this house is wrapped for insulation with newspapers that date from the 1890s and early1900s. Apparently first built as a single-family dwelling, it is now a multiple dwelling. (Larry H. Oskin photo, TKHS collection.)

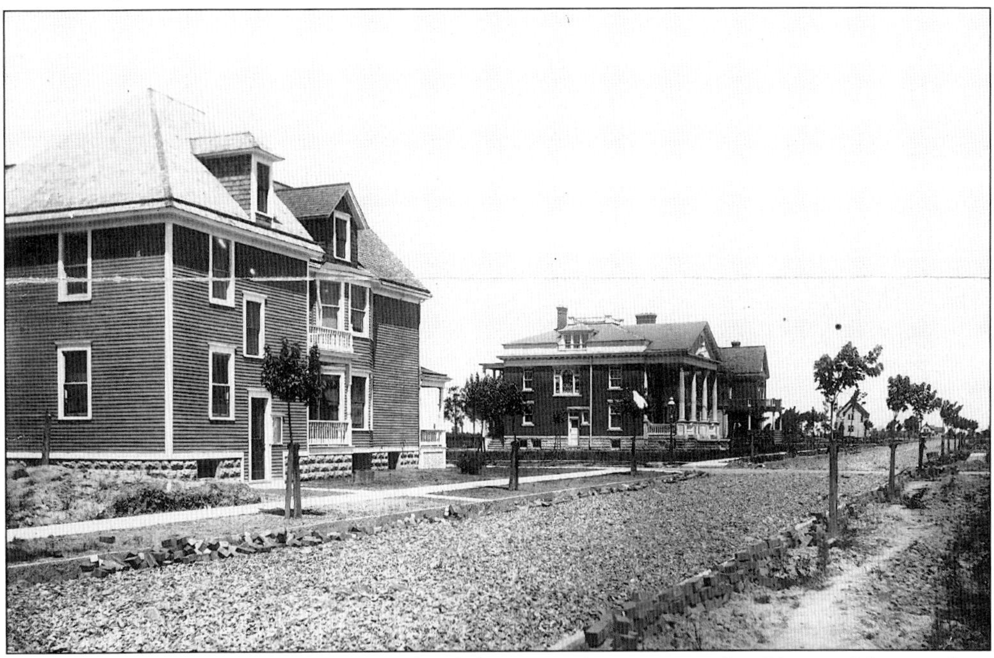

Eugene Avenue, c. 1910. The large, brick house in the center is the Olmstead house, then as now one of Kenmore's most impressive homes. Owner E.B. Olmstead was Kenmore's village president in 1912. The classical revival portico is a well-known village landmark, but other details of the home, such as the stained-glass window on the second story of the south side, are also worthy of attention. The wood frame house at the corner remains largely unchanged.

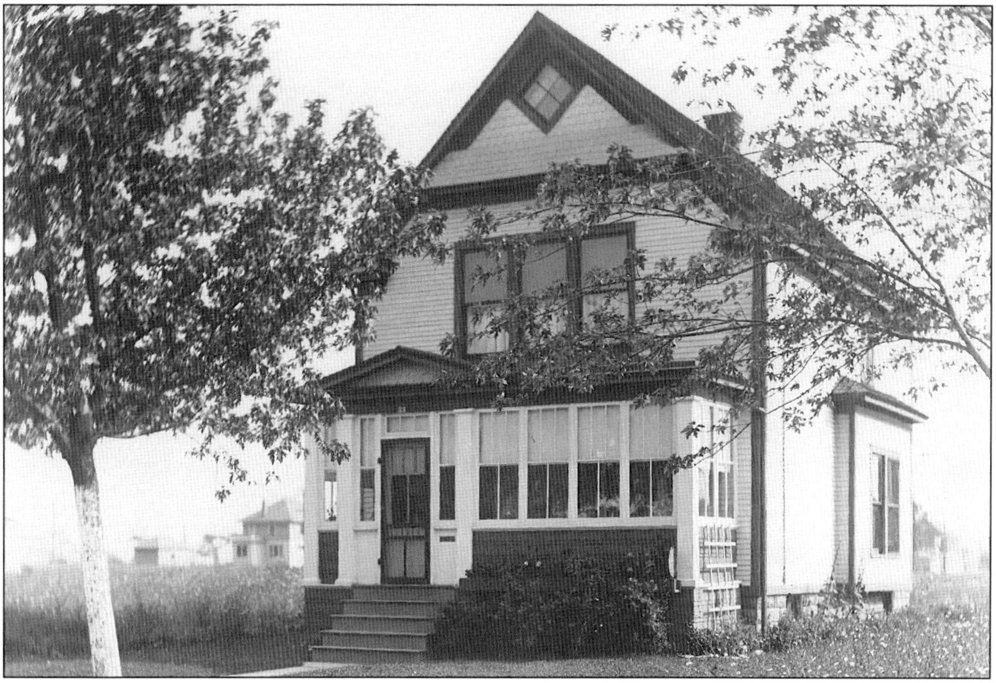

THE HOME AT 33 (NOW 31) ENOLA AVENUE. Although the siding has changed and shutters have been added on the second story, this home retains most of the original features shown here, including the window treatment on the enclosed front porch and the unusual diagonal attic window. This view, looking south, clearly shows that the northern portion of the village was only beginning to develop—open fields dominate the surroundings.

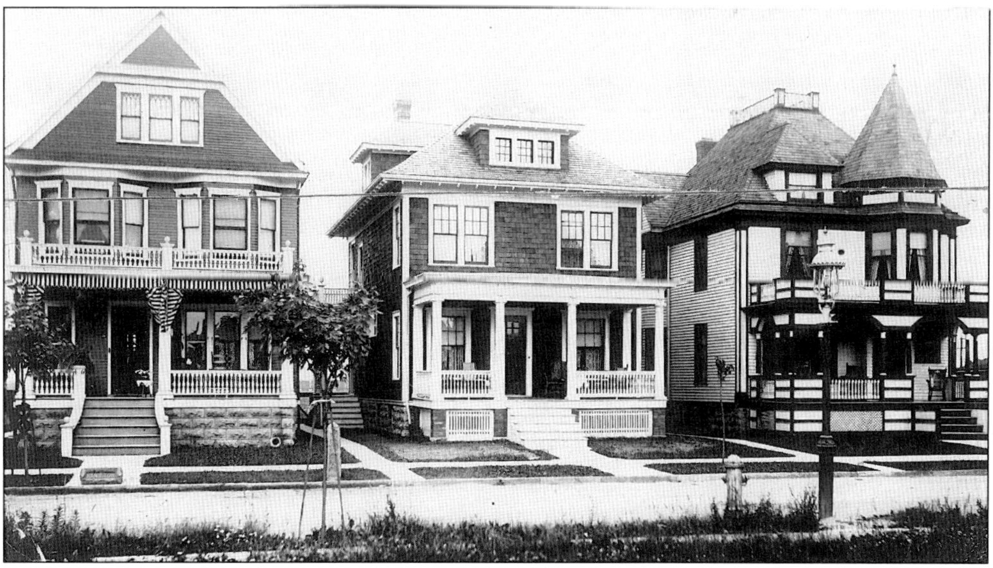

AN EARLY-20TH-CENTURY PHOTOGRAPH OF THREE OF THE ORIGINAL HOUSES ON WEST HAZELTINE, NUMBERS 40, 46, AND 54. All three stand today, though altered in appearance, especially number 54, whose conical tower roof remains, but whose ornamentation has largely been removed or covered. Note that the street already has curbs, sidewalks, gas street lights, and fire hydrants, amenities made easier to obtain by the incorporation of the village.

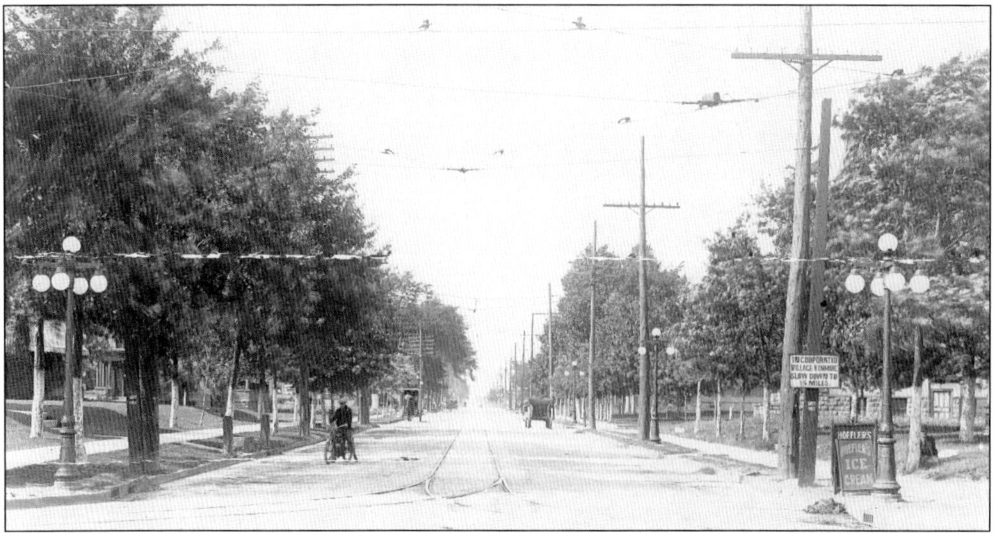

Delaware Avenue at Kenmore Avenue in 1920. Note the 15-mph speed limit, which was strictly enforced. Except for the motorcycle and one automobile in the distance, horse-drawn vehicles were still the rule, necessitating regular street cleaning. The sweepings of "horse exhaust" are neatly piled along the curb for later pick up. At left, in front of the Wheel Chair Home, are hitching posts and a carriage stone, common in that era. Ladies with long skirts needed the step to alight gracefully from a carriage or auto of the day. The trolley line ran to Tonawanda until 1926. The trees have all been whitewashed in an attempt to give the young village a neat appearance.

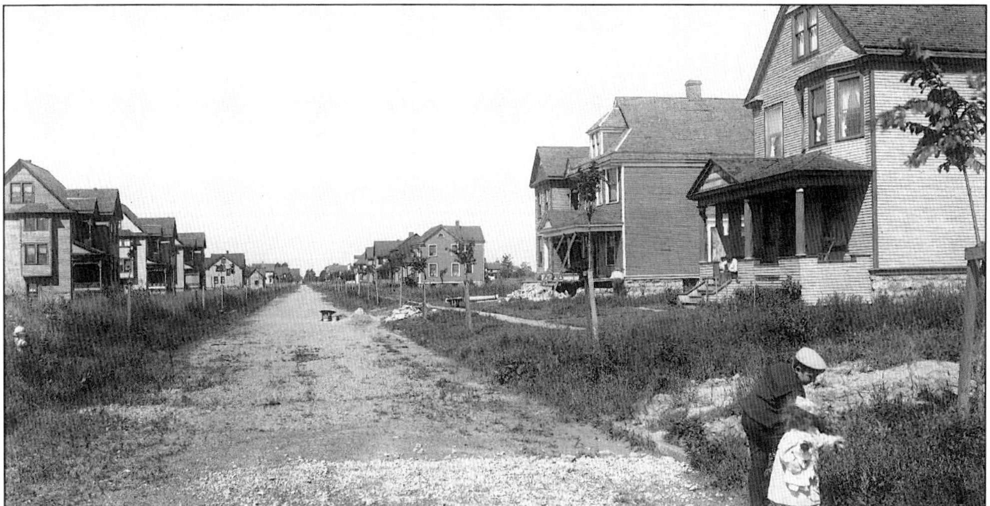

Parkwood Avenue (then called East Tremaine) looking west from Rowley Avenue, c. 1910. Brand new homes, some still getting finishing touches, are fronted by newly planted trees. Though curbs had been installed, this block of Parkwood had yet to be paved. A new fire hydrant appears at left. Construction materials were commonly dumped at the curb in the young village. Automobiles were still rare and astute drivers took great care on the rough side streets. The boy and his sister are picking wild flowers, which were widespread in the tall grasses of as yet unmowed front lawns. The little girl's doll appears to have a black face and is dressed as a cook.

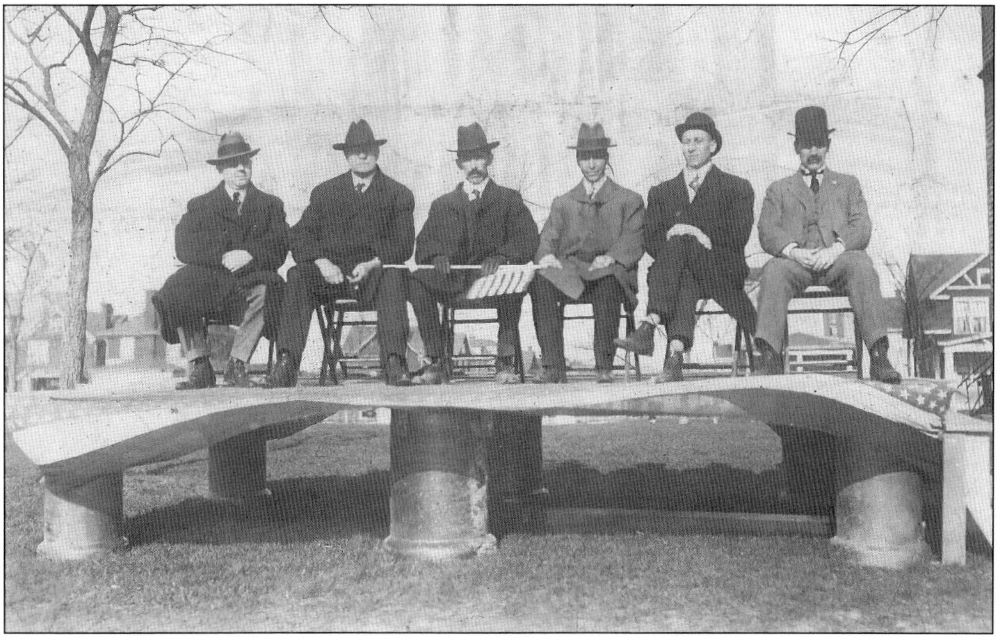

THE KENMORE VILLAGE BOARD, 1909. Seated together on this obviously temporary platform, possibly gathered to review a volunteer fire department parade or field day event, are the political leaders of the ten-year-old village. From left to right are Village Trustees Andrew Seipp and Frank Booth, Village President Matthew Young, Trustee Charles Seaman, Village Clerk Elmer Johnson, and Village Treasurer John Gilbert. (KVFD collection.)

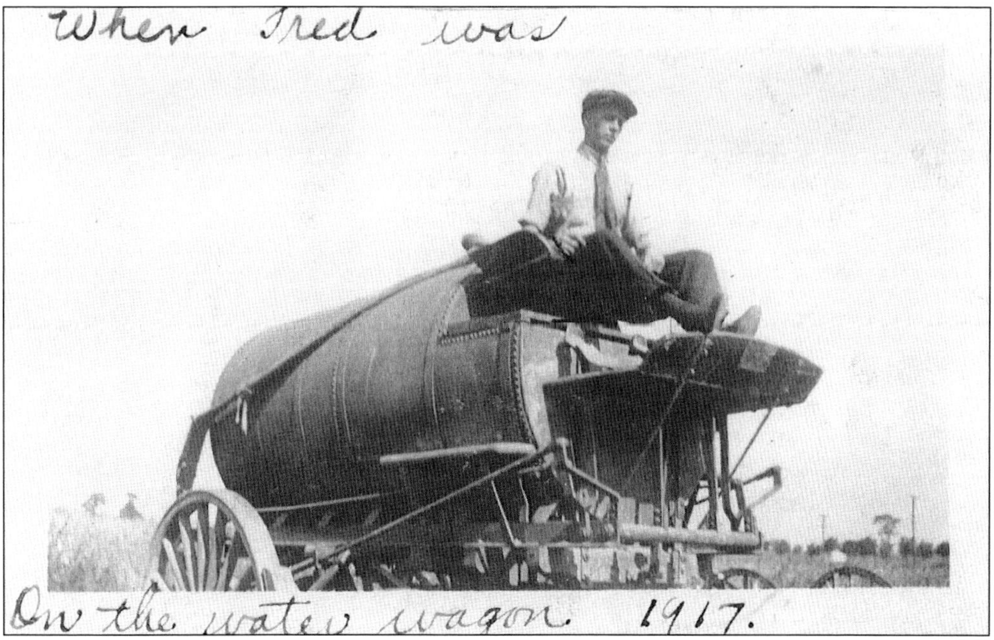

FRED EBERHARDT AND THE WATER WAGON USED TO KEEP THE DUST DOWN ON UNPAVED STREETS, 1917. Fred Eberhardt was one of the pioneer real estate developers in early Kenmore in partnership with his brother L.P.A. He was also Kenmore's second president, serving from 1901 to 1902 (the title was changed to mayor in the 1920s).

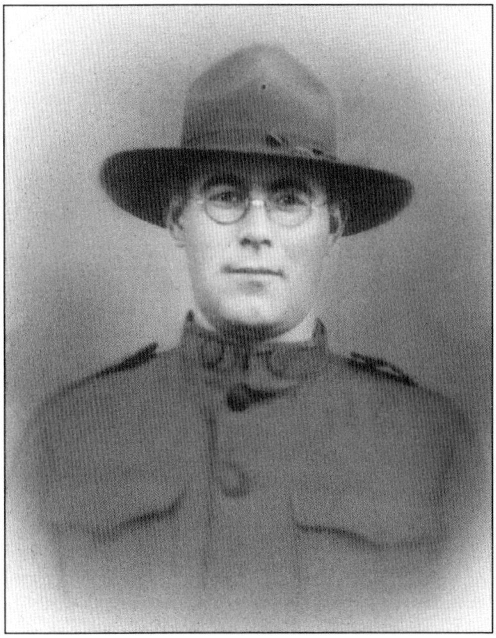

Milton Brounshidle, the first of seven young men from Kenmore who gave their lives for their country in World War I. Brounshidle, Harry Crosby, Lambert Keller, and Winfield Kimmins were killed in action. Joseph Byrnes, Frederick Eberhardt Jr., and Owen Fisher also died in service. Village streets carry the names of Crosby and Keller; all are memorialized on the monument on the village green shown on p. 66.

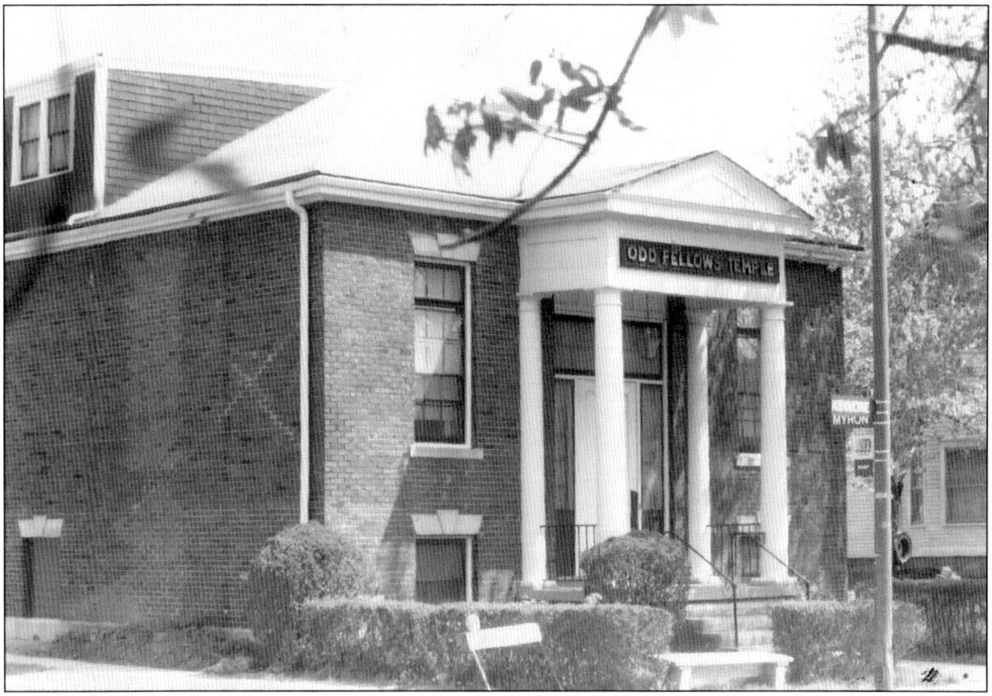

The Odd Fellows Temple/Machinists Hall at the corner of Kenmore and Myron. The first fraternal organization in the village, Kenmore Lodge No. 795, Independent Order of Odd Fellows was founded in 1913, and placed the cornerstone for this hall the next year. The building, whose outside appearance has changed little over the years, long served as a meeting place for the Odd Fellows and other organizations. It is now home to Local Lodge 447 of the International Association of Machinists and Aerospace Workers, which has preserved the exterior and some of the unique interior features.

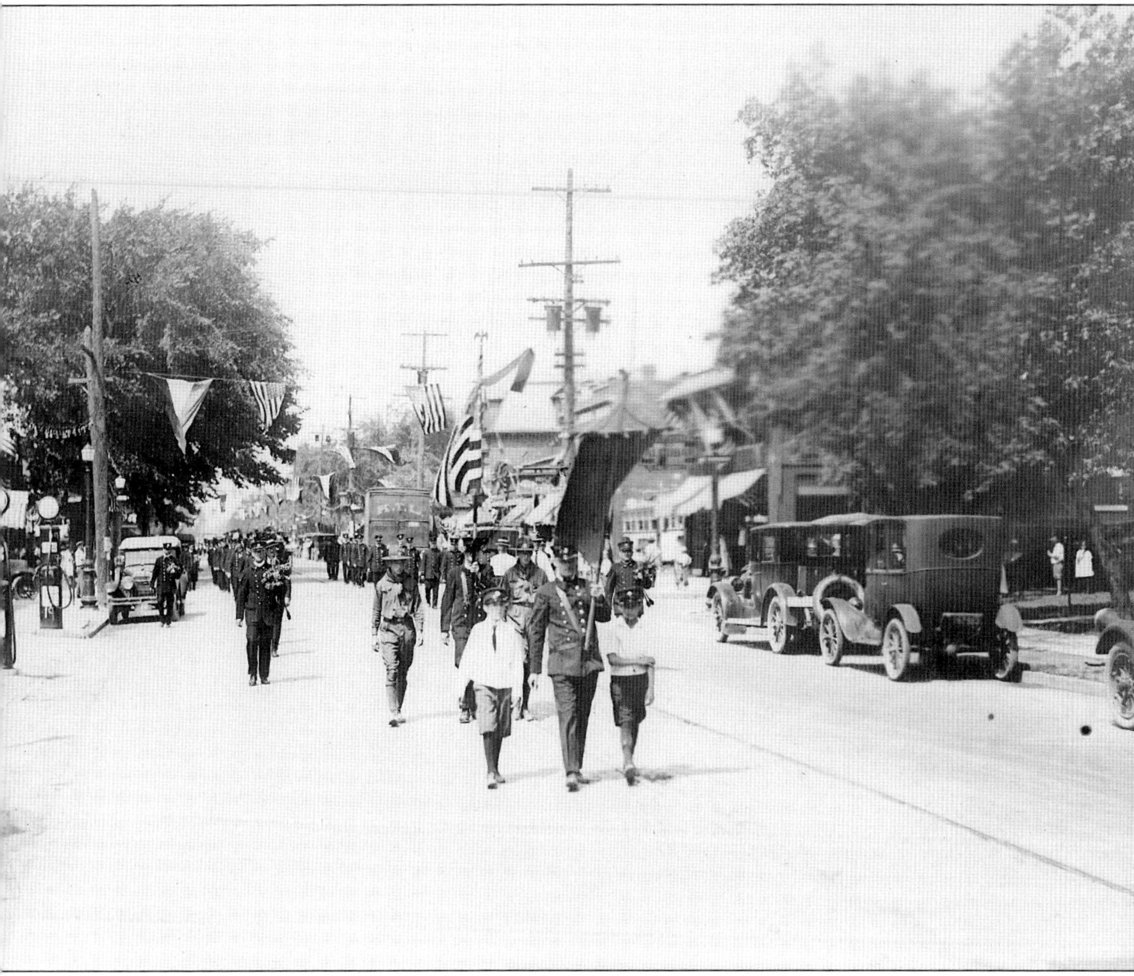

An Independence Day parade on Delaware Avenue in 1924. Volunteer firemen with two junior members and Boy Scout leaders head the parade. Forty-eight-star flags wave throughout the village. Looking north from West Hazeltine, the Alcobar can be seen at Parkwood; next to it is the Green Lantern Lunch Car. At the extreme right the front of a Pierce-Arrow motor car can be seen with its patented "bullfrog" headlights. Many Kenmorites worked at the Elmwood plant of Buffalo's most prestigious automobile company. On the left is an early gasoline filling station.

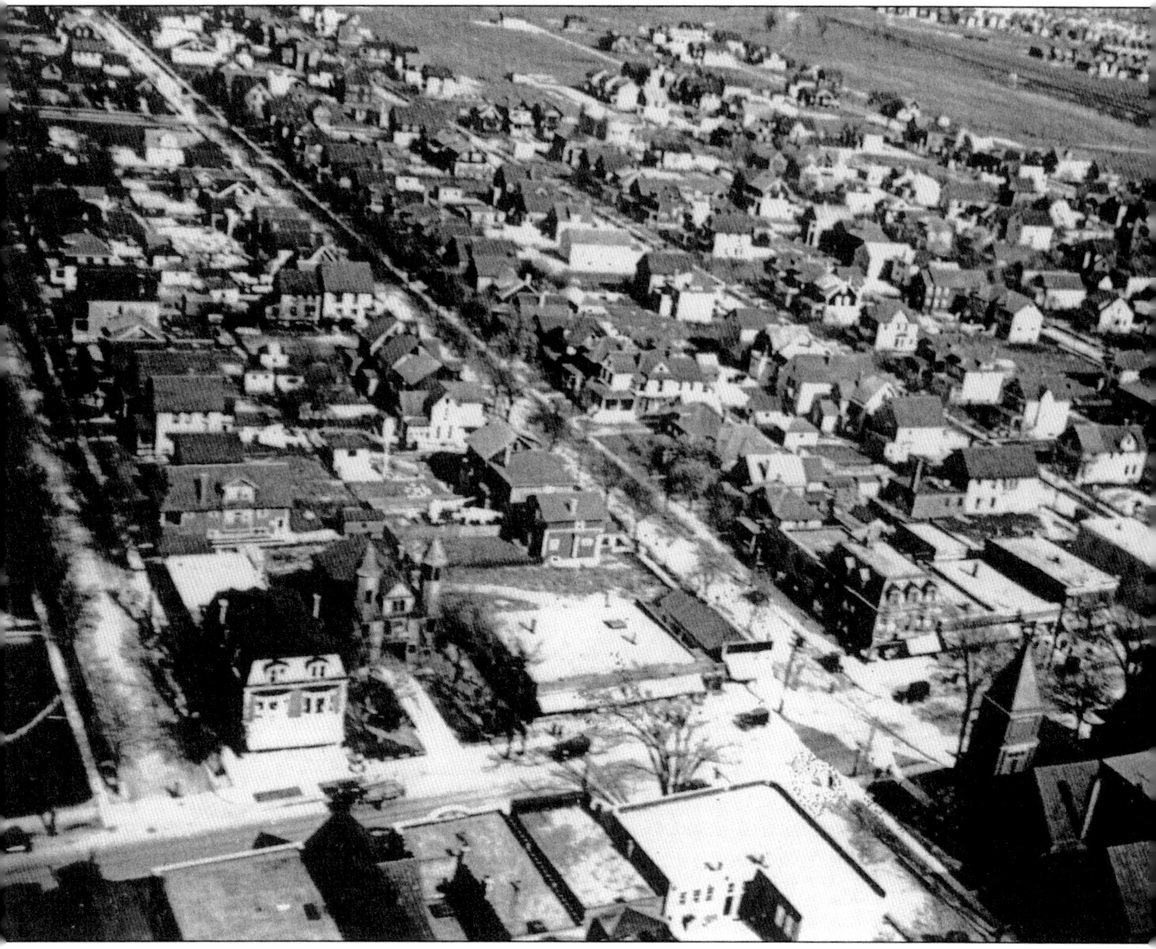

AN AERIAL VIEW OF KENMORE'S EAST SIDE, C. 1923. The Kenmore Methodist-Episcopal Church (bottom right), Donovan Bros. Drug Store (across LaSalle on the corner), and the old fire hall with its twin towers (across Delaware Avenue) can be seen here. East side streets from the left are Warren, Euclid, Parkwood, East Hazeltine, and Kenmore Avenues. In "South Kenmore," Villa Avenue and Sanders Road have been developed. The DL&W and Erie Railroad belt line tracks are at the upper right; the IRC trolley car route with its poles passes under those tracks and continues on toward Kenmore Avenue.

Three

YEARS OF GROWTH

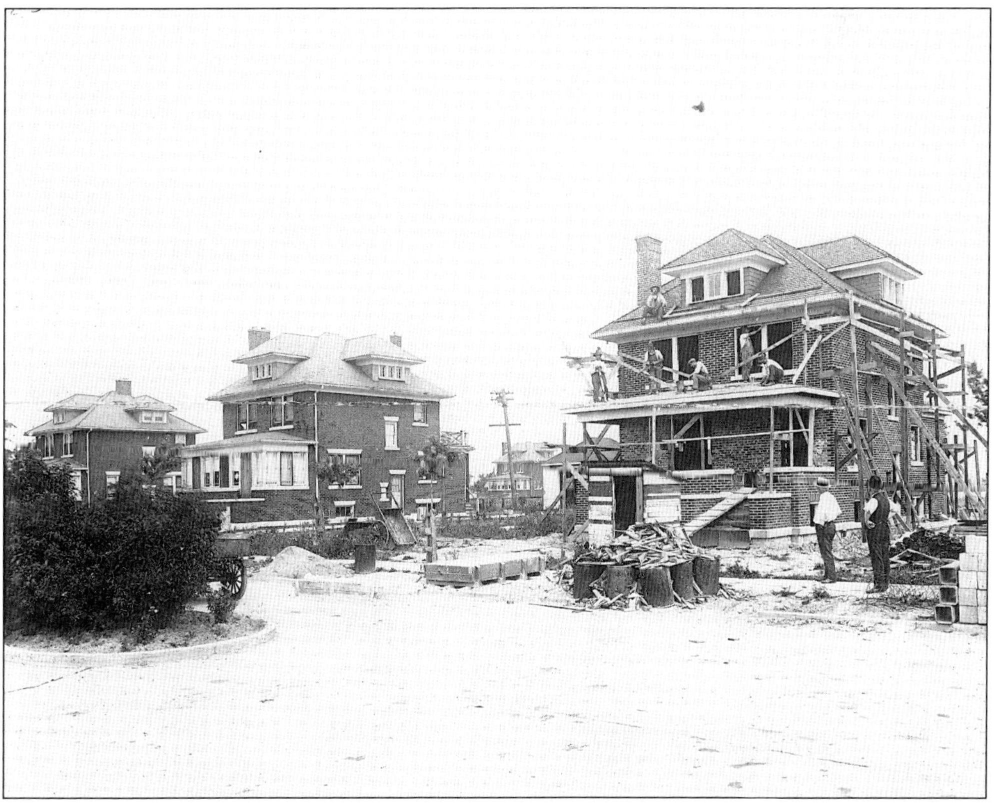

NUMBER 30 EAST GIRARD BOULEVARD UNDER CONSTRUCTION, C. 1920. This view looks northwest toward Delaware Avenue. The distinctive brick home joins two similar homes recently erected. In the background can be seen a home at Delaware and Somerton, where Paddoch Chevrolet now stands.

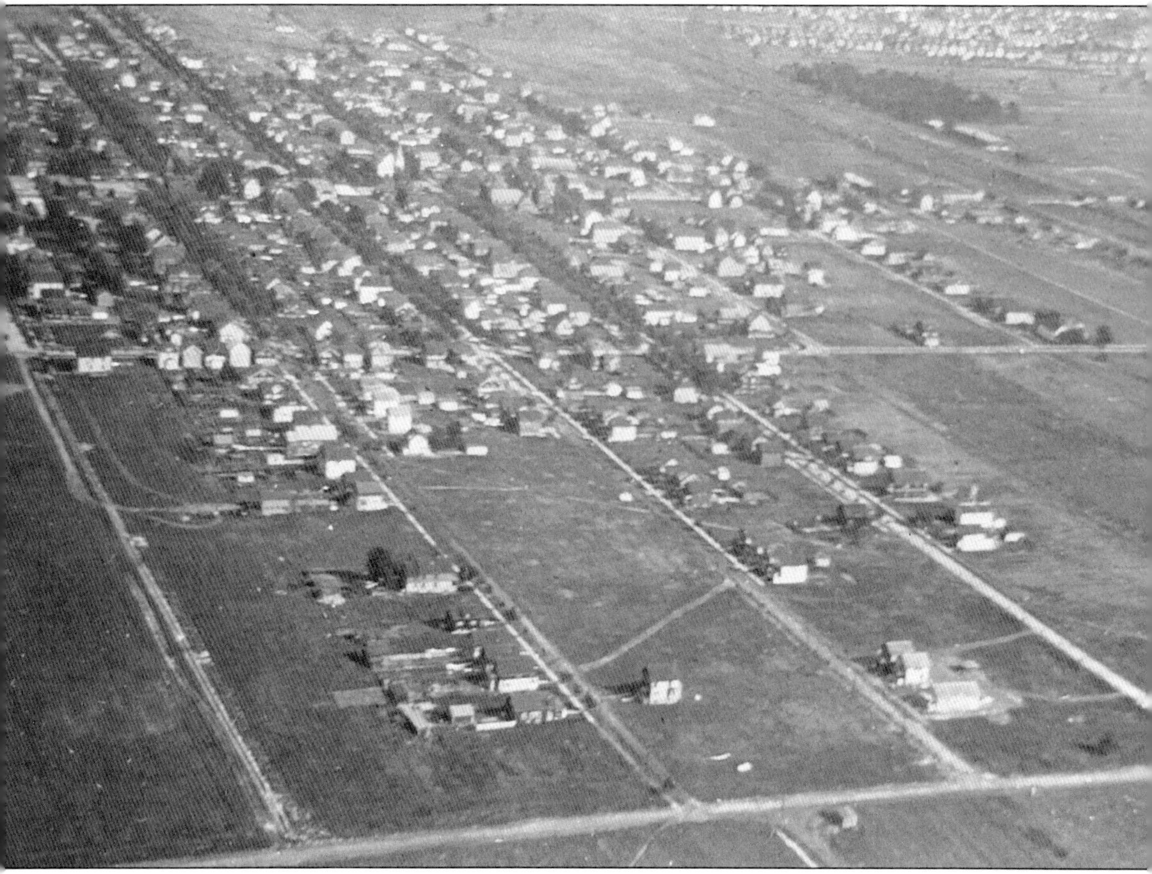

AN AERIAL VIEW OF KENMORE LOOKING EAST FROM ELMWOOD AVENUE. The formerly unpaved dirt trail was improved with concrete pavement and extended from Kenmore Avenue to Knoche Road in 1923. West Hazeltine was the principal east-west street in the village until Kenmore Avenue was paved later in the 1920s. The wooded areas near the belt-line railroads were a forbidden, yet oft-frequented, place for Kenmore boys to play. In the early 1920s, Kenmore's built-up area covered little more than a block on either side of Delaware Avenue and only as far north as Mang Avenue.

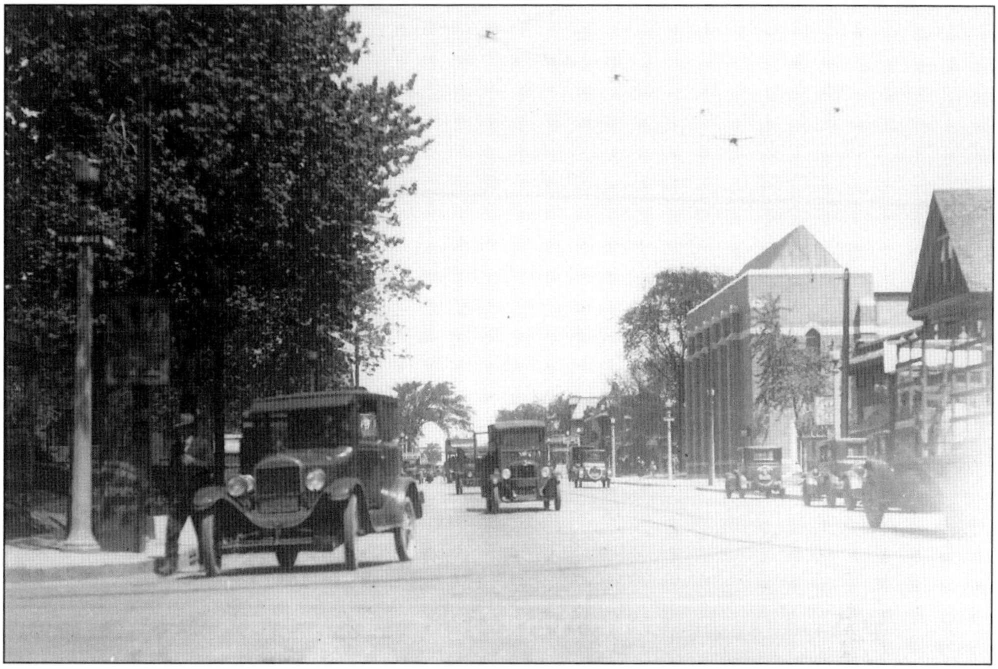

DELAWARE AVENUE IN 1928. By this time, Delaware had become a busier and more commercial street than originally envisioned. The buildings to the right, on the east side of Delaware, are businesses, the exception being the new Presbyterian church. The streetcar tracks that ran east and west on Kenmore Avenue and north on Delaware are shown clearly, as are the overhead trolley wires. Note the up-to-date concrete lampposts.

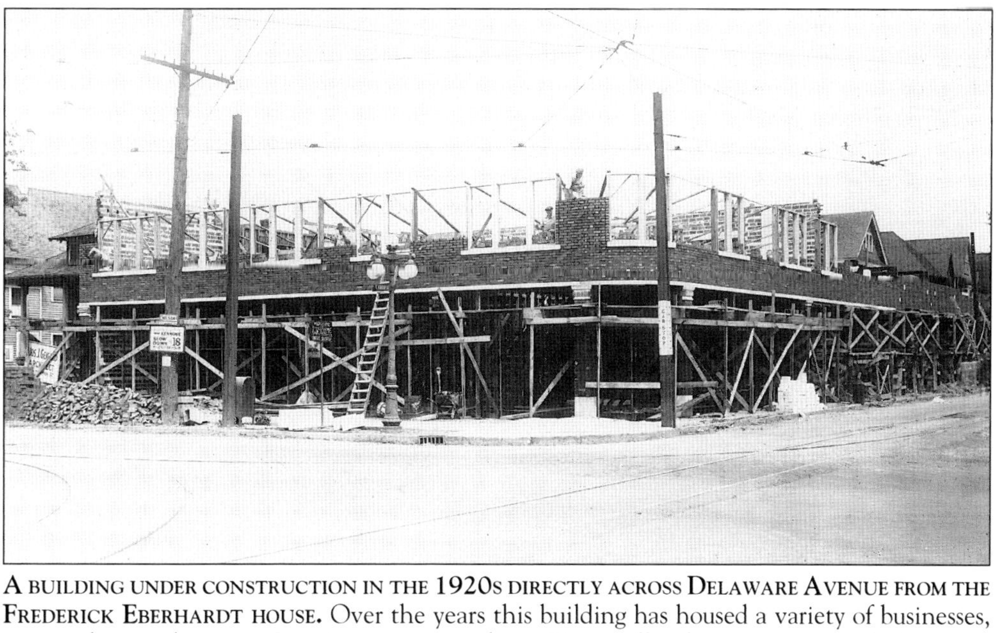

A BUILDING UNDER CONSTRUCTION IN THE 1920S DIRECTLY ACROSS DELAWARE AVENUE FROM THE FREDERICK EBERHARDT HOUSE. Over the years this building has housed a variety of businesses, among them a pharmacy, Love's ice cream parlor, a Deco coffee shop, a pizzeria and submarine shop, at least two taverns, an A&P market, barber and beauty shops, and most recently, Louie's Texas Red Hots. Notice the street car stop and the 18-mph village speed limit.

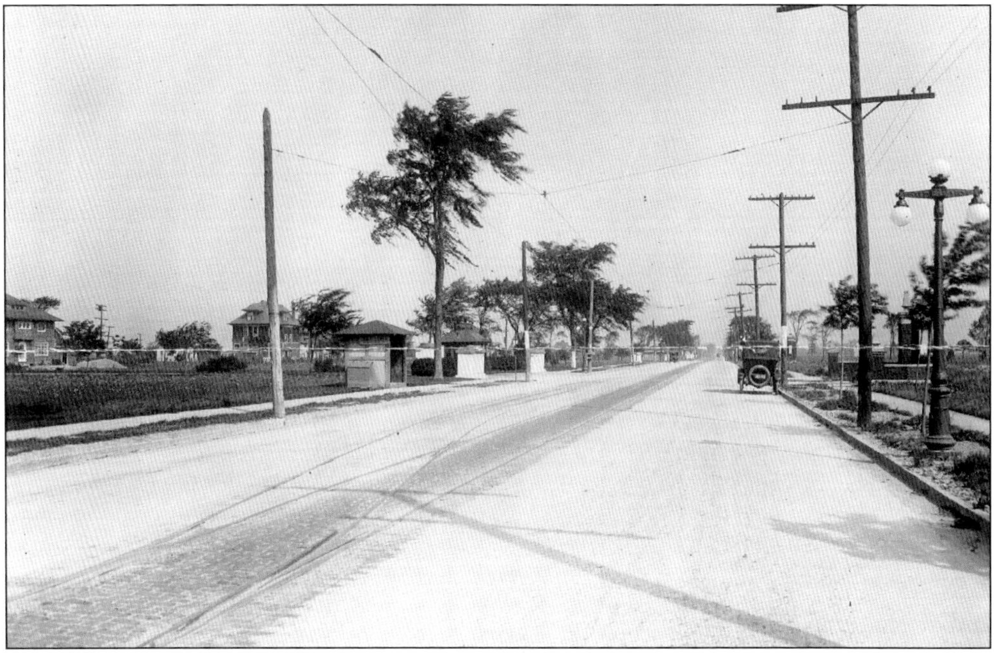

DELAWARE AVENUE LOOKING NORTH FROM COURIER IN 1924. The East Girard entrance pillars are at the right. To the left are pillars for West Girard and a trolley waiting station for "Kenmore Estates." The turnout led to one of three passing sidings for the streetcars between Kenmore and Tonawanda. Only three vehicles appear on Delaware Avenue. Driving and parking were a cinch in those days!

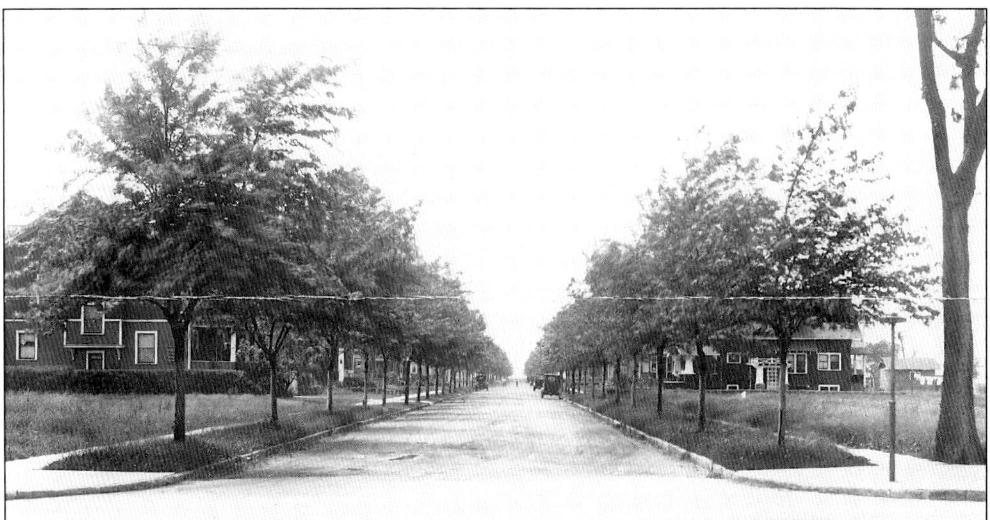

KINSEY AND DELAWARE AVENUES. Kinsey Avenue awaits pavement, but curbs and concrete sidewalks have been installed, streetlights are in place, and trees have been planted beginning at Delaware Avenue (in the foreground). The undeveloped lots at both corners of Kinsey and Delaware would eventually contain commercial structures, as the village's main thoroughfare increasingly assumed a business, rather than a residential, character.

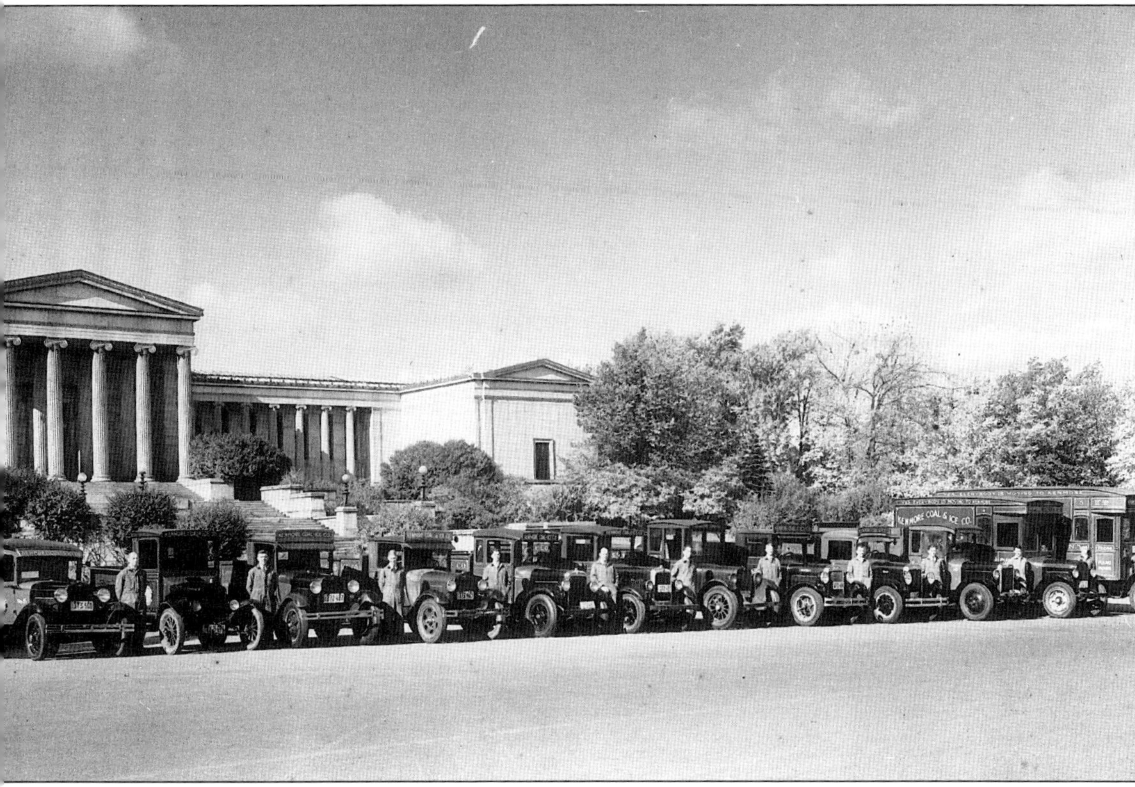

"Everybody is moving to Kenmore," c. 1930. At a time when the Great Depression was beginning to show its baleful effects on all kinds of businesses, including those connected with real estate, this publicity picture was used to entice potential home buyers to move to the village. The trucks are from the Kenmore Coal and Ice Co., which was also engaged in the moving business. They are shown lined up in front of one of the Buffalo's most famous and beautiful buildings, the E.B. Green-designed Albright Art Gallery in Delaware Park. How many potential—or actual—homeowners were attracted is impossible to tell at this point, but it certainly resulted in a unique photograph. Automotive buffs can enjoy examining the vehicles, attempting to discern the years and makes depicted; architecture fans can enjoy the view of the gallery as it looked over a half-century ago.

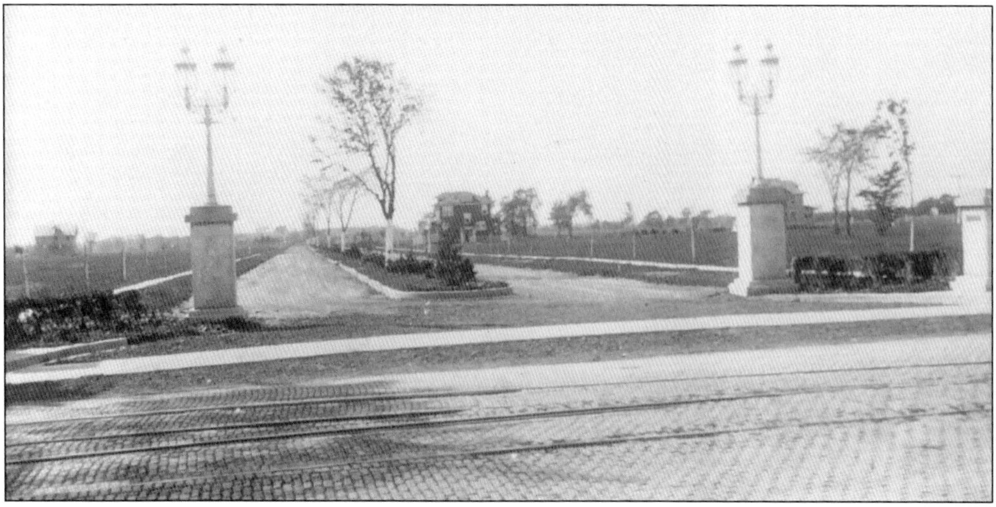

West Girard as seen from Delaware Avenue about 1920. Many of Kenmore's early streets had pillars of various designs to mark them as unique and somewhat upscale neighborhoods. West Girard's boulevard was removed many years ago, as were the pillars. The home standing alone at #71 would soon be surrounded by others built during the building boom of the 1920s. The Delaware Avenue streetcar tracks had a passing siding between Girard and Palmer Avenues so trolleys could operate both ways on the single-car track to Tonawanda.

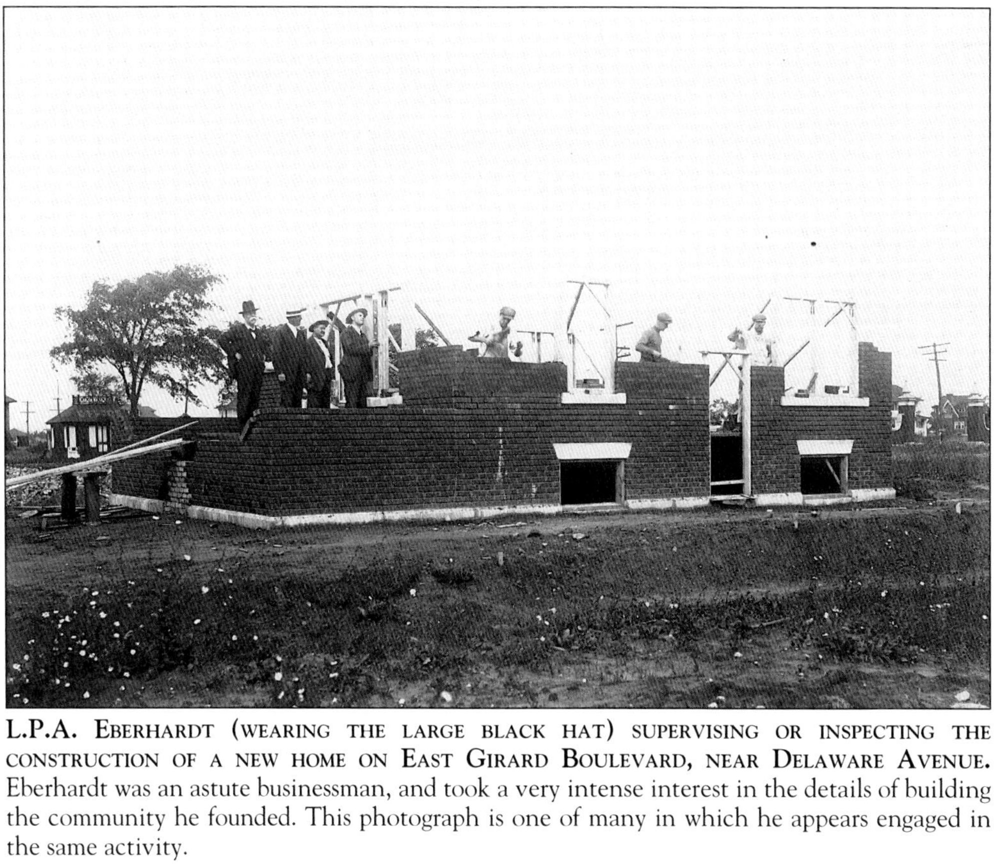

L.P.A. Eberhardt (wearing the large black hat) supervising or inspecting the construction of a new home on East Girard Boulevard, near Delaware Avenue. Eberhardt was an astute businessman, and took a very intense interest in the details of building the community he founded. This photograph is one of many in which he appears engaged in the same activity.

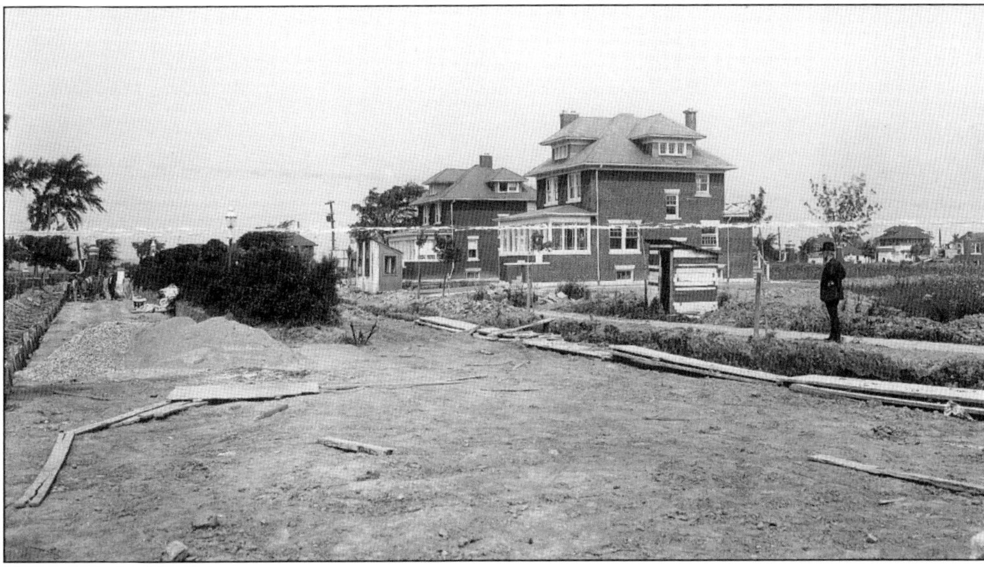

A 1920–21 VIEW OF NEW CONSTRUCTION ON EAST GIRARD LOOKING WEST TOWARD DELAWARE AVENUE. Forms for curbs have been prepared on the south side; the sand and gravel for the concrete is piled in what will be the roadway. Bushes are planted in the divider, which also has its street lighting. One of the pillars that set off the entrances to streets in the northern part of the village can be seen in the left background.

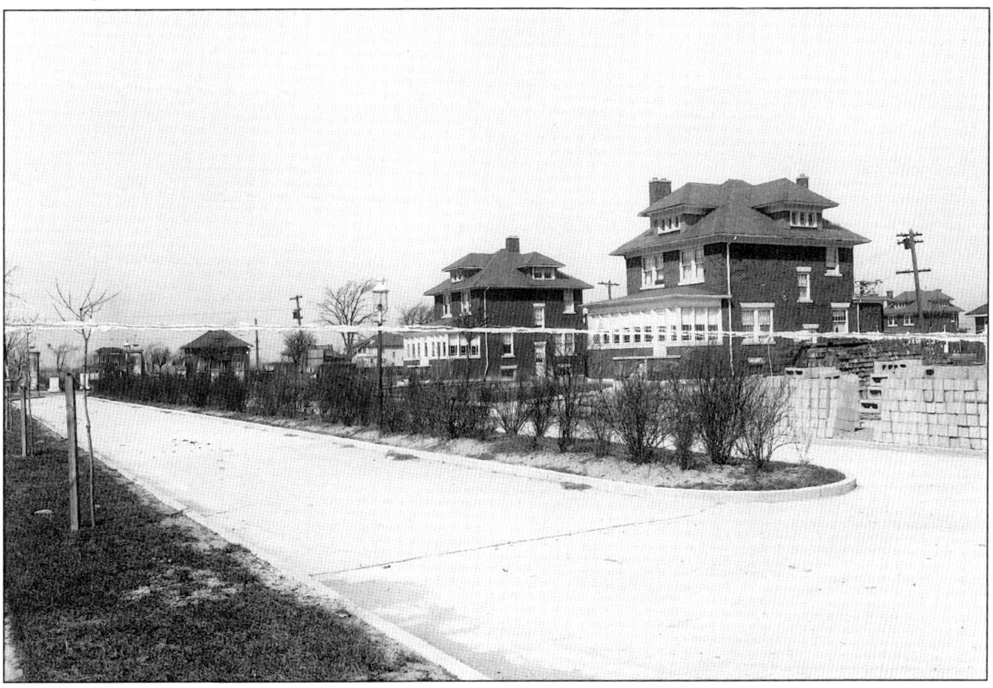

EAST GIRARD, A FEW MONTHS AFTER THE PREVIOUS PICTURE WAS TAKEN. The street already has a much more finished appearance—trees have been planted, curbs have been poured, and the roadway is paved. The houses are occupied (one has an automobile parked in front), and a stack of concrete blocks stands ready for the construction of the next dwelling to be built. The entry pillars (since removed) can be seen at the beginning of the street.

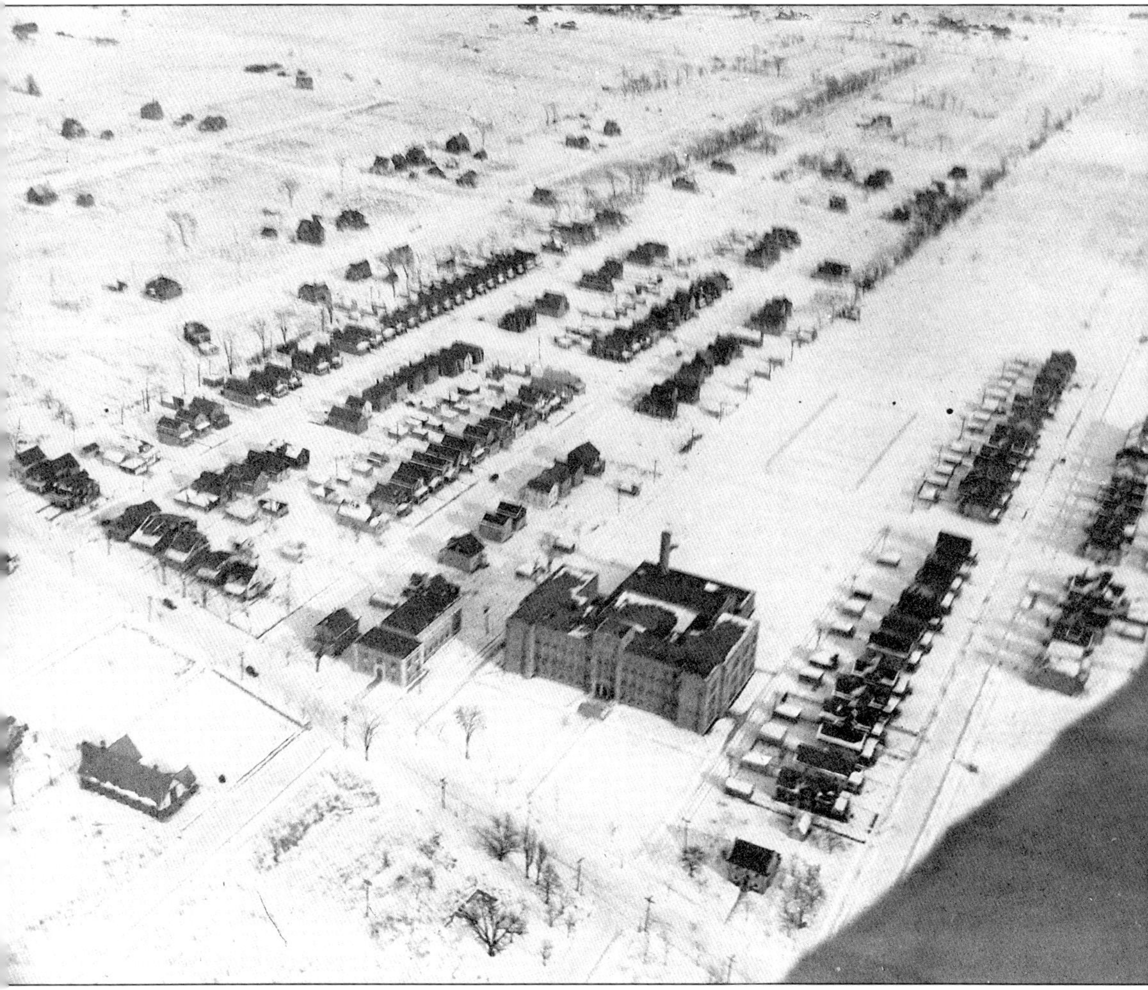

An early 1927 aerial view of the new Kenmore Junior-Senior High School and its surrounding neighborhood. When the school opened in November 1924, it was already overcrowded, and the Masonic Lodge building to its left was pressed into service as emergency classroom space. By autumn of 1927, both the new school and Washington School were on half-sessions awaiting the completion of a large addition on the rear of the 1924 building. Across Delaware Road from the Masonic building stands Pilgrim Lutheran Church, dedicated in 1925. Directly across from the school are the foundations of the former Jacob Heimiller farm. The old buildings were torn down to clear the land for the new Kenmore Methodist-Episcopal Church, which would be completed in 1928. Crosby Avenue (at right) already has 45 homes built on it, most with garages. Nassau and Stillwell Avenues have been built up, with one house even beyond Colvin. Twenty homes have been completed in the upscale Deerhurst subdivision. The fenced area on school property just east of Myron Avenue was the high school tennis courts. Lindbergh School would be built in 1931 at the east end of the school property.

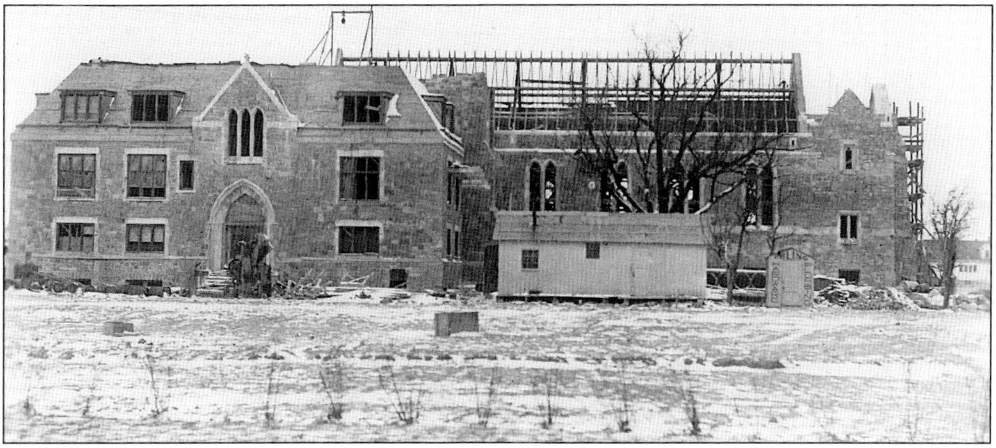

THE KENMORE UNITED METHODIST CHURCH UNDER CONSTRUCTION EARLY IN 1928. The original Methodist-Episcopal church stood at Delaware and LaSalle for 35 years. Many people in the village thought the Methodists were "a bit daft" to build so far out of the village center. Construction began in 1927 with the demolition of the old Jacob Heimiller farmhouse on Delaware Road at Madison Avenue (now Landers Road). The first sod was turned late in July and the cornerstone ceremony was held in September. The gray, stone, English Gothic church was dedicated on Sunday, June 17, 1928.

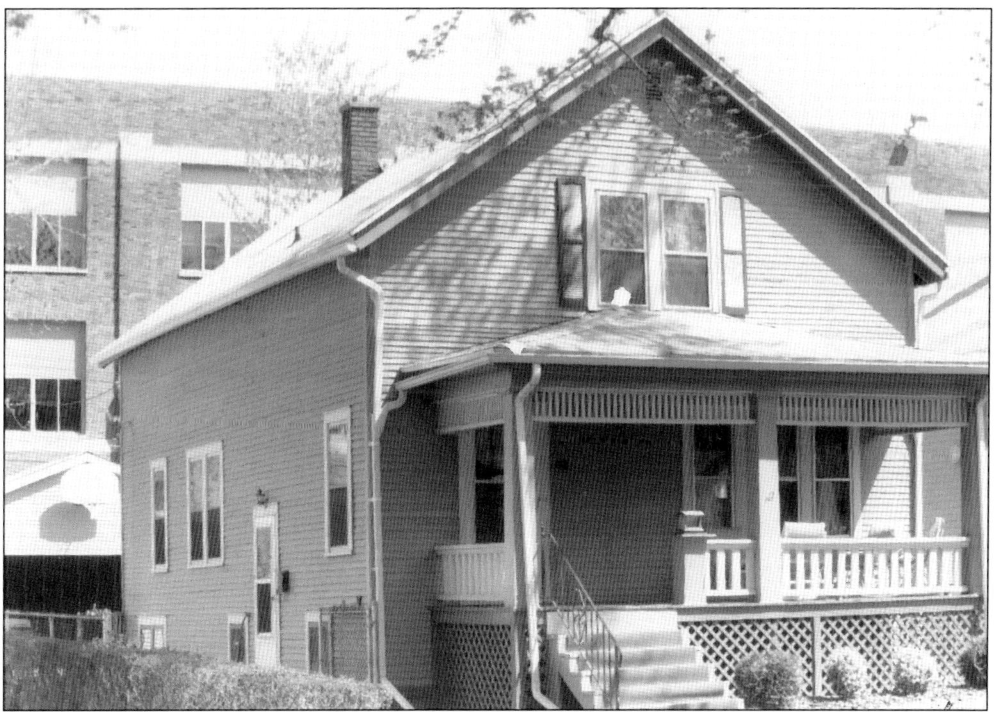

THE SINGLE-FAMILY HOME AT 42 CROSBY AVENUE, APPROXIMATELY HALF-WAY BETWEEN DELAWARE ROAD AND MYRON AVENUE. This was one of the first single-family homes to be constructed on the street formerly called East Wabash. A surviving advertisement from the realtor gives the price of the new house as $6,000. In this photo, taken some 75 years after the house was built, it is easily recognizable, its exterior appearance having changed little. The present Kenmore Middle School can be seen in the background.

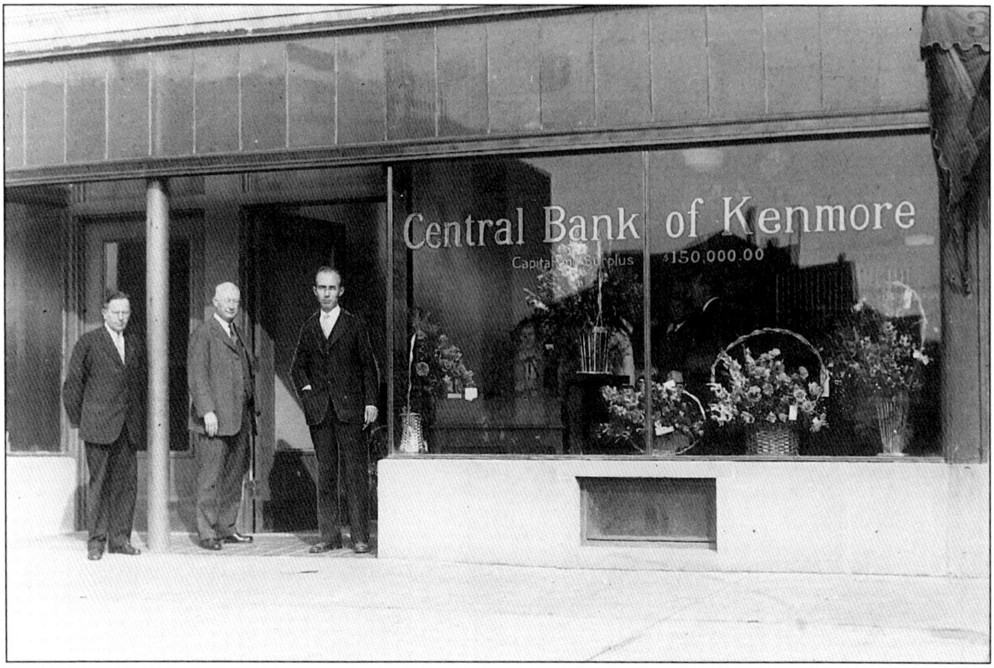

THE CENTRAL BANK OF KENMORE ON OPENING DAY, OCTOBER, 1 1927. Located in the Kenmore Theater block where Kenmore Towers stands now, this bank was actually an "uptown" branch of Kenmore's State Bank, with which it merged in 1935. The principal officers were, from left to right, Howard Inskip, George Wallace, and Leonard Rauthenberg. Their initial capitalization of $150,000 was equivalent to over a million dollars today.

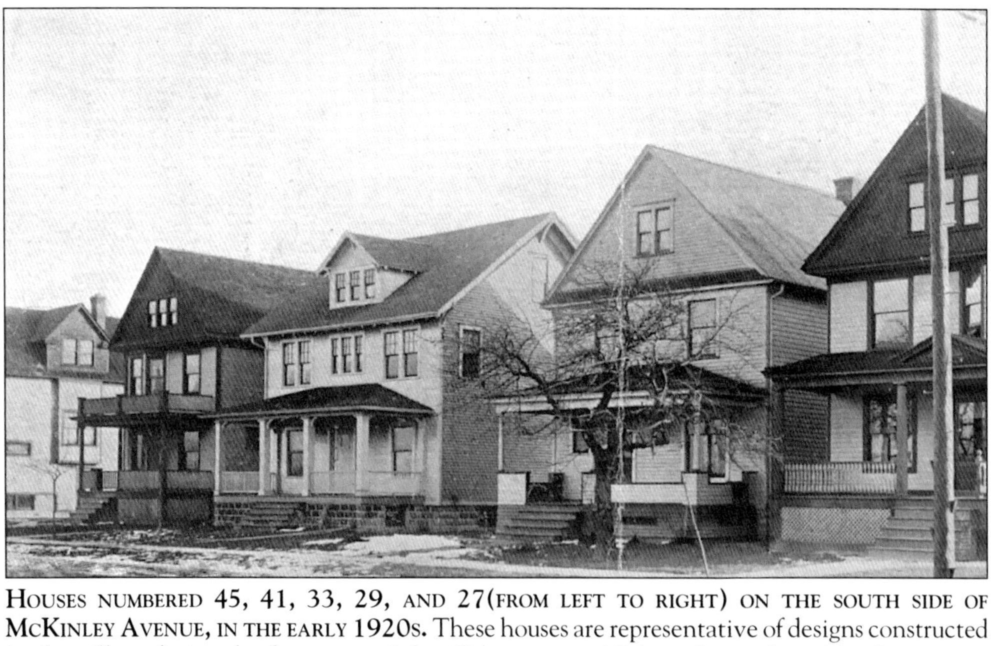

HOUSES NUMBERED 45, 41, 33, 29, AND 27(FROM LEFT TO RIGHT) ON THE SOUTH SIDE OF MCKINLEY AVENUE, IN THE EARLY 1920S. These houses are representative of designs constructed in the village during the first years of the 20th century. All have been altered in the ensuing years, some more than others, and another home was built between numbers 41 and 45. The newer house is now numbered 41; the original 41 is now 39.

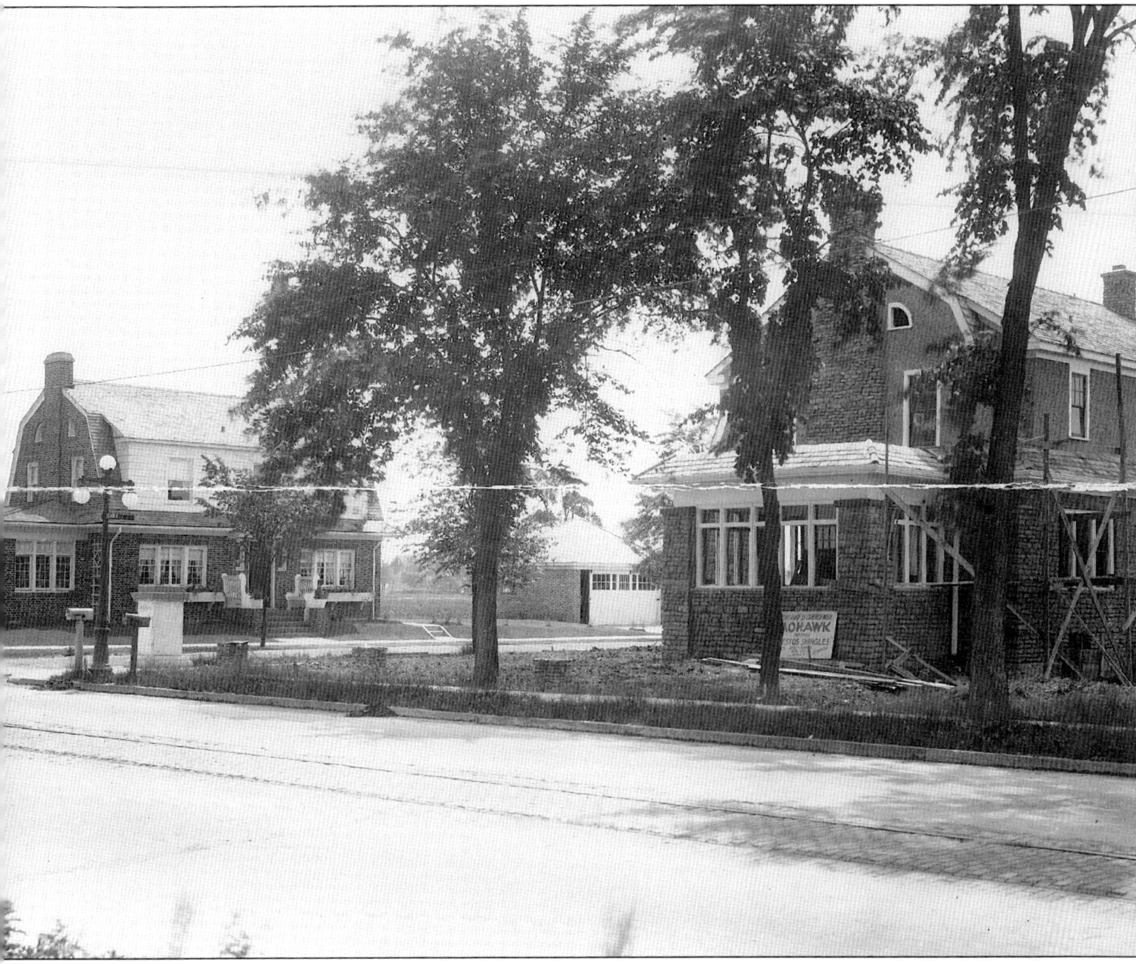

TWO "DUTCH COLONIAL" HOUSES AT THE CORNER OF PALMER AND DELAWARE AVENUES. In the middle and late 1920s, the village was growing toward its northern and eastern boundaries. These two houses are typical of the fashionable domestic architecture of the period (notice also the now long-removed entry pillars). They may represent an attempt to maintain the residential character of Delaware Avenue, but the street was destined to become mainly commercial. The home on the northwest corner was eventually adapted for business use, and for many years a large A&P market and its parking lot occupied the remainder of the block northward to West Girard. Another plaza, which for several years housed a Loblaw's supermarket, was located diagonally across the street between East Girard and Columbia. When the A&P closed, a small shopping and office plaza and a restaurant replaced it. By 1998, with the restaurant closed and the plaza largely vacated, the Walgreen's chain applied for a permit to locate a new store in its place. After considerable controversy about the character of the avenue, potential traffic, and the need for another chain drugstore (the village already had three such within its limits), permission was given for Walgreen's to utilize the entire block. Adjacent houses on West Girard and Palmer were demolished or moved. The house shown here on the left, across Palmer, remains at its original location.

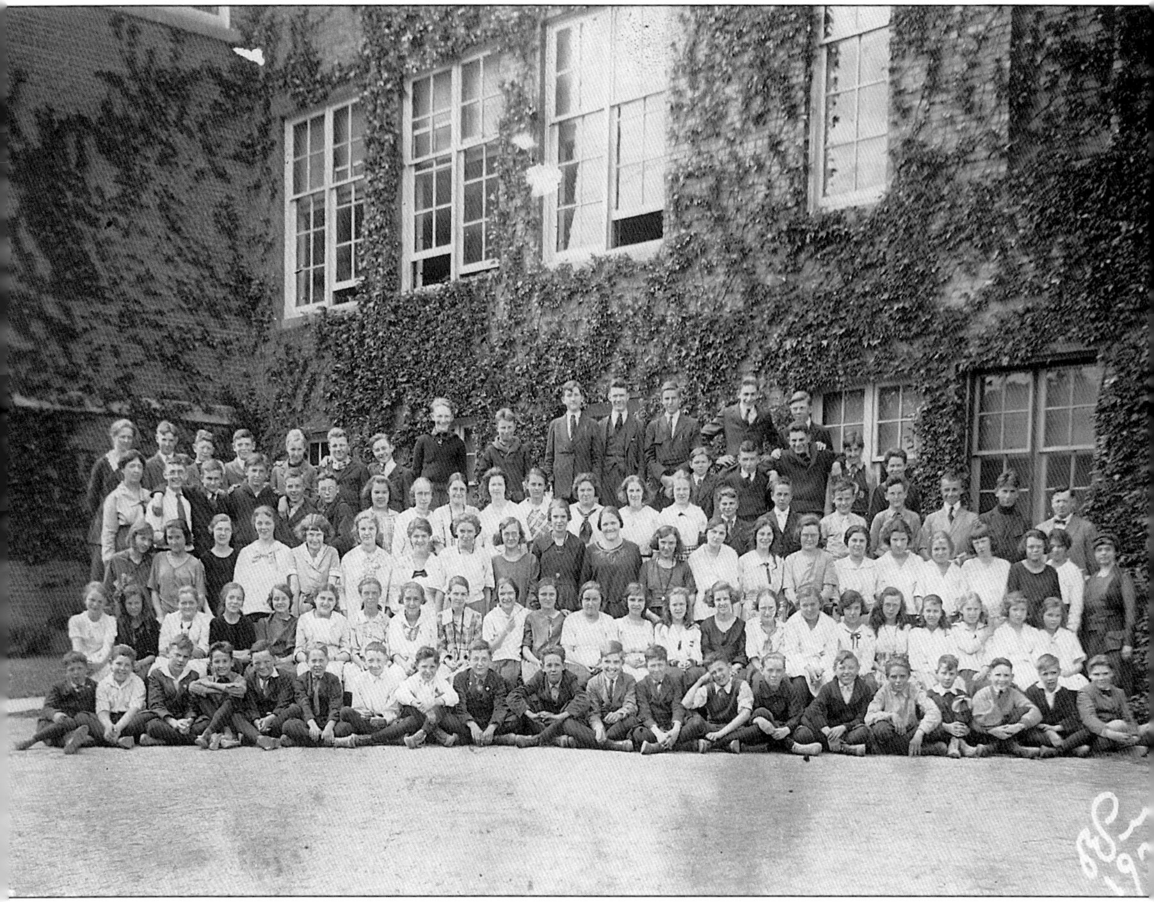

THE KENMORE GRAMMAR SCHOOL'S 7TH AND 8TH GRADES IN 1921, OUTSIDE OF THE DISTRICT SCHOOL BUILDING ON DELAWARE AVENUE AT WARREN. The grammar and high schools shared this building from the time it was constructed in 1911 until 1924, when the 7th through 12th grades were moved to the new junior and senior high school, three blocks north on Delaware Road. At that time the district school building became the George Washington Elementary School. This photograph is one of the clearest available of the school during the last few years it served multiple functions. The pupils are not identified on the photograph, but their teachers are. In keeping with the customs of the time, when teachers' first names were never spoken aloud—at least to their faces—by the children they taught, the four teachers are identified simply as Miss Veile, Miss Babcock, Miss Stinnard, and Mrs. Moore. Washington School underwent major renovations in 1957–58; it was closed in 1982 and subsequently sold to Heritage Centers. (Readers who can identify any of the pupils are invited to contact the Tonawanda-Kenmore Historical Society, which will be pleased to add the names to those of the teachers listed on the back of the photo.)

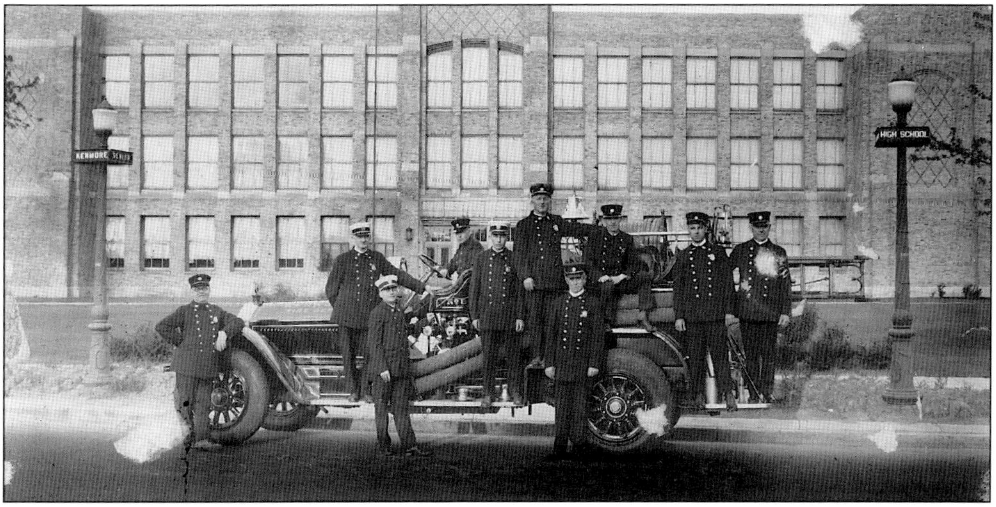

A 1926 PHOTOGRAPH OF VILLAGE VOLUNTEER FIREFIGHTERS AND THEIR EQUIPMENT IN FRONT OF THE ALMOST NEW JUNIOR AND SENIOR HIGH SCHOOL ON DELAWARE ROAD (NOW THE MIDDLE SCHOOL). In 1924 this school replaced the former high school three blocks south at the Delawares and Wardman. Look closely at the street signs mounted on the lampposts; they are labeled "Kenmore" and "High School." (KVFD collection.)

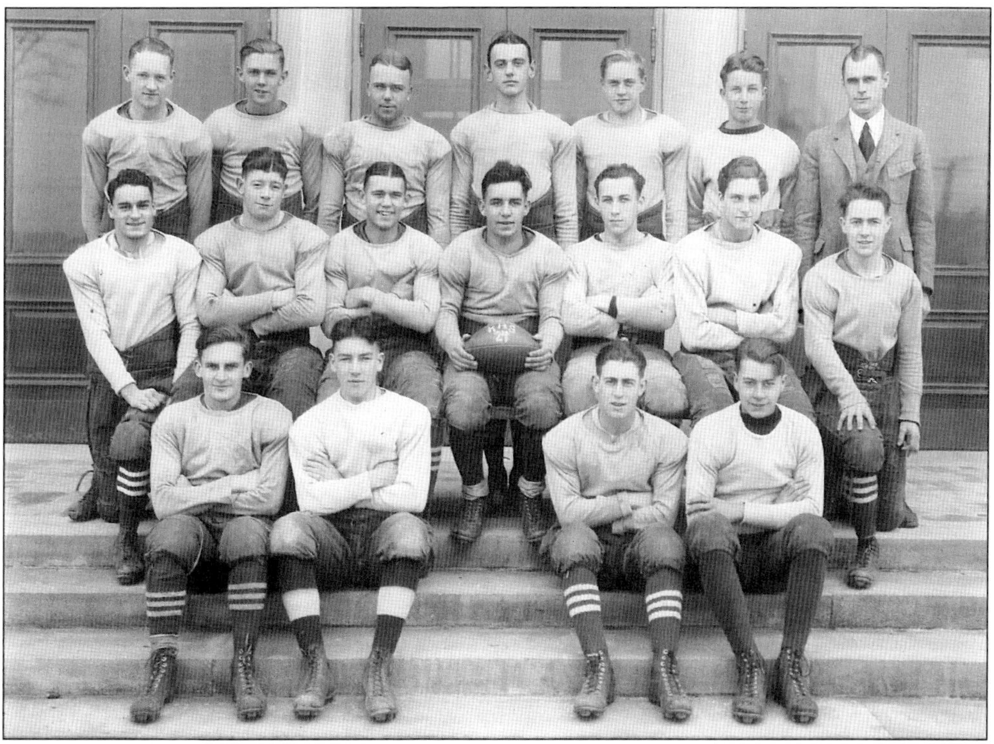

THE UNDEFEATED 1924 KENMORE HIGH FOOTBALL TEAM POSING FOR THE KENITORIAL WITH COACH ANDREAS ("ANDY") SCHULTZ IN FRONT OF THE NEW HIGH SCHOOL. The team's 6-0-1 record included a scoreless tie with Fredonia in its first game, and victories over the alumni team, Springville, Lackawanna, Leroy, Batavia, and East Aurora. The season was celebrated with a dinner and a student-faculty billiard match at Gandy's Oyster House in Buffalo.

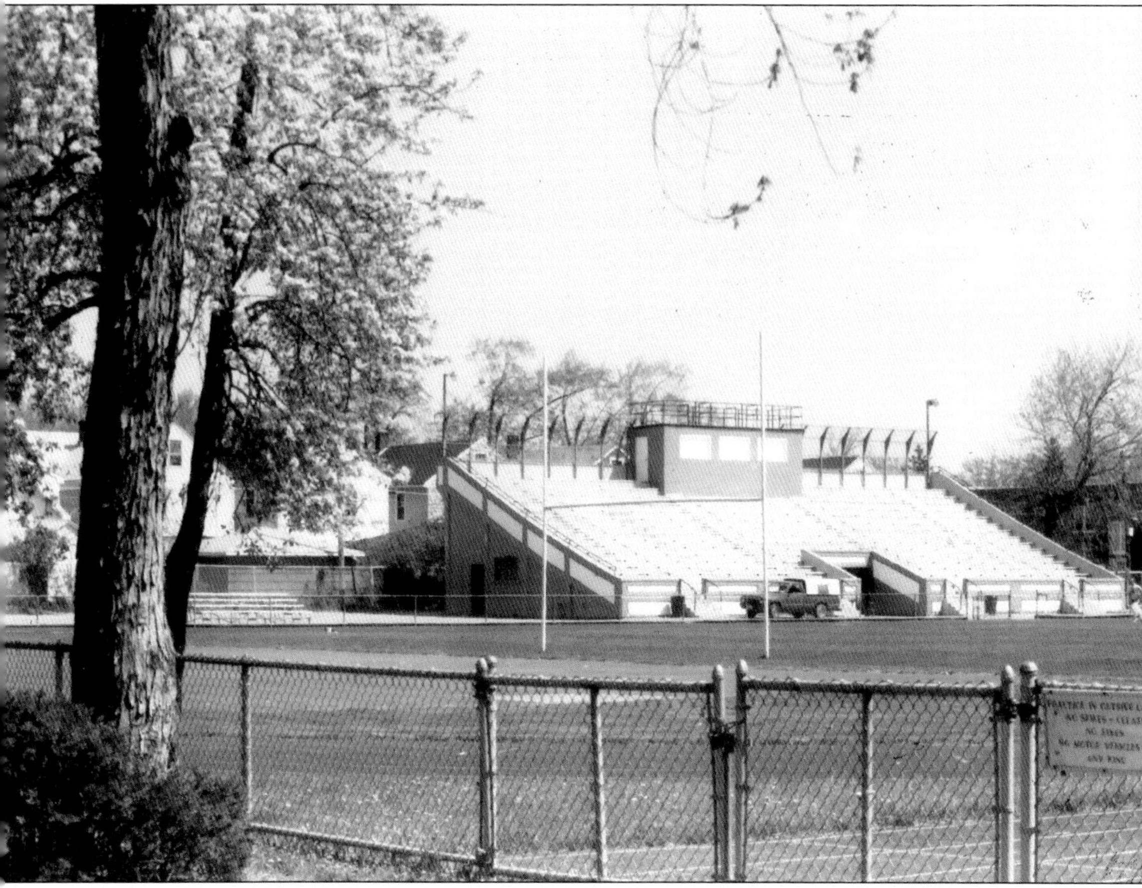

CROSBY FIELD. Located on the central portion of a plot of land between Crosby and Nassau Avenues, stretching from Delaware Road across Myron Avenue and Colvin Boulevard to Irving Terrace, the land was purchased by the school district in 1921 in anticipation of the need for expanded facilities as the village population grew. Three schools—the present Kenmore Middle School and the Lindbergh and Longfellow elementary schools—have been built on the land, along with playground facilities and additional buildings used for school district maintenance and to support athletic events. Village residents make much recreational use of the field, basketball courts, baseball diamonds, quarter-mile track, and tennis courts (which opened in 1982 just east of Colvin). The concrete stands shown here on the north side of the field were constructed in 1927, when the space was developed as the athletic field for the high school, then located on Delaware Road. Another set of stands was subsequently erected on the south side, to the concern of some Crosby Avenue residents who worried about noise and litter. The wooden bleacher seats on those stands were replaced by metal ones in 1982. Crosby Field remains the home field of the Kenmore West Blue Devils. The track was given a synthetic surface in 1983, was resurfaced in 1992, and has become a frequent venue for regional track and field events.

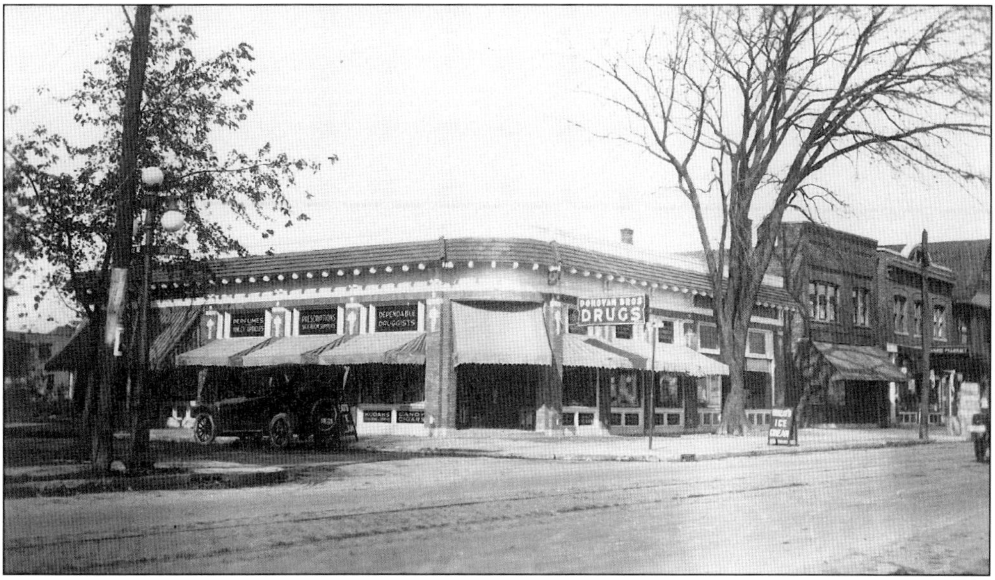

Donovan Brothers Drug Store. George and James Donovan opened this drug store at Delaware and LaSalle on September 1, 1921, and operated it for over a half-century. A sidewalk sign advertises "Wheat's Ice Cream." The Kenmore Pharmacy competed just two buildings away at right. Kenmore's "Big Tree," an elm in the sidewalk in front of Donovan's, was finally condemned as a nuisance and cut down by the village DPW in April 1929.

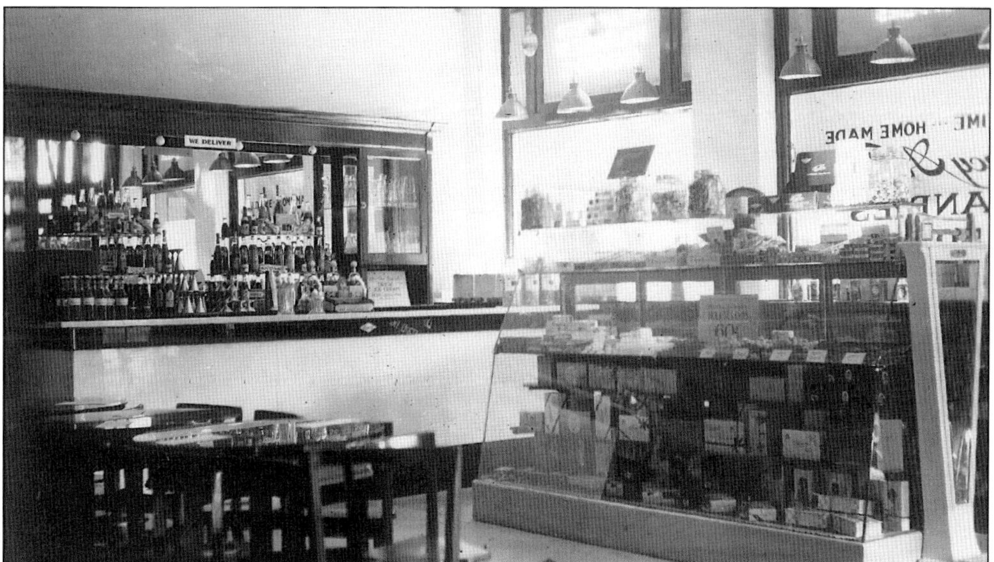

Inside Donovan Bros. Drug Store in 1921. The soda fountain at left was popular with young and old, who could enjoy their ice cream treats at the tables in the foreground. A sign behind the counter advertises "Try our Special Brick Ice Cream For your Sunday Dinner." In the case at right is a sign for "Molasses Chip—60¢"; below that are some Whitman's candy boxes that look little different from today's Whitman's. At top center a window advertises Wearever Rubber Goods to passersby. The scale at right would give you your weight and fortune for a penny. The Bermondsey gift shop now occupies the store.

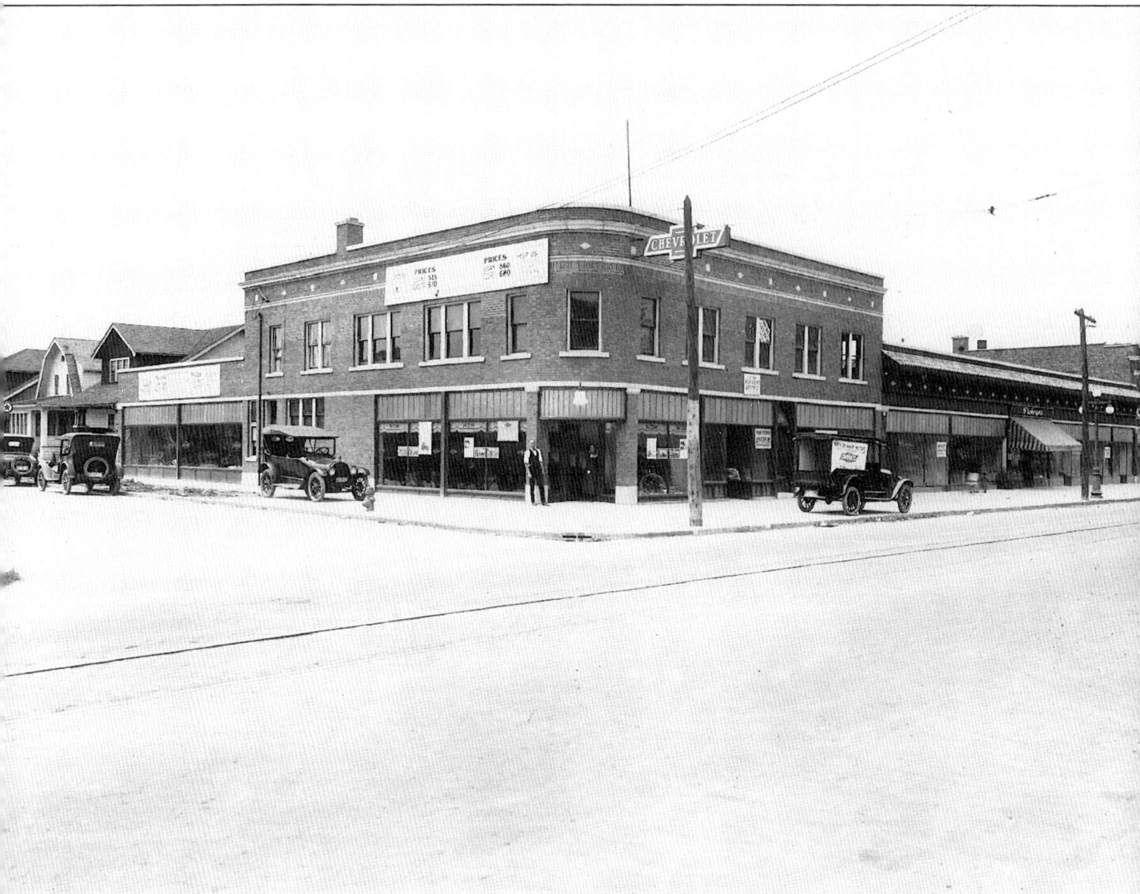

THE FIRST CHEVROLET DEALER IN THE VILLAGE, NORTH DELAWARE MOTORS, C. 1920. This Delaware-Lincoln corner building houses CVS Pharmacy now. To the right, the store with the awning extended was Flickinger's grocery store. Most of the store fronts in the new building were still for rent. Parked on the Delaware Avenue sidewalk is a covered delivery wagon with roll-down canvas sides, and there is a gasoline pump on Lincoln Boulevard. Prices for new cars were as follows: Roadster (far left) $510; Touring Car (parked on sidewalk) $525; Coupe $680; and Sedan $860.

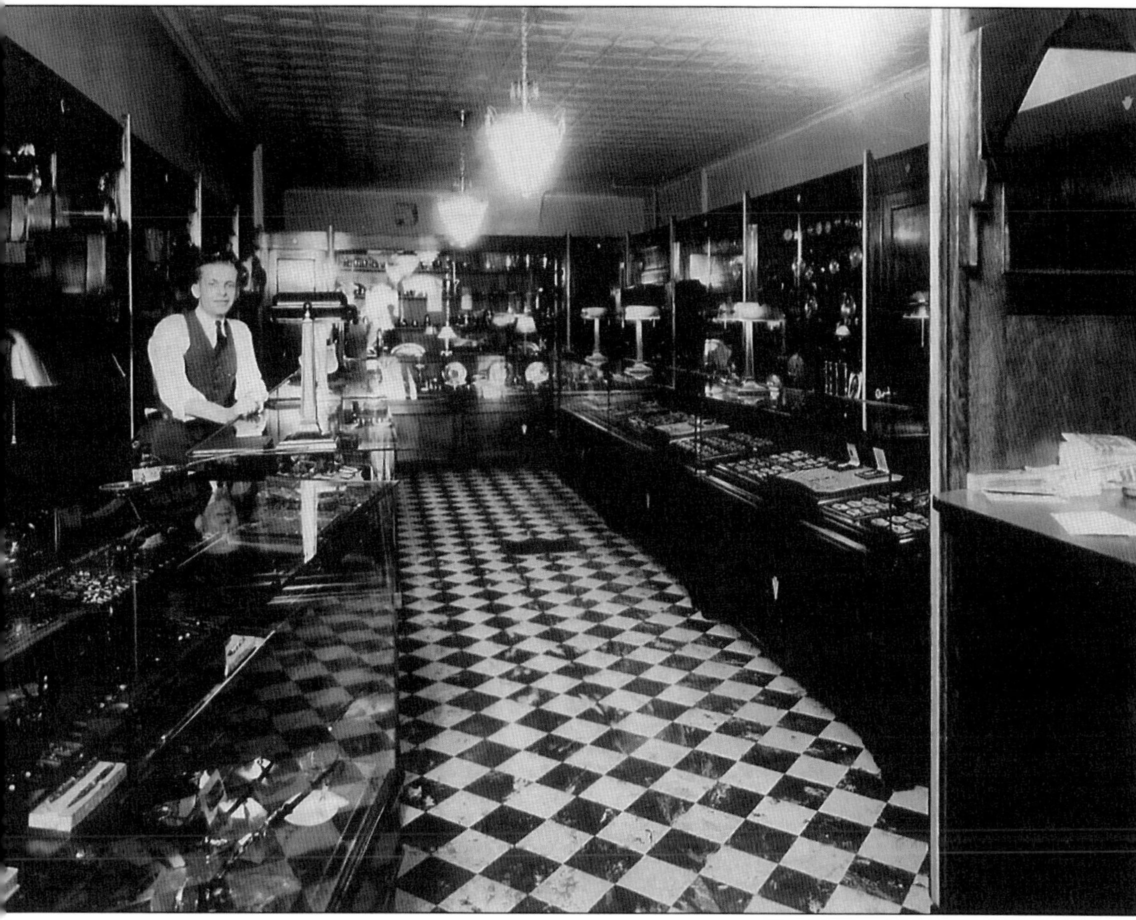

Hofert Jewelers, one of Kenmore's oldest businesses. Jeweler Ed Moeloth and watchmaker Herbert Hofert had been employed in downtown Buffalo before deciding to open their own store. It is said that both looked for a likely place to locate, and independently of each other selected Kenmore as the most promising site. Their judgment turned out to be correct, for the firm that opened its doors as Moeloth and Hofert in 1929 has been located in the village business section ever since. This photograph shows the original shop at 2892 Delaware Avenue, north of Lincoln, with one of the founders, Herbert Hofert Sr., behind the counter. Herbert Jr. and his brother William worked in the store for some 40 years, retiring about 1993. In the 1950s, the Hoferts bought out the Moeloth interest, and when the business moved a block south to 2876 Delaware in 1970, only the Hofert name was retained. The present store has retained much of the appearance of the original; the display cases, with their arrowhead decoration, were moved to the new facility, and the pattern of the floor tiles is similar to that of the old. The business is now operated by Pepper (Herbert III) and Dominic Hofert, grandsons of the founder. (Photo courtesy of Hofert Jewelers.)

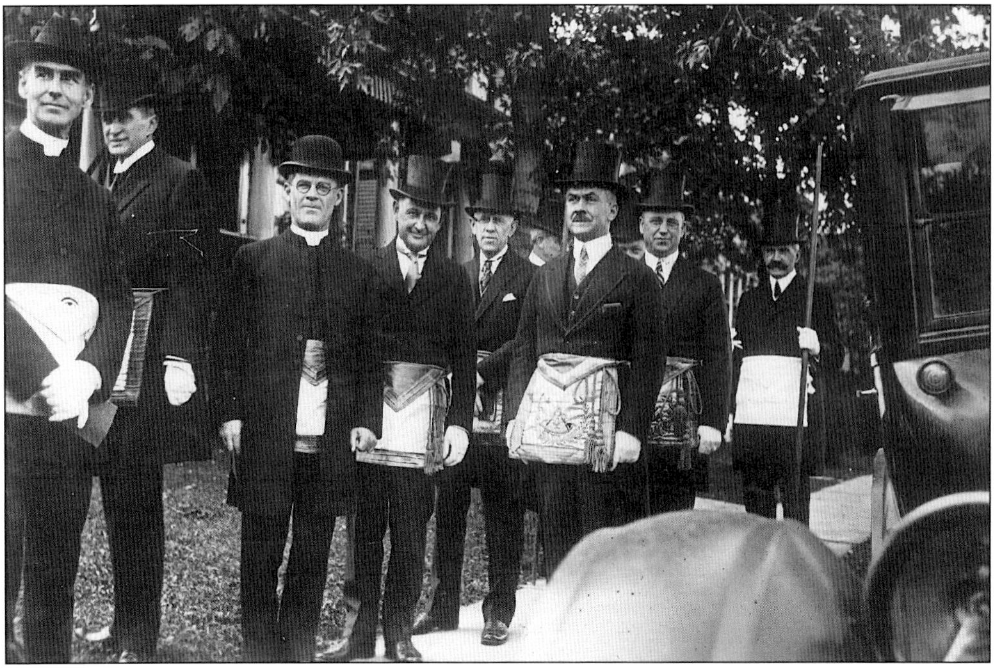

MASONS GETTING READY FOR SOME KIND OF CEREMONY, PERHAPS THE GROUNDBREAKING OR DEDICATION OF THE LODGE ON DELAWARE ROAD. There are ten Masons in this undated snapshot (you need to look carefully to find all of them). At least two of them appear to be members of the clergy.

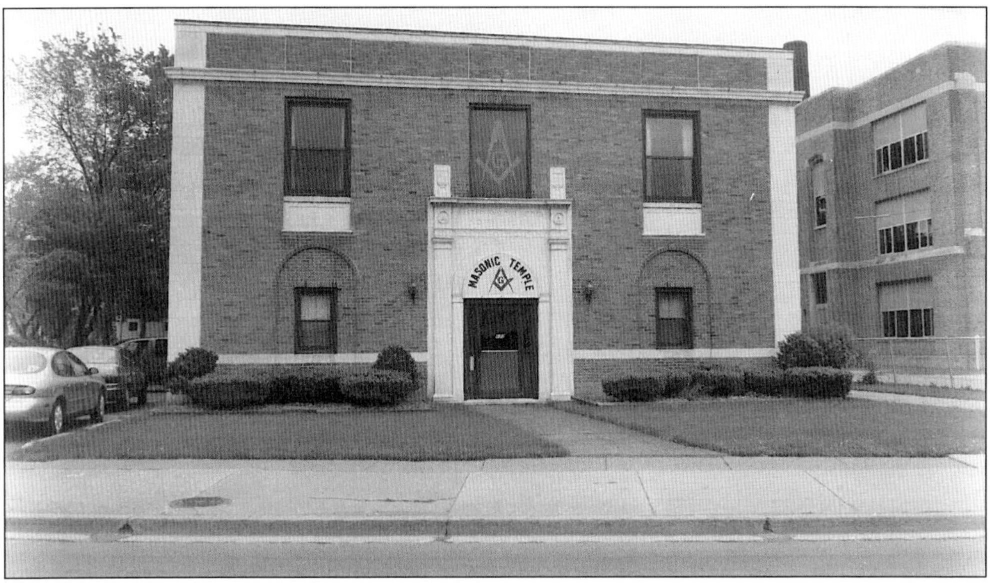

THE MASONIC TEMPLE ON DELAWARE ROAD NEAR NASSAU AVENUE HOUSING MASTER BUILDER LODGE, ORDER OF THE EASTERN STAR, AND OTHER MASONIC-RELATED ORGANIZATIONS. Master Builder Lodge 911, F&AM turned the first sod for the construction of this building in February 1926. Rev. Dr. Frederick Parkhurst, the town and village historian and former minister of the Methodist-Episcopal Church, offered the prayer. The cornerstone laying took place in April. The building is used on Sundays by a church, the House of Eternal Truth.

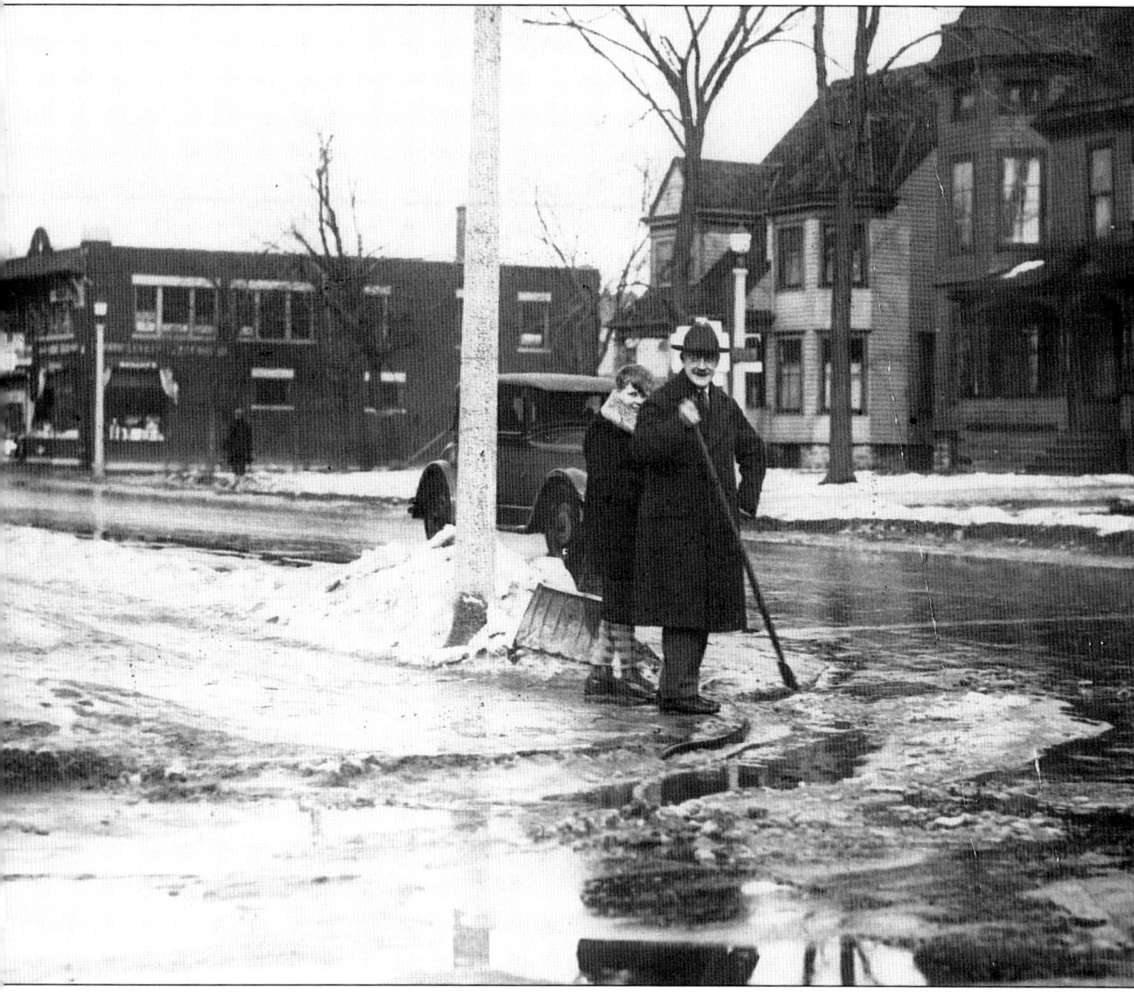

Henry A. Brown and his son, Robert L. Brown, at Delaware and West Hazeltine Avenues, clearing ice from a c. 1929 winter storm. Henry Brown was a captain in the U.S. Army during World War I; Robert is a grandson of L.P.A. Eberhardt. Across Delaware Avenue, from left to right, are the Kenmore Green Lantern Lunch Car operated by Madeline Moore, the Alcobar Candies and Ice Cream shop at Parkwood Avenue, the home of Dr. Gideon D. Smith, the home of William Gudgel, and a corner of Kenmore Presbyterian Church.

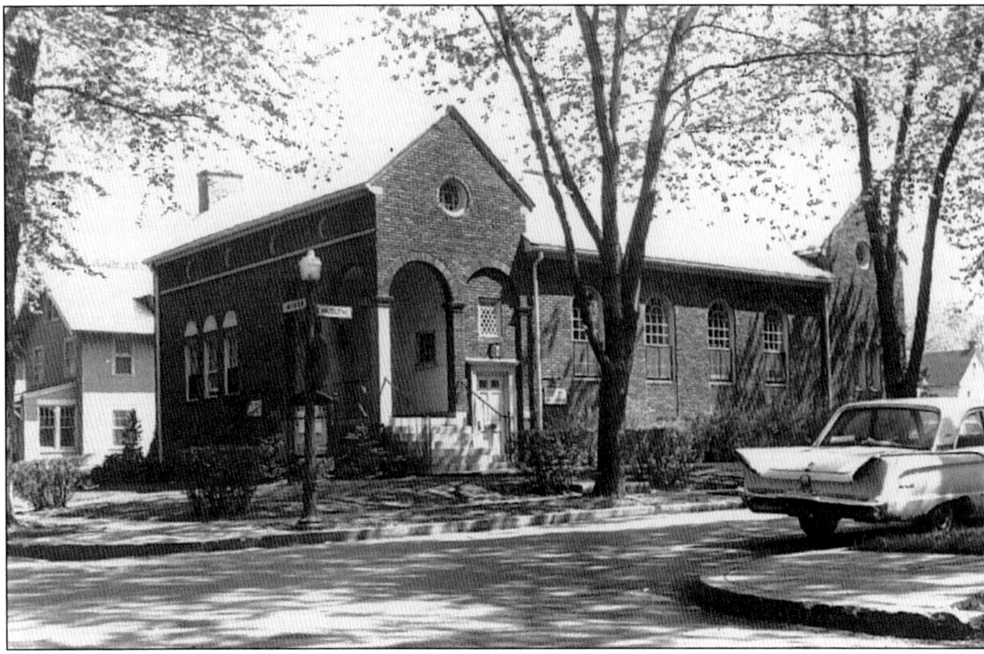

The First Church of Christ, Scientist in Kenmore, organized in 1919 in the village hall. In 1921, the congregation purchased two lots at East Hazeltine and Myron Avenues. The first service in this brick-and-stone Italian Renaissance church was held on Easter Sunday, 1922. For many years the denomination also maintained a reading room in the Hitchcock Block at Delaware and Euclid. In 1996, the Kenmore congregation and the remaining Buffalo congregation merged as the Buffalo-Kenmore First Church of Christ, Scientist, which remains based in this building. (Larry H. Oskin photo, TKHS collection.)

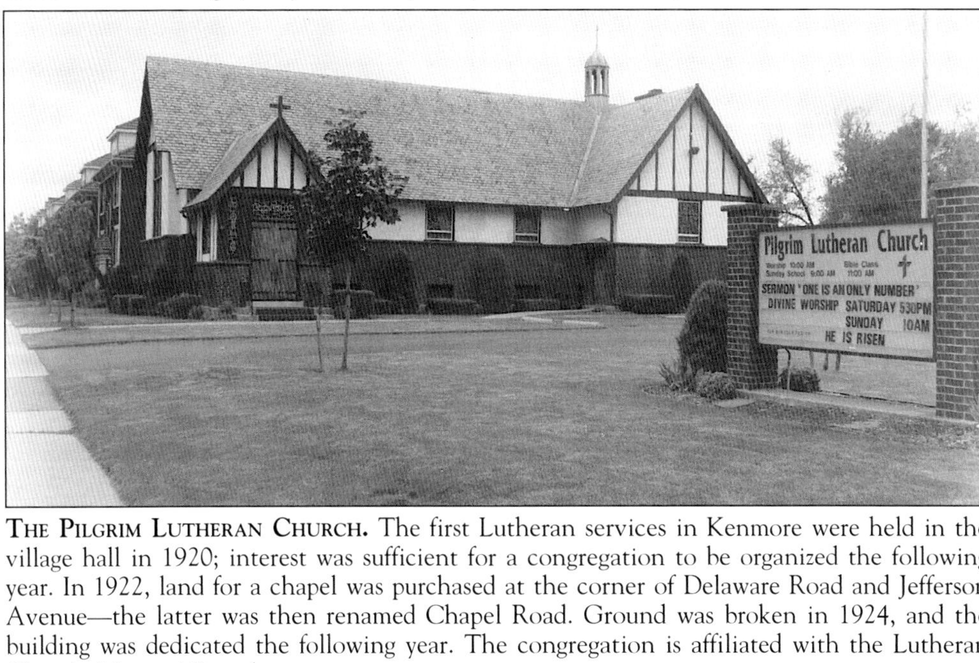

The Pilgrim Lutheran Church. The first Lutheran services in Kenmore were held in the village hall in 1920; interest was sufficient for a congregation to be organized the following year. In 1922, land for a chapel was purchased at the corner of Delaware Road and Jefferson Avenue—the latter was then renamed Chapel Road. Ground was broken in 1924, and the building was dedicated the following year. The congregation is affiliated with the Lutheran Church, Missouri Synod.

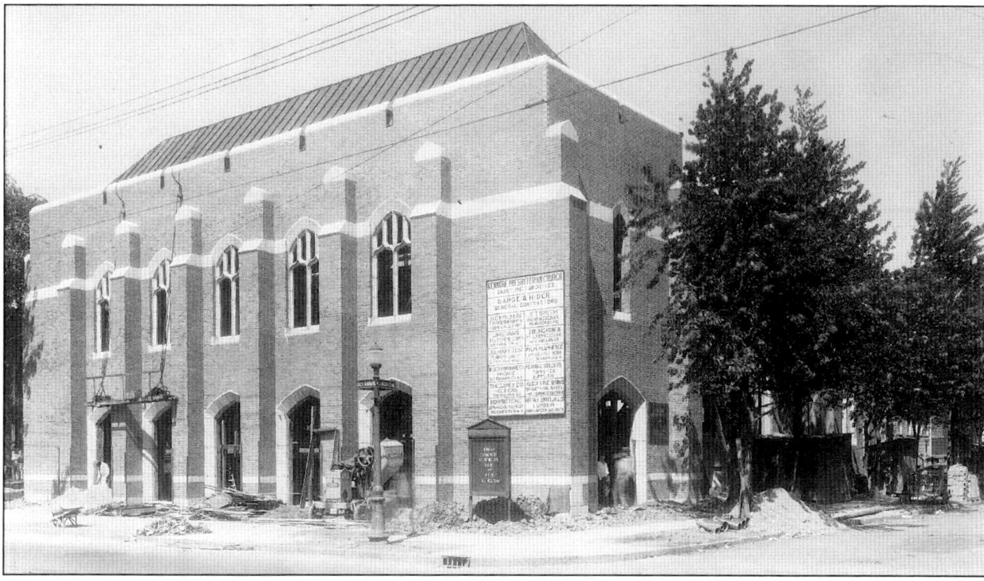

THE PRESENT KENMORE PRESBYTERIAN CHURCH UNDER CONSTRUCTION. In 1926 it was determined that the original building was no longer adequate for the growing congregation. The new church, built around the old one, accommodated 1,100 worshippers. Major alterations in 1948, 1966, and 1982 removed the original gabled roof section, demolished the Hazeltine Avenue gym, and reduced the seating capacity, but expanded the chancel and the Christian education and fellowship facilities, and added a chapel.

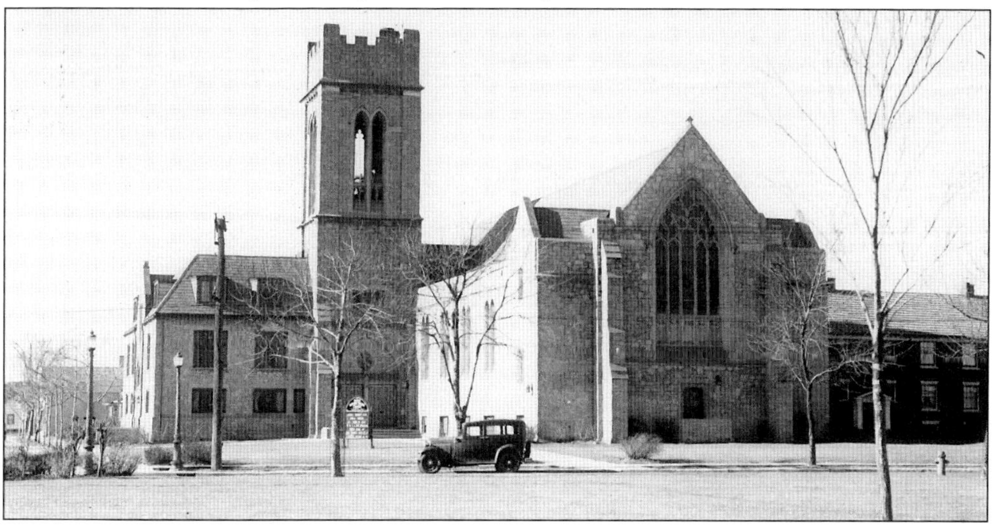

THE KENMORE METHODIST-EPISCOPAL CHURCH SHORTLY AFTER BEING COMPLETED IN 1928. The Model "A" Ford parked on Delaware Road was built the same year. The bell had not yet been hung in the tower when this photo was taken. In 1939 the northern and southern Methodist churches unified and the building was renamed Kenmore Methodist Church. The Chapel Road apartment buildings to the right of the church were purchased and developed as a church education center in 1951. In 1968 the name was changed to the Kenmore United Methodist Church following an international union of Methodist and Evangelical United Brethren churches. By this time it had become the largest congregation in the Buffalo District. (KUMC.)

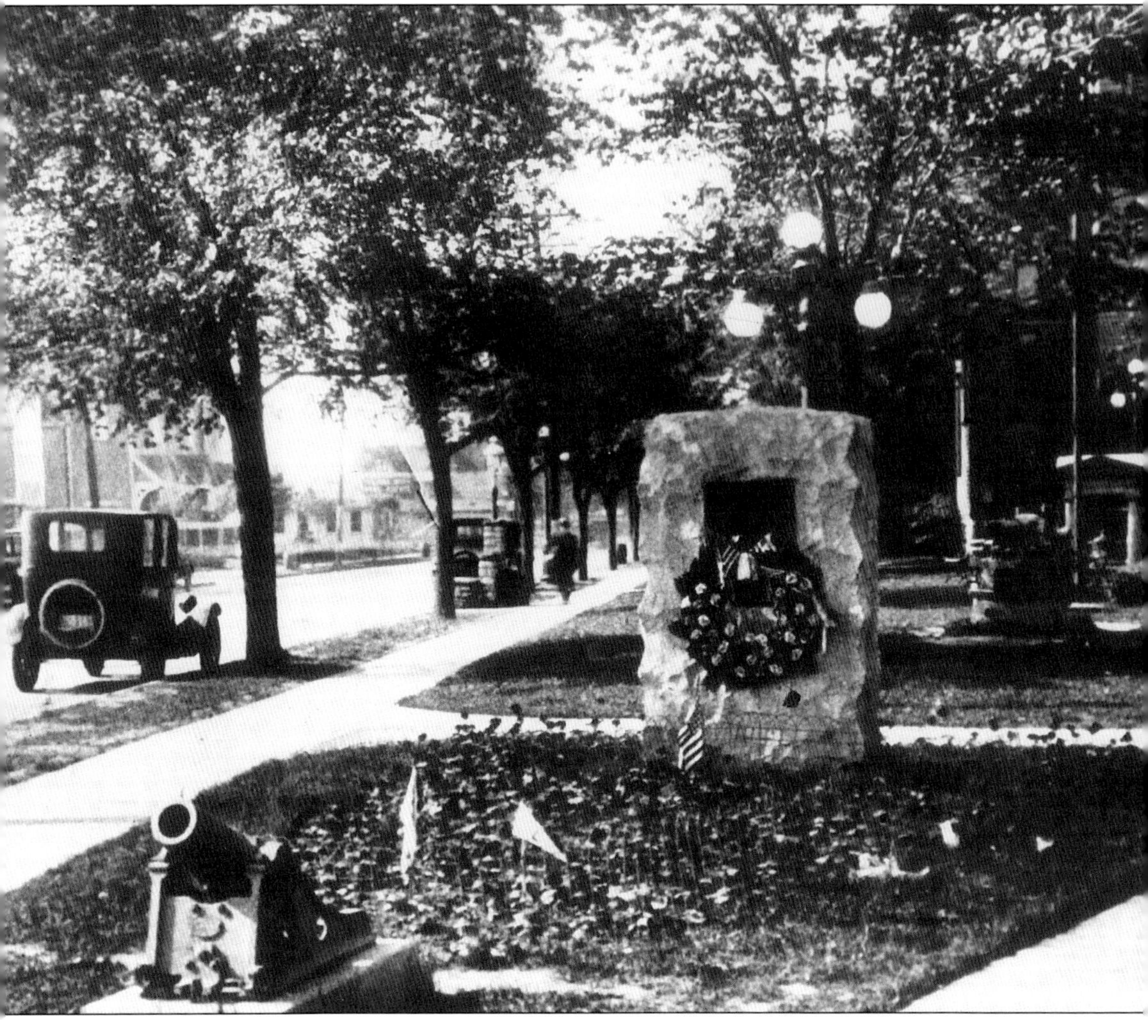

The World War I Memorial on the village triangle. This rough-faced granite stone memorial with its bronze tablet was unveiled and dedicated on Memorial Day, 1920, to those who gave their lives in the Great World War. Two years later the American Legion added a German naval gun and the mortar in the foreground as additional memorials of "the war to end all wars." They were popular village landmarks until 1936, when the guns were moved to Sheridan Park to make room for construction of the municipal building. Between the sidewalk and Delaware Avenue is the water fountain installed by the WCTU here in pro-temperance Kenmore. It had a drinking fountain on one side for pedestrians and fresh water for horses on the other side.

FRED EBLING, TEDDY JONES, AND FRED EBERHARDT ENJOYING A RARE LEISURE MOMENT IN THE RAPIDLY GROWING VILLAGE DURING THE 1920S. Fred Ebling was the superintendent of Kenmore's water department.

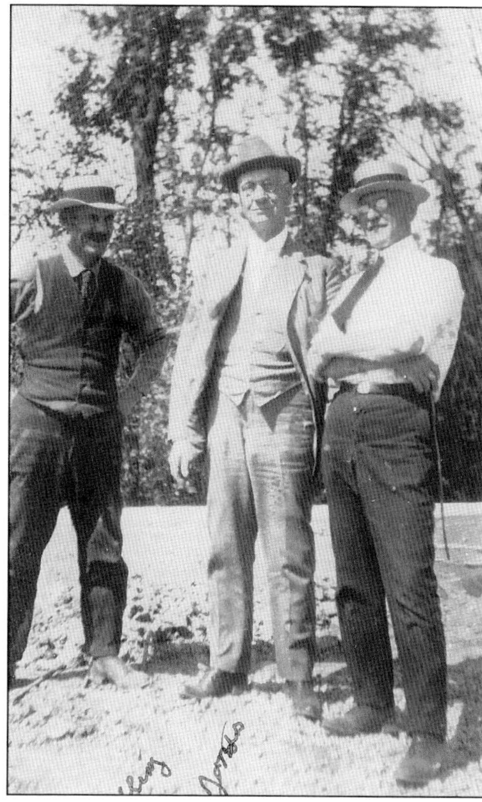

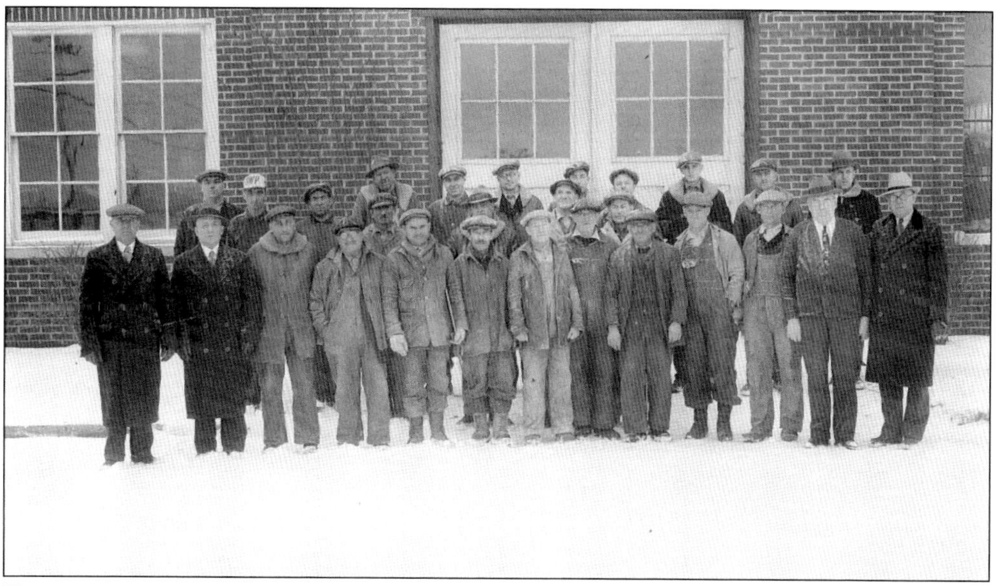

THE VILLAGE OF KENMORE DEPARTMENT OF PUBLIC WORKS. The department was located on Elmwood Avenue at the corner of Mang when this undated group portrait of its workers and supervisors was taken. By the time the village celebrated its centennial, the building had been enlarged and modernized, another structure had been added at Elmwood and Keller, and the number of employees had greatly increased.

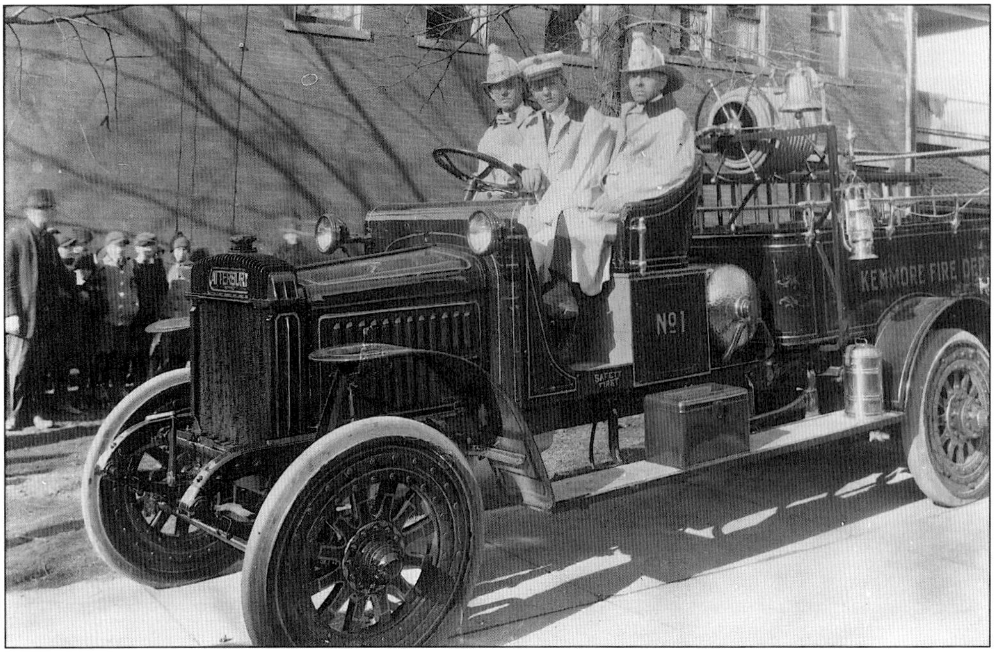

The first motorized piece of fire-fighting apparatus of the Kenmore Volunteer Fire Department. Purchased in response to the need for something more modern than the existing hand-drawn equipment, the 1.5-ton Atterbury combination chemical and hose truck cost $2,925 when delivered in 1919. In 1922, a 350-gallon pump was installed on the vehicle for an additional $1,850. The photo shows the truck on parade in 1927. (KVFD collection.)

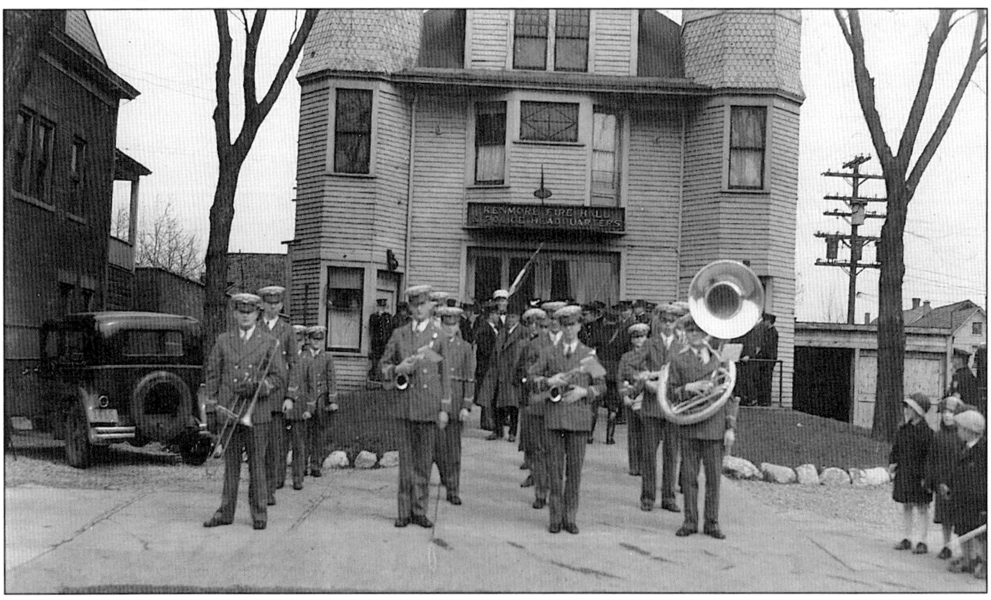

The cornerstone ceremony for Kenmore's new fire hall, April 21, 1929. Following a marching band, firemen and police paraded from the original combination fire hall/village hall/police station (shown here) up Delaware Avenue to Nash Road, where the cornerstone ceremonies were held. The old building was razed five months later when the new building was completed.

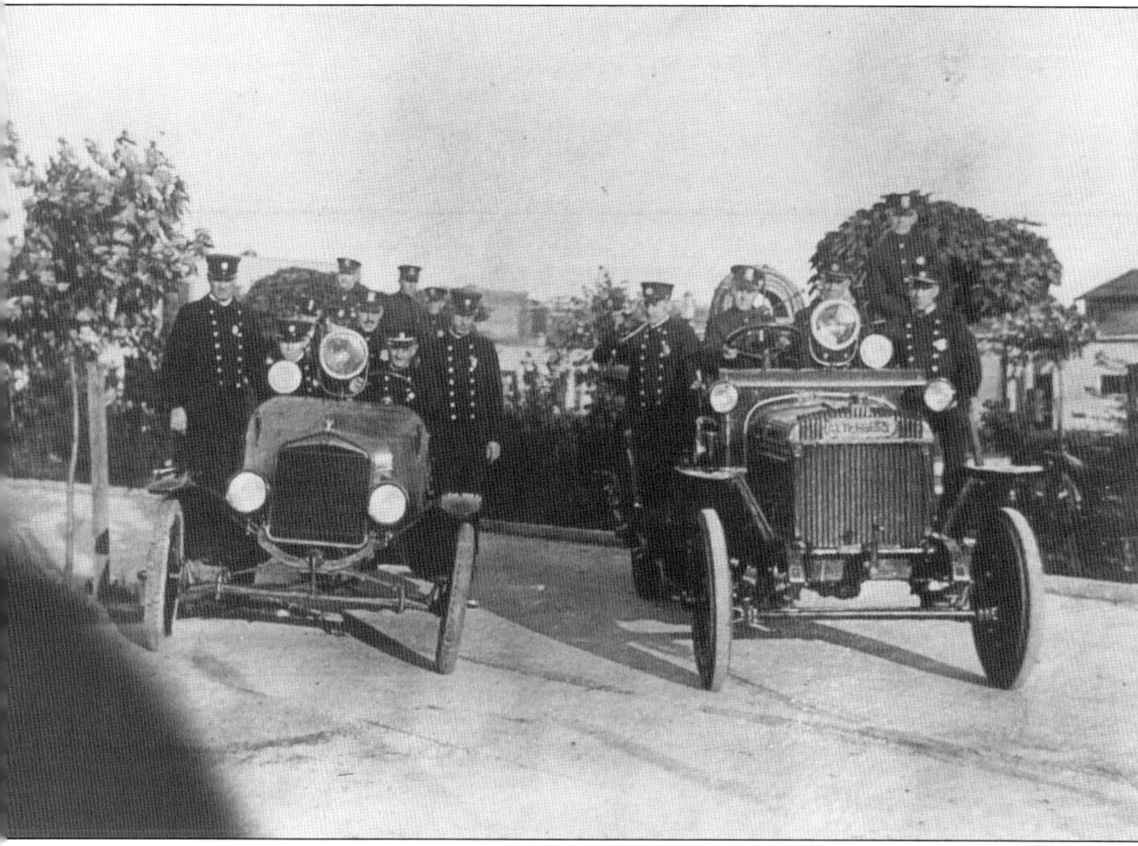

The Keystone Kops? No, they are Kenmore Volunteer firemen showing off the village's first two motorized firetrucks in 1924. The Atterbury fire engine at right was put into service in 1919. It was originally a combination chemical and hose truck, upgraded three years later. At left is the Ford Model "T" that was modified in 1922 to pull the 1868 hook-and-ladder apparatus acquired by the village in 1905.

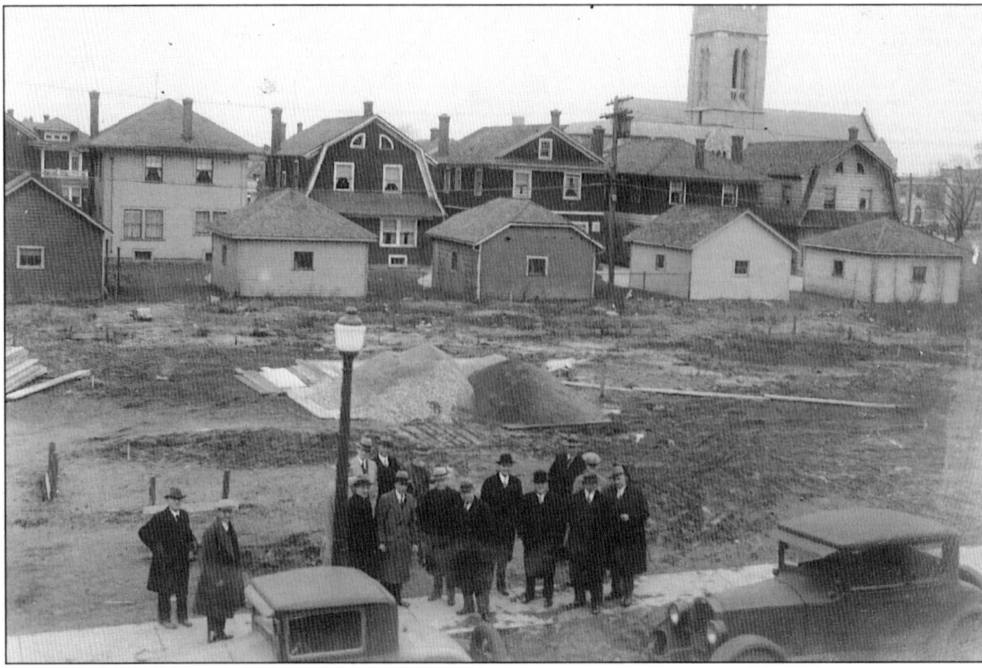

VILLAGE OFFICIALS AT THE NASH ROAD SITE OF KENMORE'S NEW POLICE AND FIRE HALL, MARCH 22, 1929. Everyone is dressed in an overcoat and wearing a hat. No well-dressed man of that era would be seen in public without a hat, no matter the time of year. In the background are the homes and garages of Landers Road, erected in the 1920s, as was the Methodist-Episcopal church at Delaware Road.

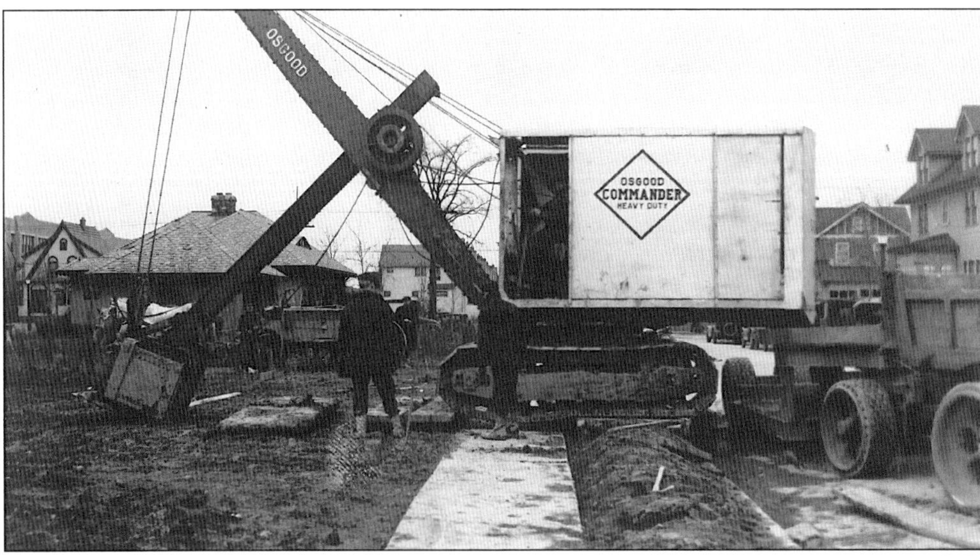

CONSTRUCTION ON NASH ROAD IN APRIL 1929. The first earth is about to be turned for Kenmore's new fire and police station. Large and Hider was the contractor for the project. An almost new Osgood gasoline-powered shovel has just been unloaded at the site. Most projects in that era still used traditional "steam shovels" for digging foundations. The home at left would soon be moved to Landers Road to make way for a new post office building, erected later that year.

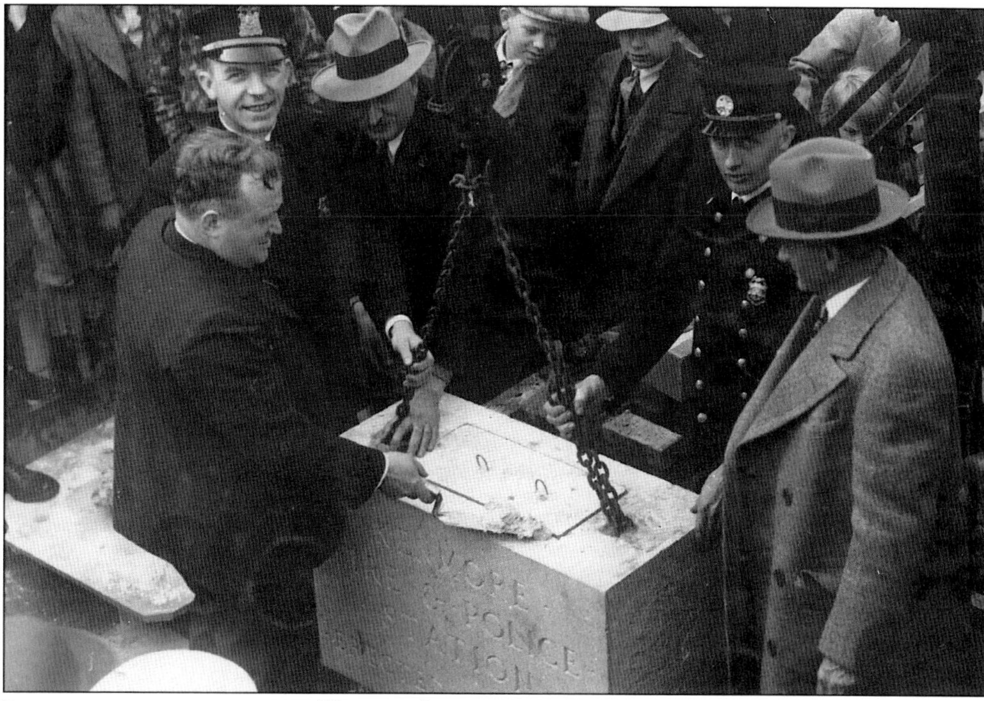

LAYING THE CORNERSTONE OF KENMORE'S NEW FIRE AND POLICE STATION ON APRIL 21, 1929. Participants include Mayor Roy Brockett (left), Police Chief Clarence Yochum (behind Mayor Brockett), and Fire Marshal Raymond Kirsch (second from right). The building was ready for occupancy by August 28, 1929.

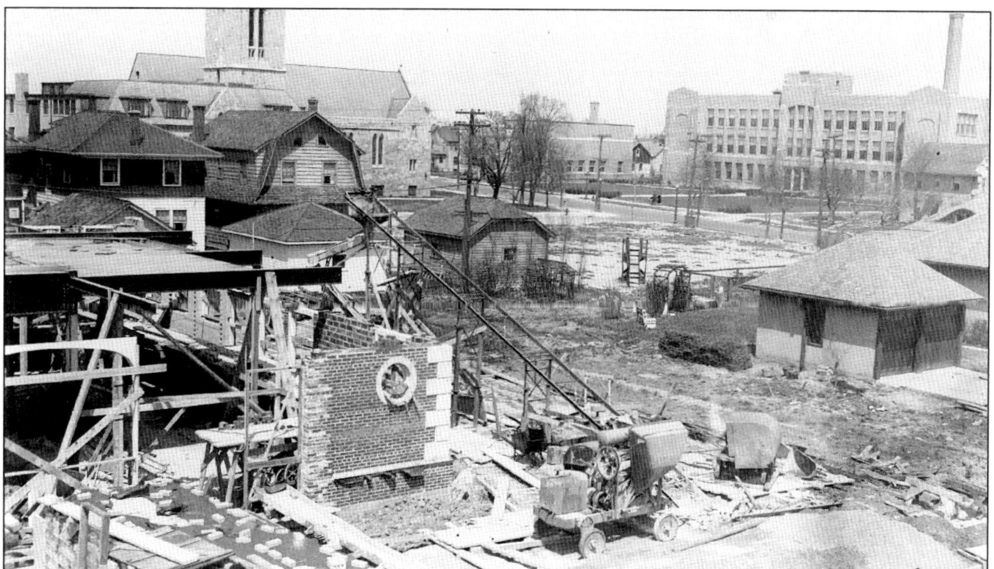

KENMORE'S NEW NASH ROAD POLICE AND FIRE HALL ON MAY 1, 1929. Later that year the home at right was moved directly to the rear and turned to face Landers Road to allow the construction of Kenmore's new post office building on the site. The Kenmore Methodist-Episcopal Church (in the left background) had been erected the year before as had a huge new addition to the Kenmore Junior-Senior High School (across Delaware Road at right).

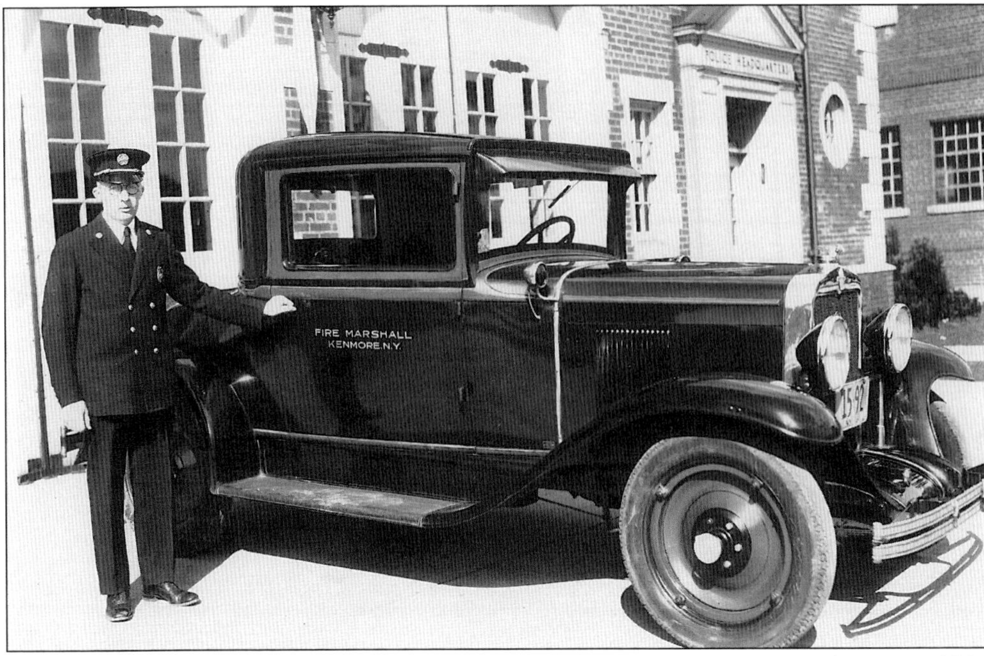

VILLAGE FIRE MARSHAL RAY KIRSCH POSING ALONGSIDE HIS NEW FIRE MARSHAL'S CAR, A 1931 DODGE, IN FRONT OF THE TWO-YEAR-OLD FIRE HALL ON NASH ROAD. The village sign painter seems to have been so impressed that he added a second "l" on the end of "marshal." Notice the sign for police headquarters on the right-hand door, an indication that the fire and police departments shared the building. (KVFD collection.)

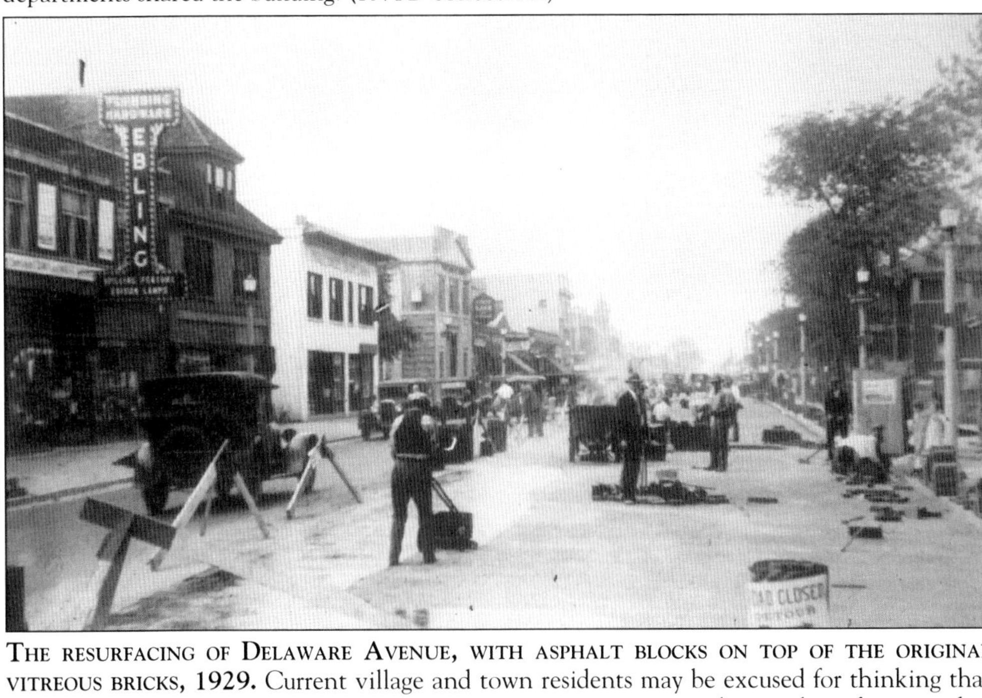

THE RESURFACING OF DELAWARE AVENUE, WITH ASPHALT BLOCKS ON TOP OF THE ORIGINAL VITREOUS BRICKS, 1929. Current village and town residents may be excused for thinking that the resurfacing of Delaware Avenue is a permanent process, given the number of times it has occurred and the resulting necessary inconvenience for pedestrians as well as motorists.

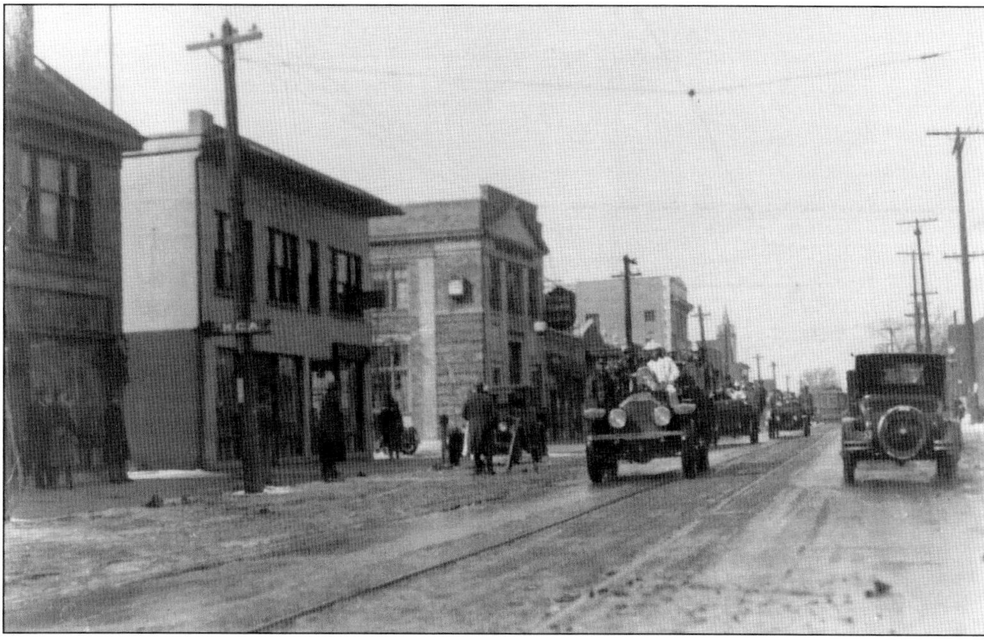

Three vehicles of the Kenmore Volunteer Fire Department returning to the fire hall on Delaware Avenue, c. 1925. They have just passed the State Bank of Kenmore at the intersection of Mang Avenue. The bank's sign hangs over the sidewalk. Notice the trolley in front of St. Paul's in the background, and nearer, the sign for the YMCA and the gas pump alongside the street. (KVFD collection.)

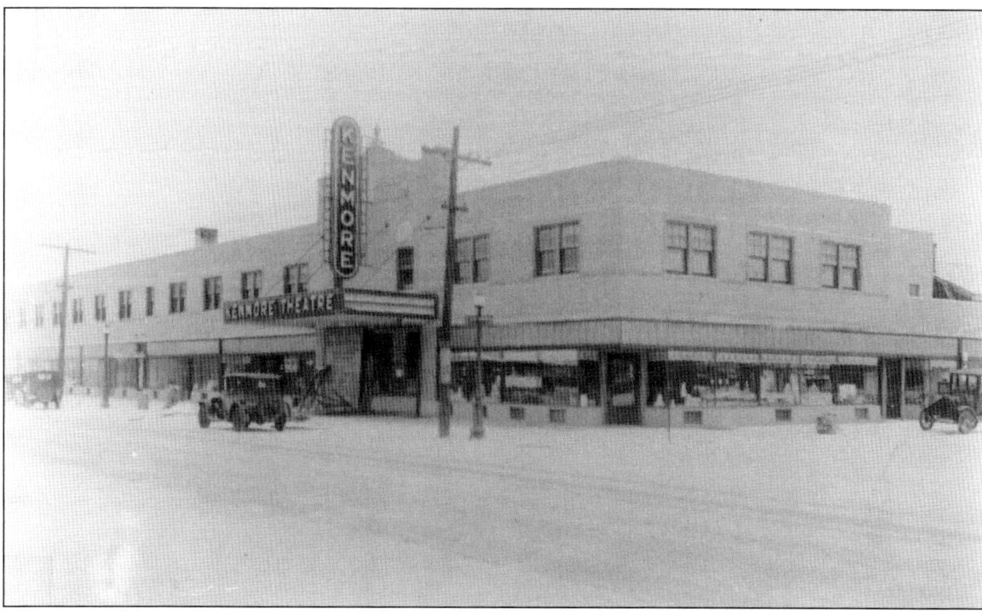

The Kenmore Theater, on Delaware Avenue between Landers and Chapel Roads. The theater was built in 1925 and showed its first motion picture early the following year. In addition to a 1,600-seat movie house and stores on the ground floor, the building contained a billiard hall and a seven-lane bowling alley. By 1965, the theater had ceased operations, and the building, renamed Kenmore Plaza, was converted into an apartment block. (KVFD collection.)

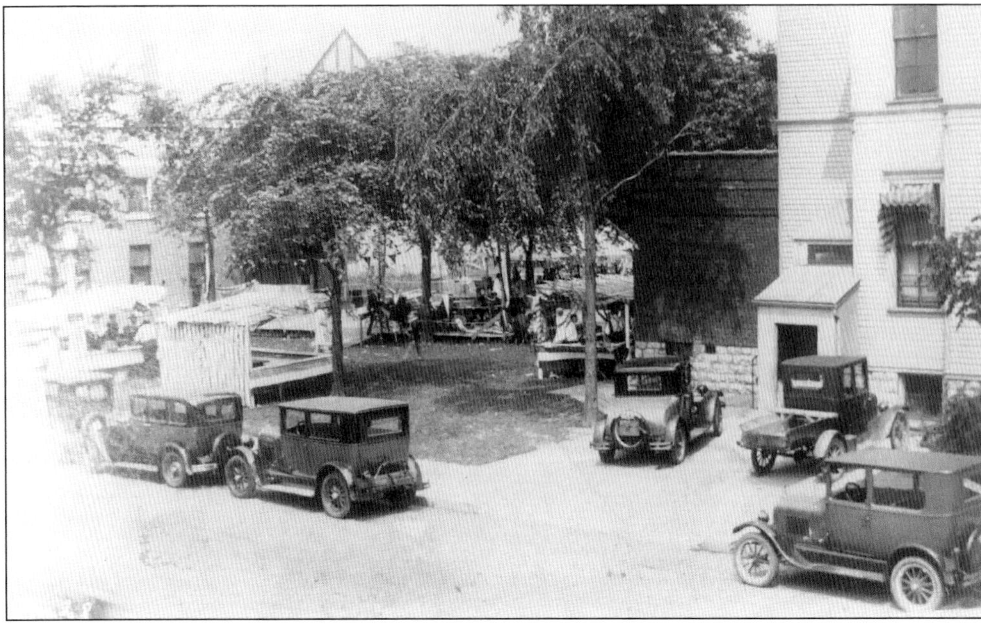

One of the Kenmore Volunteer Fire Department's field days on the lawn behind what was then the village hall between the Delawares. The styles of automobiles and the gable of the Church of the Advent (opened in 1924) date the photograph to some point in the late 1920s. The lawn vanished when the present municipal building was constructed in 1936. (KVFD collection.)

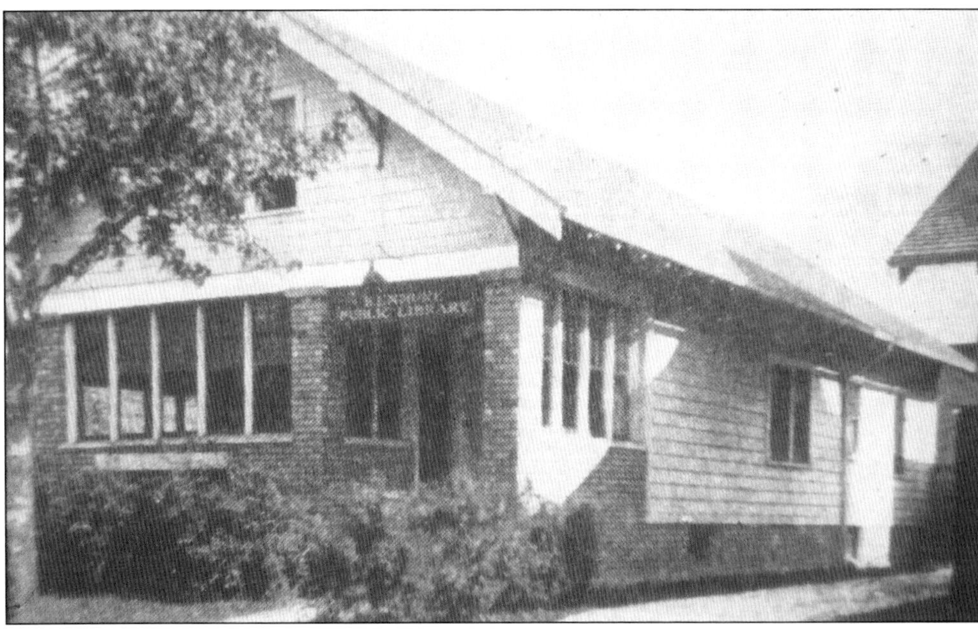

The Kenmore Free Library, founded in 1916 and housed in the village hall until 1918. After two years in the YWCA, it returned to the village hall in 1920. By then, growing patronage indicated the need for a larger facility, so in 1924 the home of Edward Ebling, at 18 Mang Avenue, a few doors west of Delaware, was purchased for $6,000 and converted to library use. Notice the sign over the front door. The library remained here until 1929.

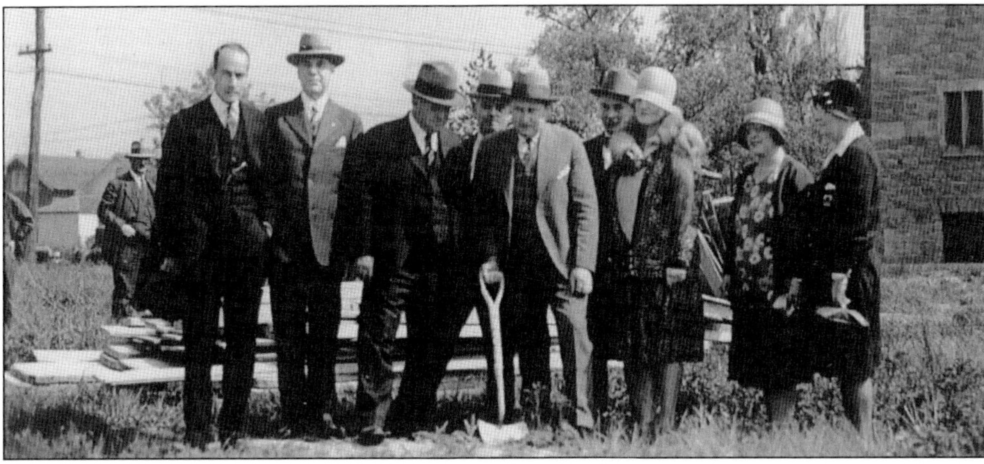

KENMORE LIBRARY TRUSTEES IN MAY 1929, TURNING THE FIRST SOIL FOR THE VILLAGE'S NEW LIBRARY, LOCATED AT CHAPEL AND DELAWARE ROADS. Village Historian Frederick S. Parkhurst (second from left) and Mayor Roy Brockett (third from left) are among those shown here. The cornerstone was laid two months later and the building opened on December 21. The new Methodist church appears at the right. The present library building is located on this same site.

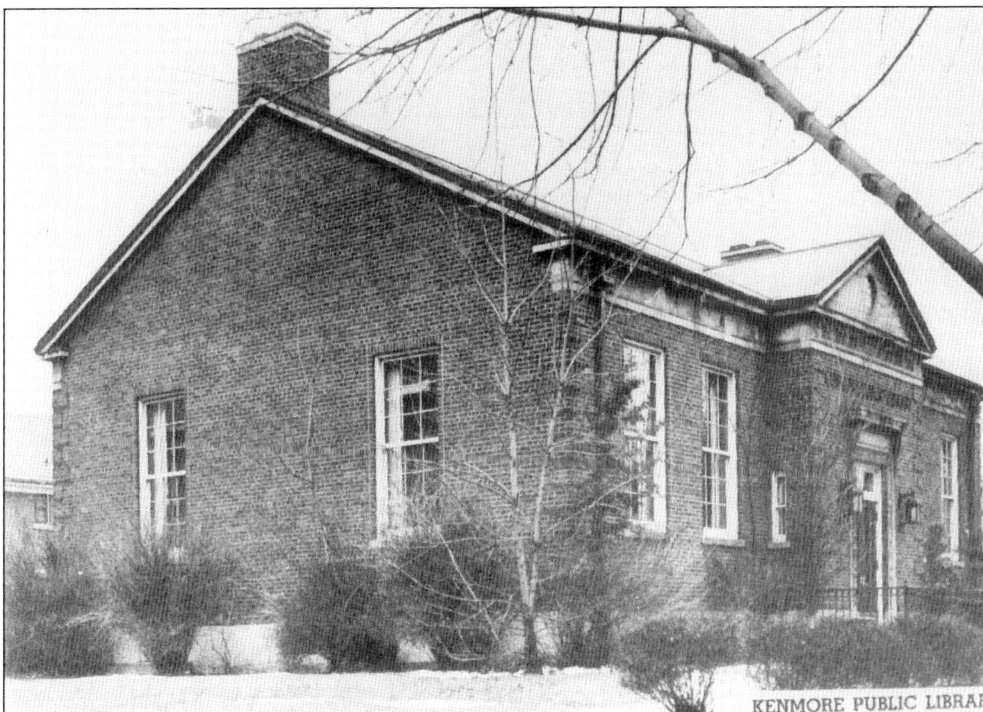

THE COLONIAL REVIVAL LIBRARY AT THE SOUTHWEST CORNER OF CHAPEL AND DELAWARE ROADS. As the village grew, so did the needs of the public library, and the house on Mang Avenue became inadequate. The building shown here, located directly across the street from the recently completed junior and senior high school, was dedicated in 1929; it remained the village's library until it, too, had been outgrown. It was replaced by the present building in 1977.

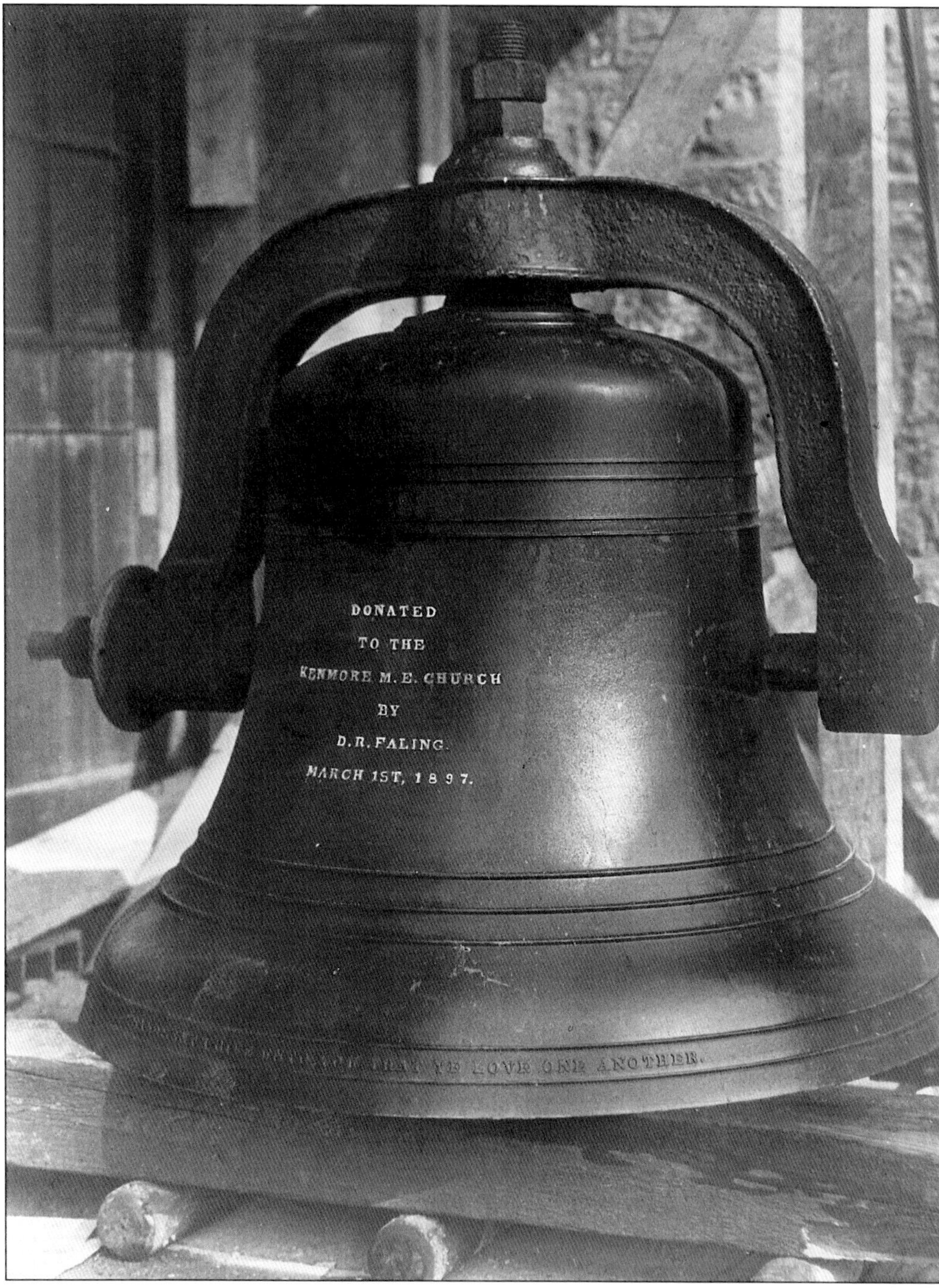

THE 2,500-POUND BELL AT THE KENMORE UNITED METHODIST CHURCH. The bell was donated to the old Kenmore Methodist-Episcopal Church in 1897 by David R. Faling, a prominent member. It was used as the village fire bell until the 1903 fire hall was built. In 1928 the bell was removed from the old church tower and installed in the tower of the new church at Delaware and Landers Roads. The movement of the bell through a half-mile of village streets attracted a large crowd. This photo shows the bell as it was being prepared for re-installation. (KUMC.)

Four

TIMES OF CHALLENGE

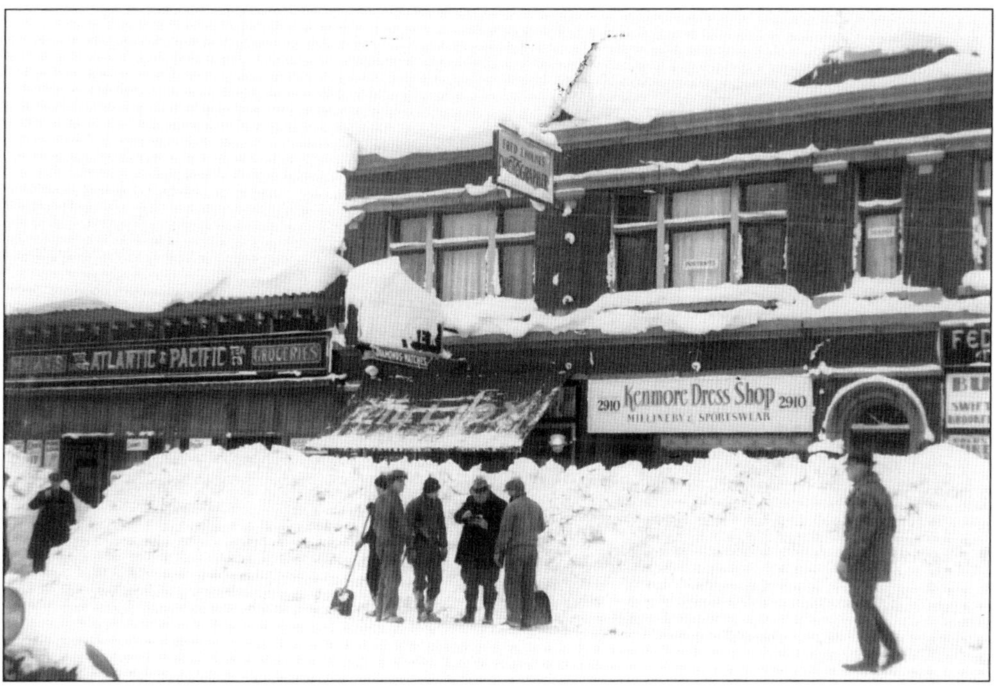

SNOW PILED IN FRONT OF STORES ACROSS DELAWARE AVENUE FROM THE MUNICIPAL BUILDING IN DECEMBER 1937. The "Great Snowstorm" of 1937 buried North Buffalo, Kenmore, and the Town of Tonawanda with 4 to 5 feet of snow, with wind-piled drifts of up to 15 feet in open areas. As usual, Kenmore cleared its streets quickly in contrast to those in Buffalo, which remained uncleared for days. The *Buffalo Evening News* printed a letter stating that "Utopian Kenmore might be compelled some day to annex Buffalo to reform it . . ." The store block included an A&P grocery store, a jeweler, a photographer, a dress shop, and a Federal meat market.

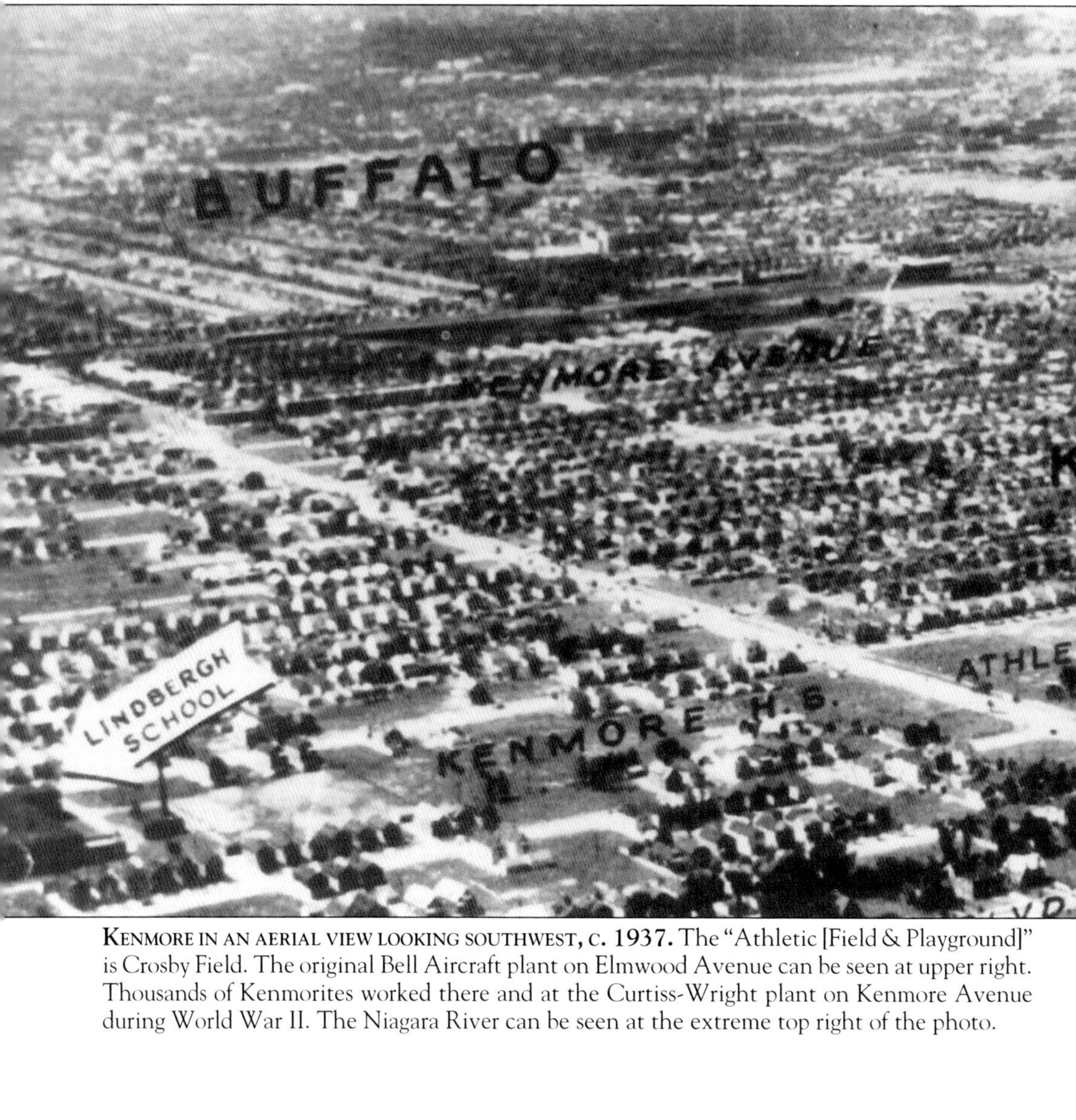

KENMORE IN AN AERIAL VIEW LOOKING SOUTHWEST, C. 1937. The "Athletic [Field & Playground]" is Crosby Field. The original Bell Aircraft plant on Elmwood Avenue can be seen at upper right. Thousands of Kenmorites worked there and at the Curtiss-Wright plant on Kenmore Avenue during World War II. The Niagara River can be seen at the extreme top right of the photo.

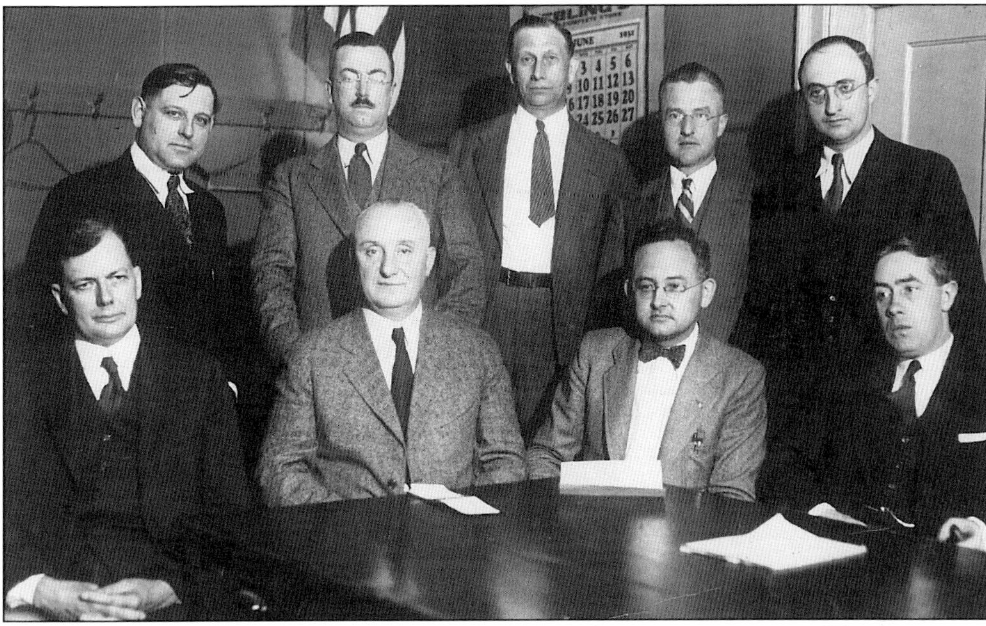

THE COMMITTEE TO INVESTIGATE FORMS OF VILLAGE GOVERNMENT, 1931. This committee was formed to look into possible alternatives to the then-existing structure of government in the village of Kenmore. The end result was that the political structure remained basically as it had been. Frank C. Moore (standing below the flag) later served as comptroller and lieutenant governor of New York State, chaired the 1937 state constitutional convention, and later chaired the State University Board of Trustees.

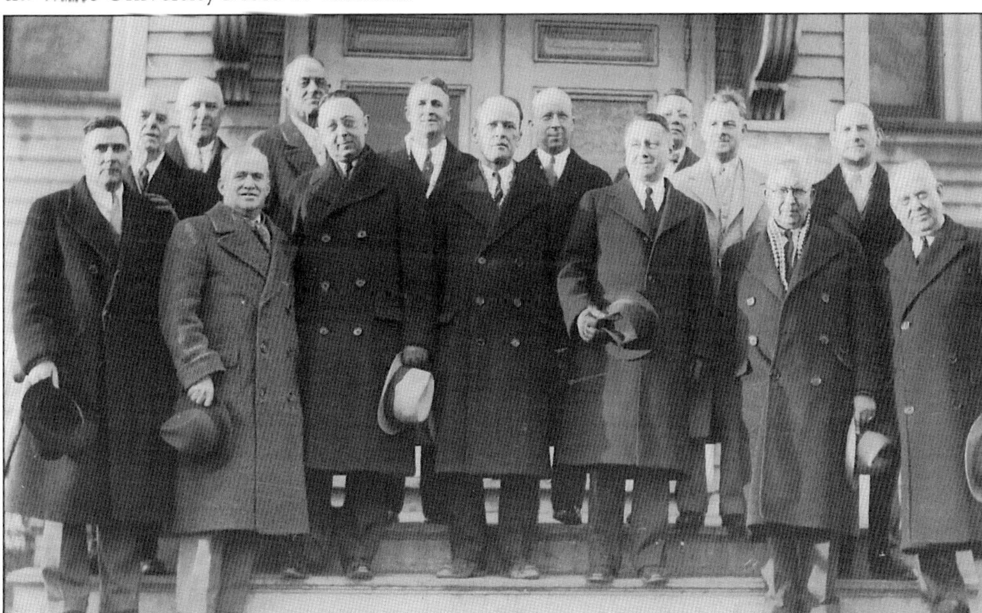

VILLAGE AND TOWN OFFICIALS ON THE FRONT STEPS OF THE OLD VILLAGE HALL JUST PRIOR TO ITS DEMOLITION IN 1936. Those identifiable are Town and Village Historian Frederick S. Parkhurst (second from left), Town Supervisor Roy R. Brockett (fourth from left), and Mayor Clifford F. Lane (sixth from left).

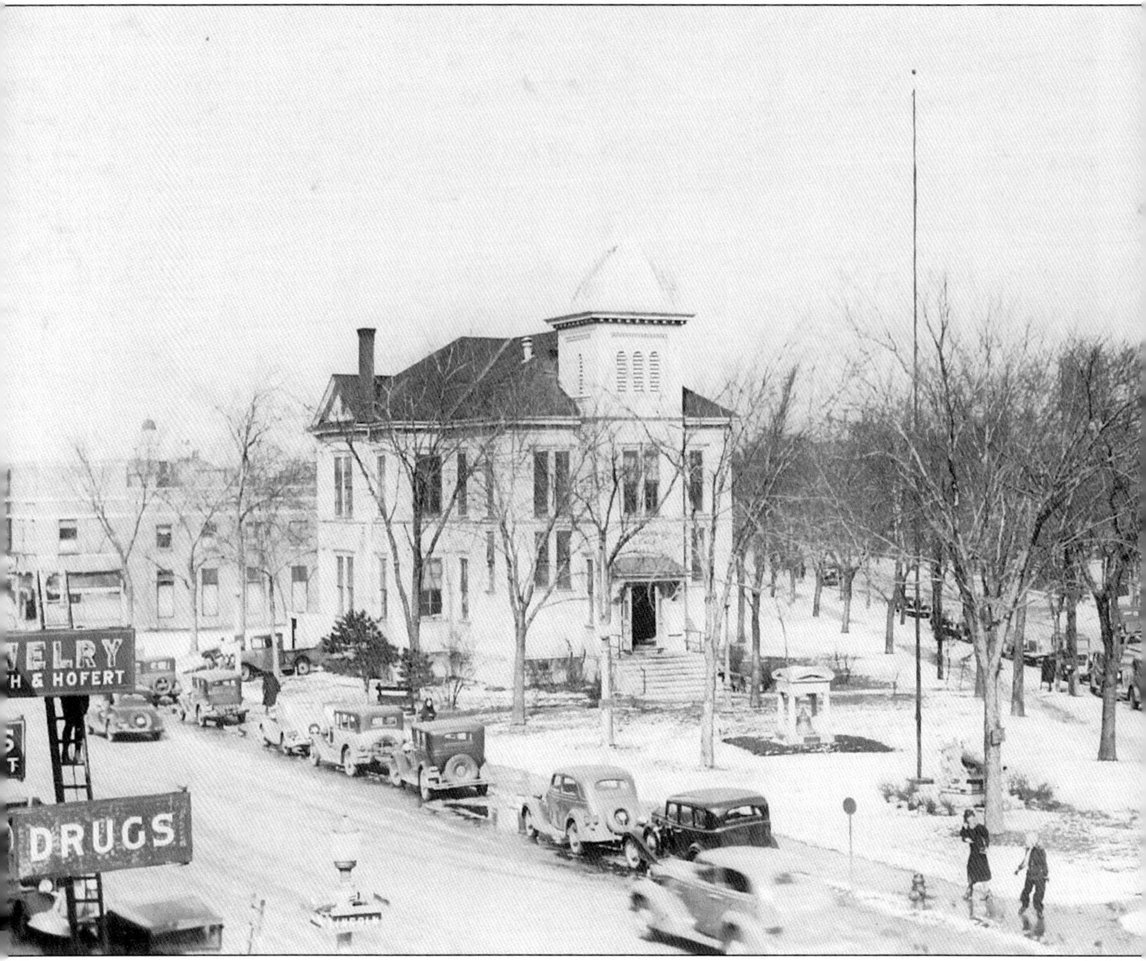

Kenmore Village Hall in March 1936. The one-time school building is shown here vacated prior to demolition. A new municipal building would soon rise on the site. The fire bell monument and the naval gun would be moved to make way for the larger building. Behind the village hall is the Arms & Bronson department store; at left signs can be seen for Moeloth & Hofert Jewelry, Siefert Shoes, and George W. Annis Drugs. A man on a ladder is replacing lights in the jewelry store sign.

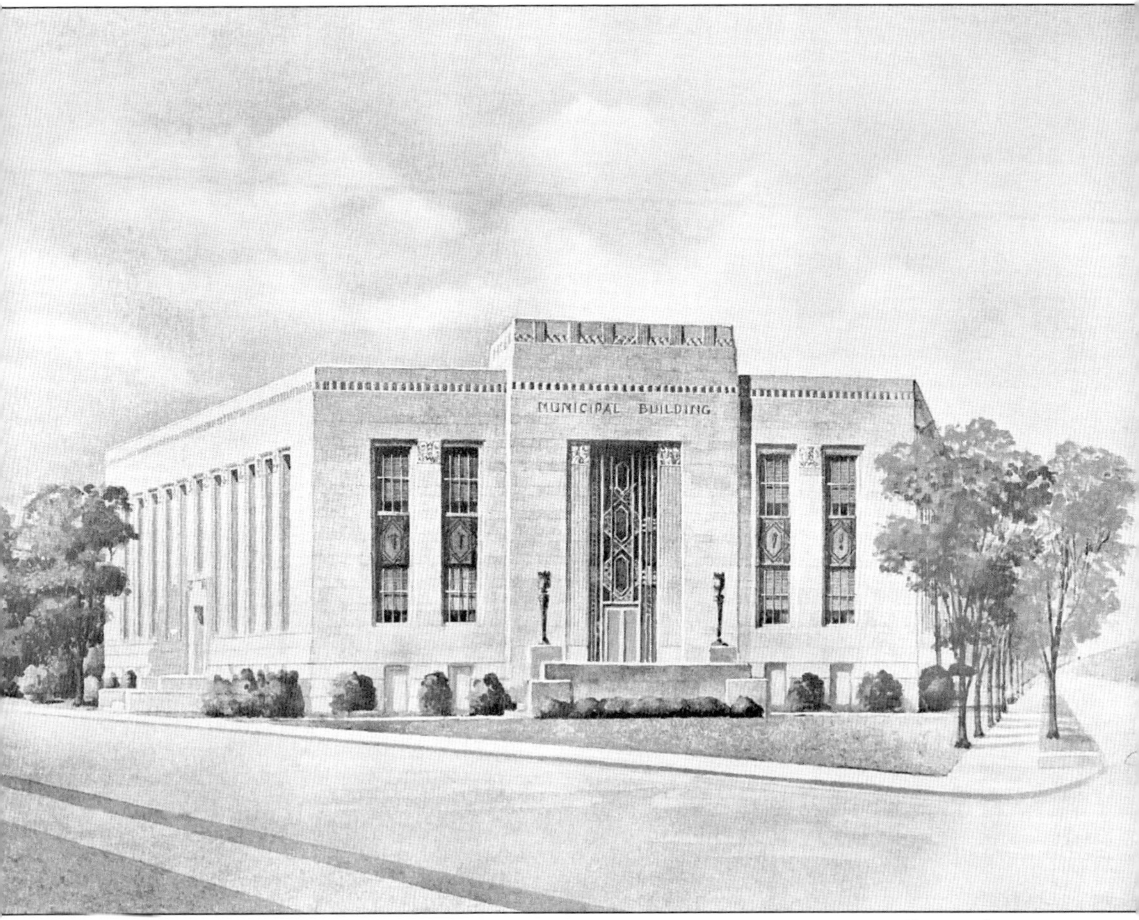

THE MUNICIPAL BUILDING, KENMORE'S MOST RECOGNIZABLE PUBLIC STRUCTURE. Situated on the village green where Delaware Avenue and Delaware Road divide, the municipal building houses the chambers of the Village of Kenmore Board of Trustees and the Town of Tonawanda Council, plus the village court, along with the offices of the village mayor and the town supervisor, both the village and town clerks, and other central offices of both municipalities. It was designed by preeminent Buffalo architect E.B. Green, and is an outstanding example of the "Classical-Monumental" style, which was favored for public edifices in the 1930s. Particularly interesting are the Art Deco aluminum ornamentation on the exterior, and the overall plan, which neatly fits the triangular lot on which it is situated. The courtroom and the council chamber on the second floor can be combined into a single room if needed. Constructed in 1936 as a replacement for the old village and town hall located on the same site, it was funded by the federal government's Public Works Administration, and dedicated by Governor Herbert Lehman. In recent years, it has been made handicapped accessible. There is a table in the town supervisor's office that once stood in the law office of Millard Fillmore. The Buffalo & Erie County Historical Society has acknowledged the historic value of the building with a marker.

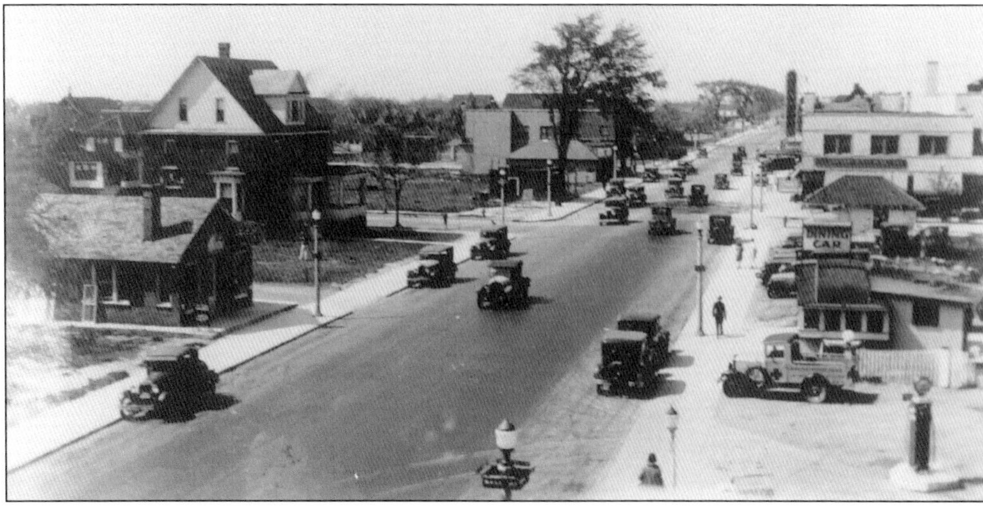

BUILDINGS ON DELAWARE AVENUE NEAR THE INTERSECTIONS OF TREMONT AVENUE AND LANDERS ROAD IN THE 1920S. The large gabled house eventually became the William Rolling Funeral Home, now the Dengler & Roberts Funeral Home. In the vacant lot just to the north now sits the 1960 post office. Two taverns and professional offices occupy the rest of the block. Across the street is the Kenmore Theater building (top right) and the Kenmore Diner (south, across Chapel). The diner was demolished in 1969.

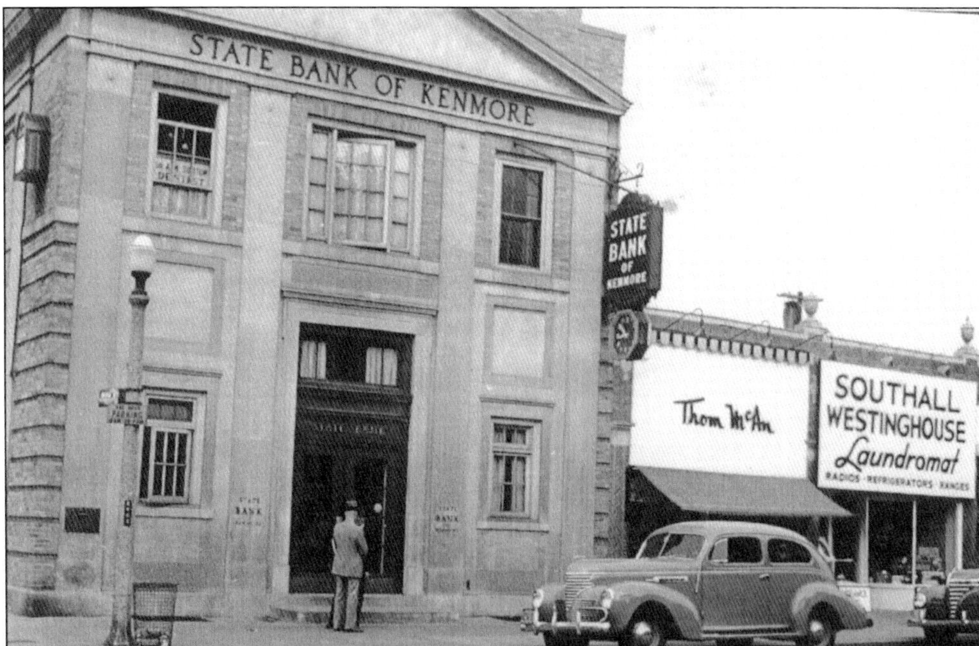

THE STATE BANK OF KENMORE AT MANG AND DELAWARE, C. 1941. It was issued a state charter and moved into this building in October 1924. After 40 years, State Bank was bought out by larger firms; the Bank of Buffalo, then the Bank of New York, and now Key Bank. Thom McAnn shoes was part of the village scene for many years. There were no parking meters in Kenmore until 1948. The DeSoto parked in front of the bank cost less than $1,000 brand new in 1939.

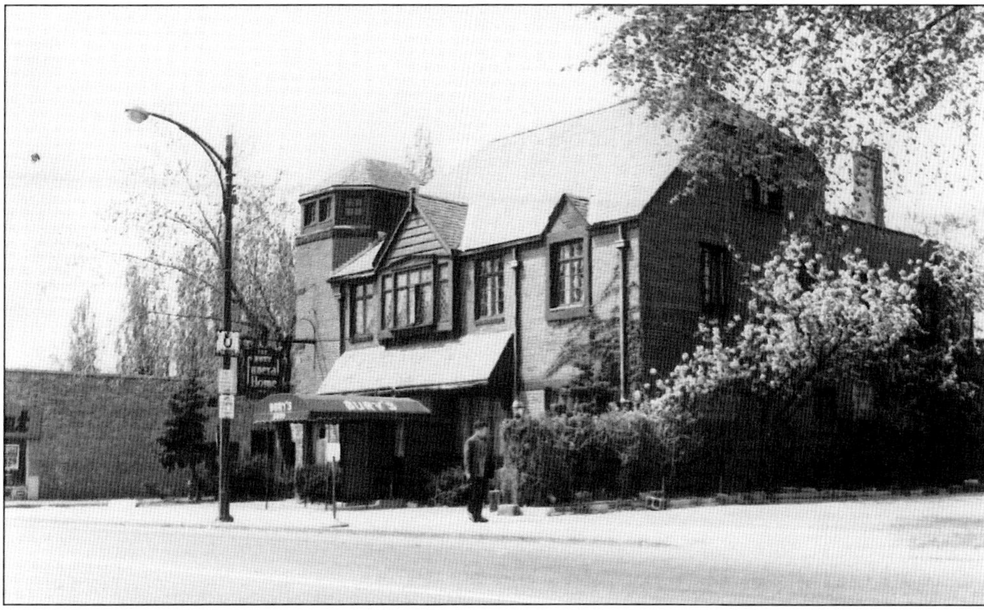

THE KENMORE STAMP COMPANY. During the 1930s, the Kenmore Stamp Company served a nationwide clientele, operating out of this Tudor Revival building at the corner of Delaware and Kinsey Avenues. When the stamp business moved out, the structure became the Bury Funeral Home (the name drew the attention of Ripley's "Believe It or Not"). It subsequently became the Bury-Roberts Funeral Home. (Larry H. Oskin photo, TKHS collection.)

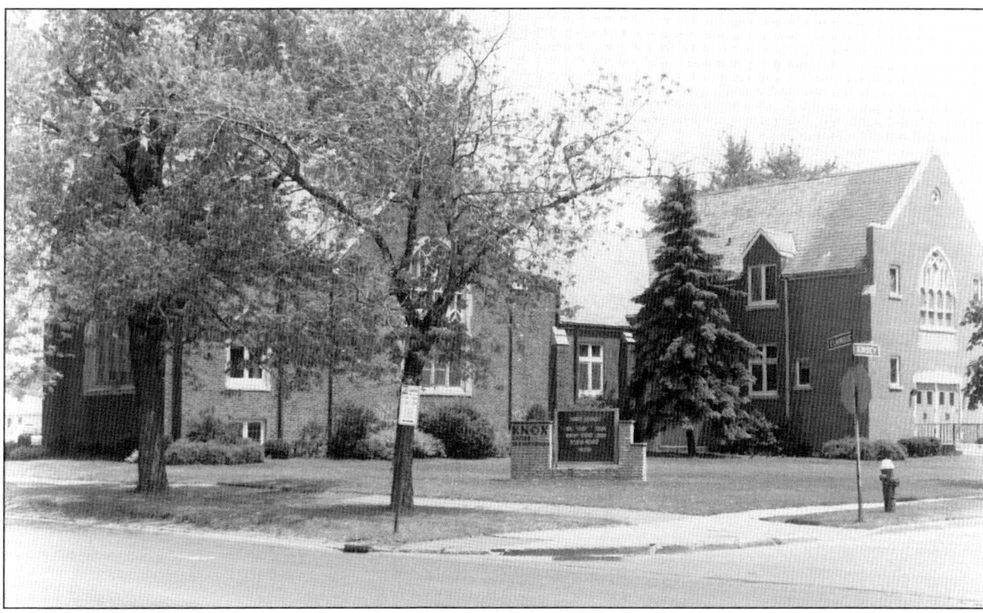

KNOX PRESBYTERIAN CHURCH. Originally a mission of the Riverside United Presbyterian Church, the congregation was founded in 1927 by 47 charter members as the Kenmore United Presbyterian Church. The building at Elmwood and Kinsey Avenues was constructed in 1928, enlarged in 1938, and enlarged again in 1956. The name, honoring the founder of Presbyterianism, was changed in 1968 after a merger of Presbyterian bodies in the United States temporarily resulted in two congregations named Kenmore United Presbyterian Church.

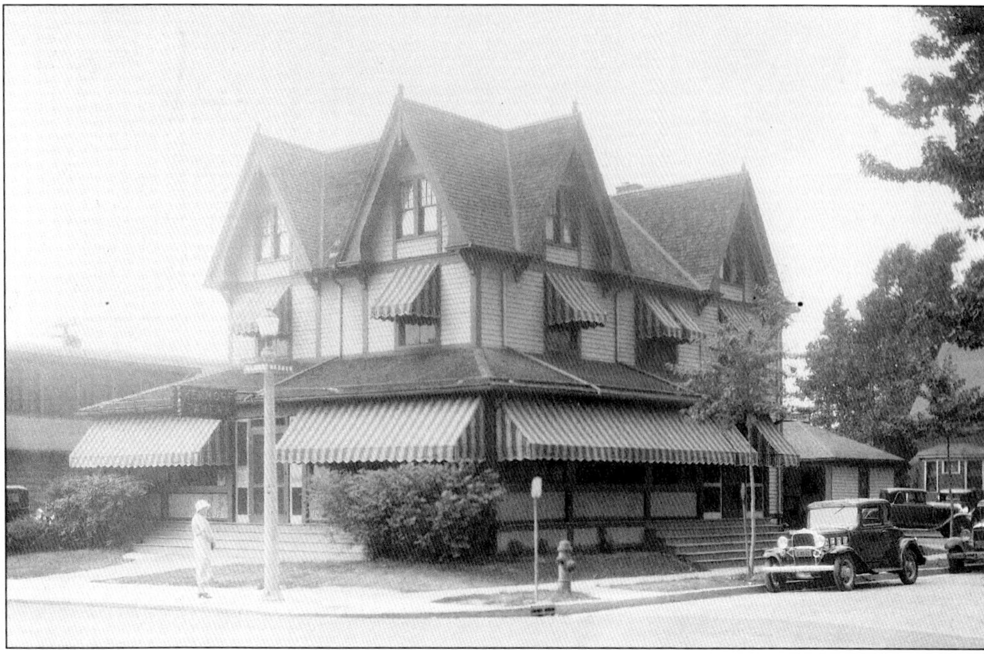

THE KENMORE TAVERN AT DELAWARE AND WABASH AVENUE, C. 1932. Opened as Bleyle's Kenmore Hotel in 1893, it was a "half-way house" serving travelers between Buffalo and Tonawanda along the newly paved Delaware Avenue.

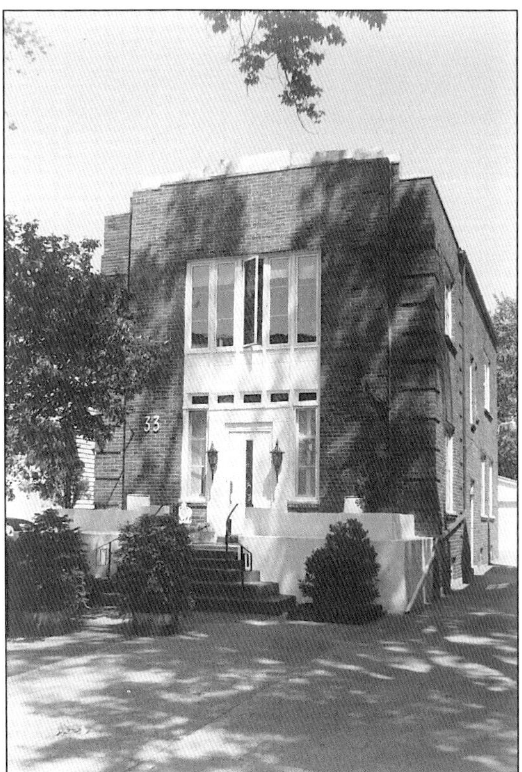

THE UNIQUE 1930S ART DECO HOME AT 33 DELAWARE ROAD. Designed by noted local architect Duane Lyman, this home was built as a doctor's office, with a small apartment upstairs to comply with the residential zoning designation of the street. For many years it was utilized as the medical office of Dr. Ralph Argen, and has more recently been adapted as the home and art studio of the Auerbach family The original interior decoration, much of it carefully preserved, reflects the style of the exterior.

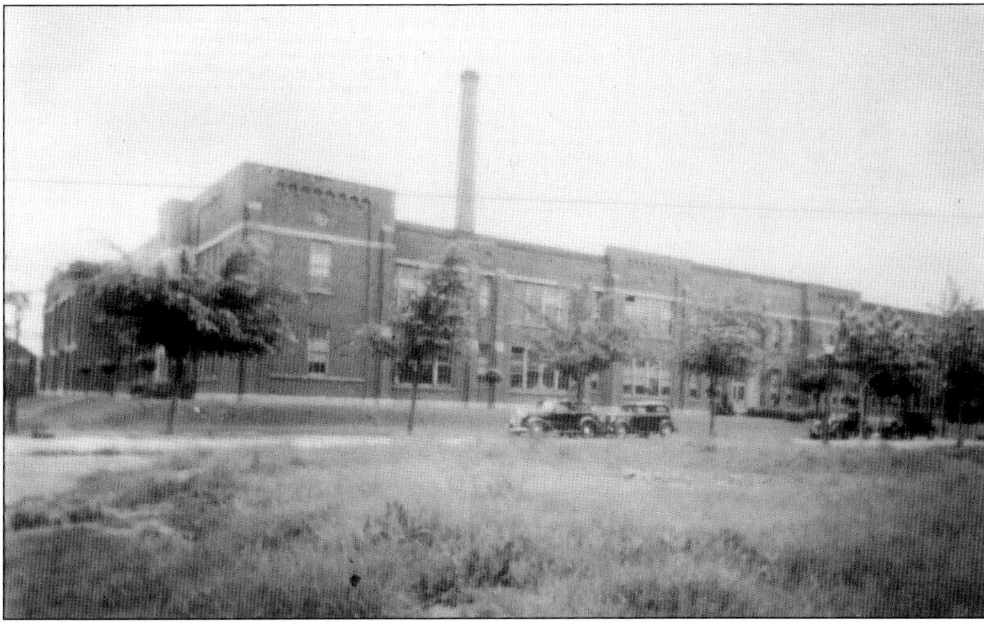

THE THEODORE ROOSEVELT ELEMENTARY SCHOOL FACING WASHINGTON AVENUE AT WILBUR. This school opened in 1928 to serve the children who lived in the expanding residential areas in the western portion of the village. Previously, they would have had to walk half-way across Kenmore to attend Washington School. Currently the oldest active elementary school building in the Ken-Ton district, it has kept up with the times through considerable renovation and modernization. This is a 1977 photo.

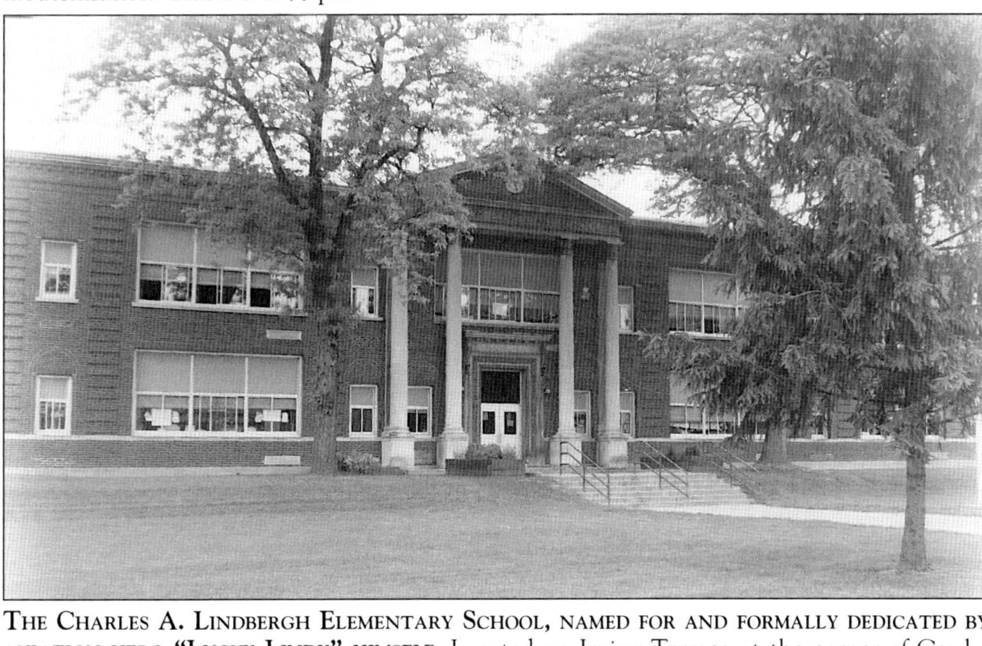

THE CHARLES A. LINDBERGH ELEMENTARY SCHOOL, NAMED FOR AND FORMALLY DEDICATED BY AVIATION HERO "LUCKY LINDY" HIMSELF. Located on Irving Terrace at the corner of Crosby Avenue, just east of the village line in the Town of Tonawanda (the playground is within the village), Lindbergh has educated thousands of village children since it opened in 1931. Its best-known alumnus, appropriately, is astronaut Edward Gibson.

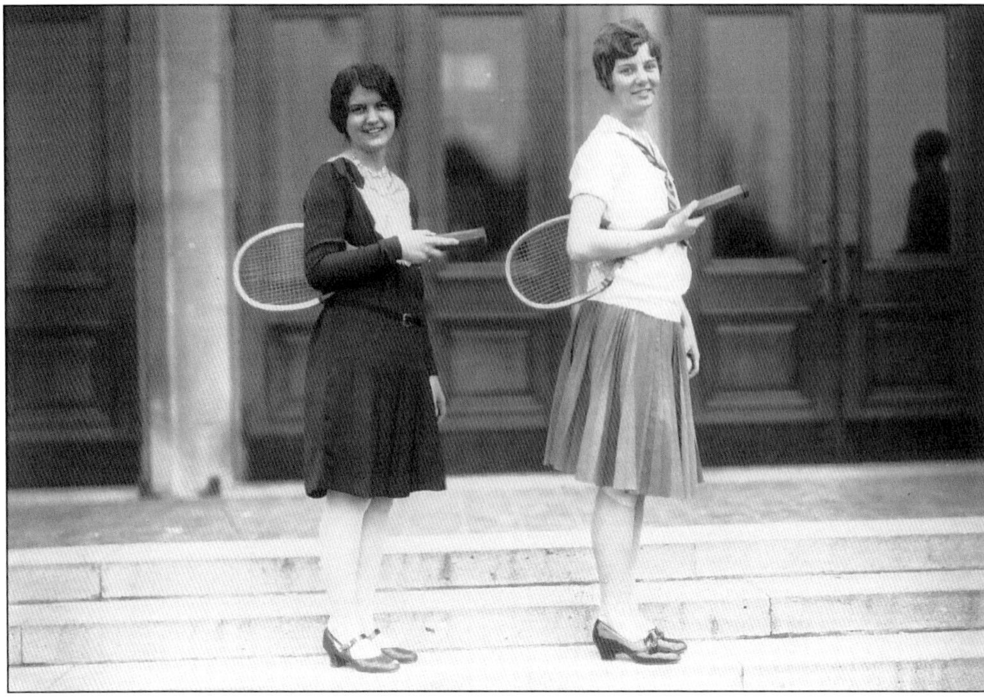

CO-CHAMPIONS POSING PROUDLY ON THE SCHOOL STEPS. The caption of this picture from the 1929 *Kenitorial* reads, "According to custom a girl's tournament was held last fall, and K's awarded the winners. As 'Jupiter Pluvius' prevented the final playoff, Lenore Scanlon and Mary Budik are tied for first place."

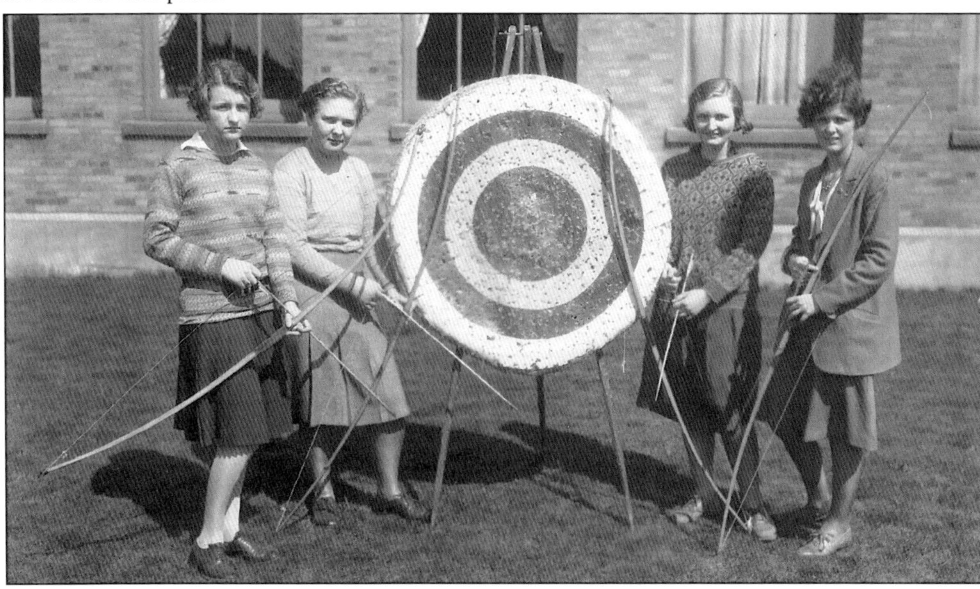

THE KENMORE HIGH SCHOOL GIRLS' ARCHERY TEAM OF 1929. From left to right are Alice Wiser, Edith DeVine, Ruth Penman, and Helen Harper. All four were awarded letter K's "for their prowess," having accomplished much during what was only the second year of the sport at Kenmore. The accompanying caption states that "unusual scores were obtained" during interscholastic competition.

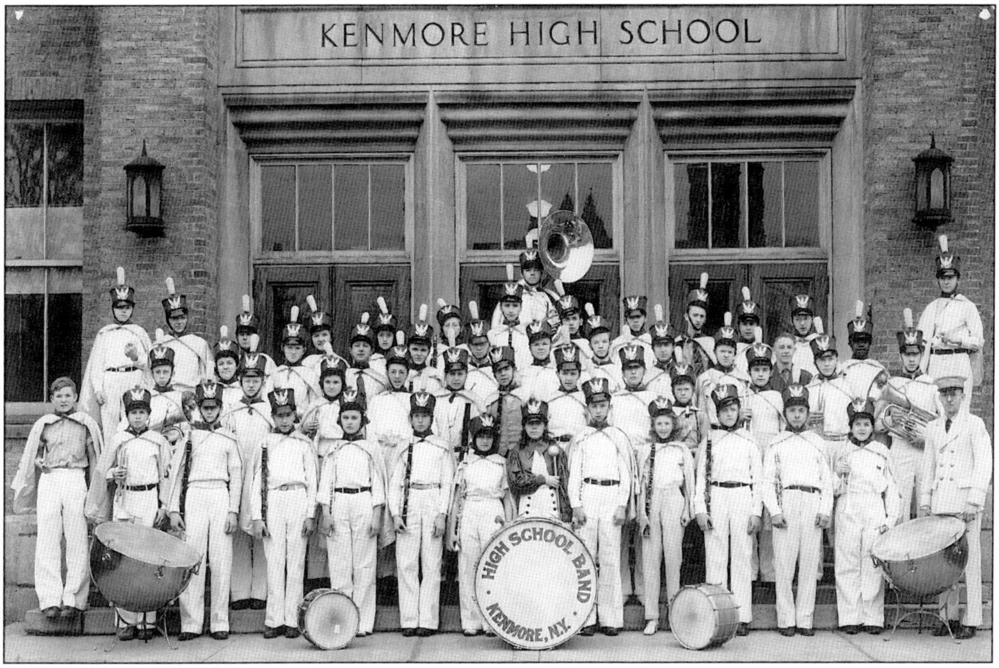

Members of Kenmore High School's "B" and "C" bands in a photo from the 1938 *Kenitorial*. The caption notes, "Because of outstanding talent in the 'C' or beginners' group, the 'B' and 'C' bands merged to form a unit of contest size and ability." The combined bands subsequently competed in a music festival at Fredonia. The conductor, standing at the far right in the front row, was Mr. Carl Hann.

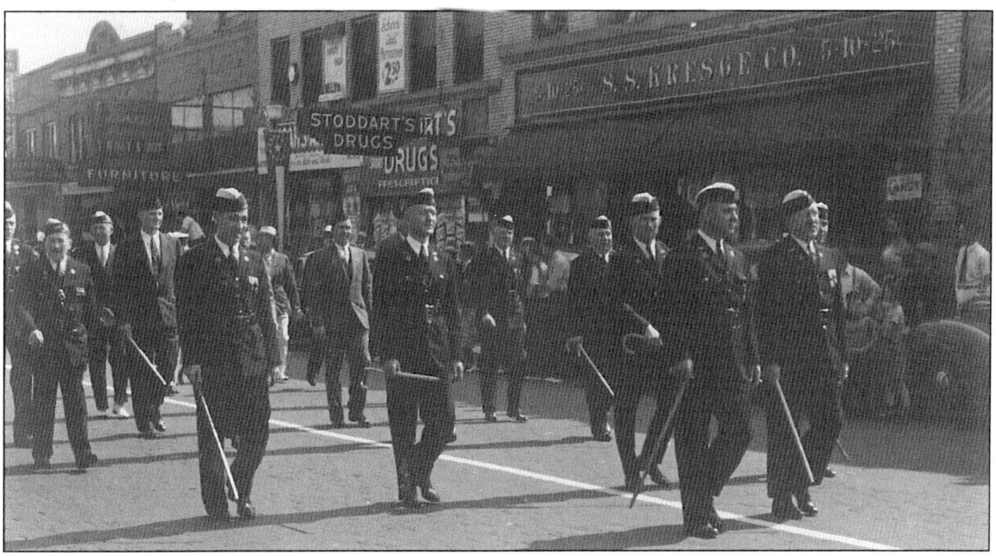

Members of the American Legion (almost certainly members of the Brounshidle Post) marching north on Delaware Avenue between LaSalle and Mang around 1940. By then a smoother surface had been applied over the paving blocks. The Kresge's store in the picture was later replaced by Fishman's, and Stoddart's Drugs became Nalbach's. The Noah's Ark auto supply store, Les Wheeler's furniture and appliances, and the Kenmore Liquor Store can be seen farther south.

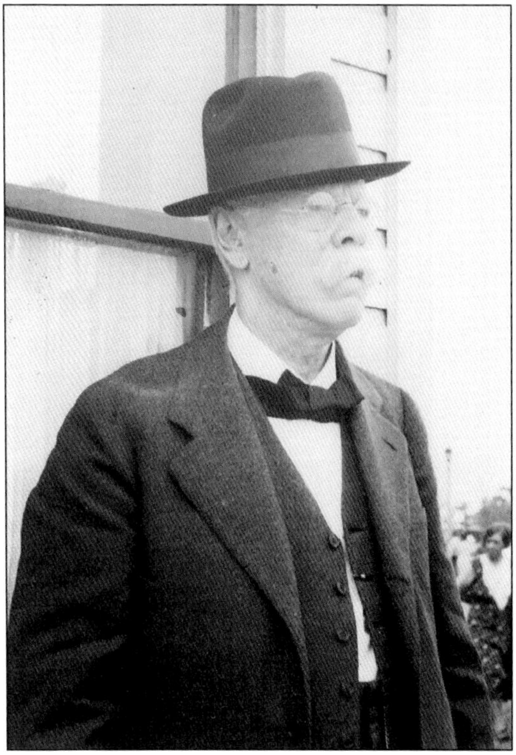

LOUIS PHILLIP ADOLPH EBERHARDT, C. 1936. L.P.A. Eberhardt nearly always appeared in public in a black suit and vest, white shirt (with starched collar), black hat, gold watch and chain, and gold-rimmed spectacles. Even at the age of 76 he was frequently seen throughout the village supervising his many enterprises.

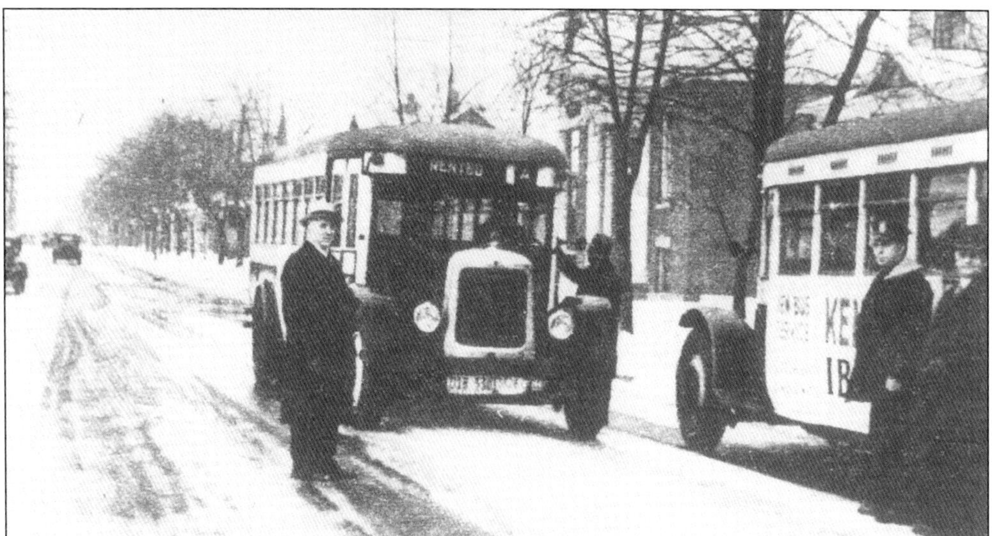

TWO BUSES AND THE ODD FELLOWS HALL (IN THE BACKGROUND BETWEEN THE TWO) AT MYRON AVENUE. The International Railway Company inaugurated service along Kenmore Avenue from Delaware to Colvin, then north on Colvin in 1931, the forerunner to today's #11 route. The new service was welcomed by the rapidly expanding village but had not gained approval by the City of Buffalo when the service was begun on January 15. Therefore, buses had to run in both directions on the village side of Kenmore Avenue until the city granted approval a short time later. Busses of this type had gasoline engines which generated electricity used by electric motors to power the wheels.

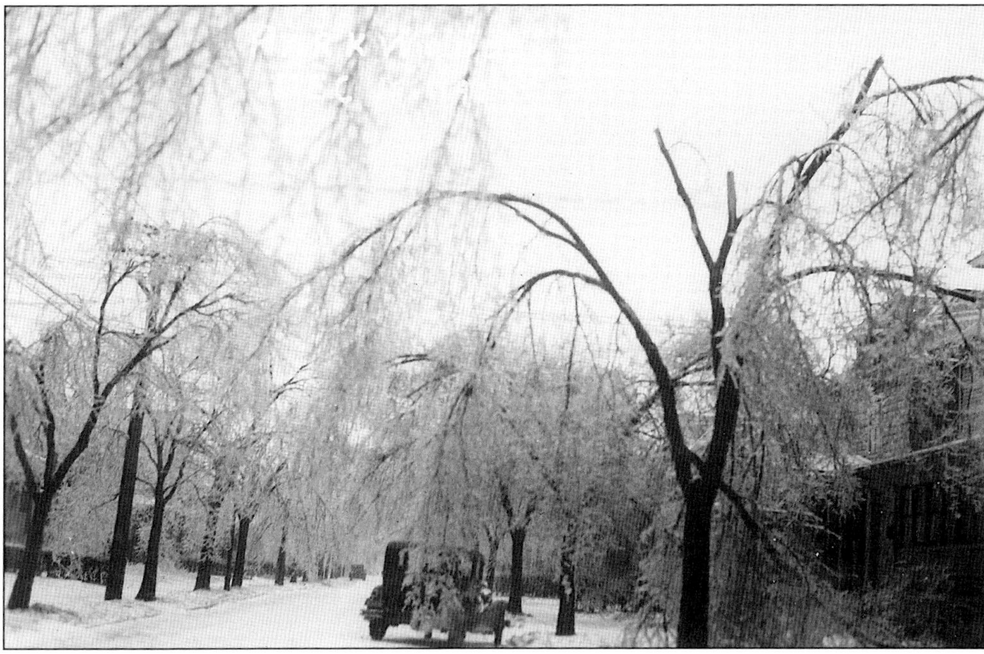

THE AFTERMATH OF AN ICE STORM, PARKWOOD AVENUE, 1929. Although Kenmore was spared the devastation of the major ice storm that paralyzed much of the northeastern United States and Eastern Canada in 1998, as this photograph shows, it has not always been immune from frozen precipitation. A similar storm struck Kenmore in 1976, resulting in downed power lines, numerous residential and business power outages, and the closing of some of the village's schools.

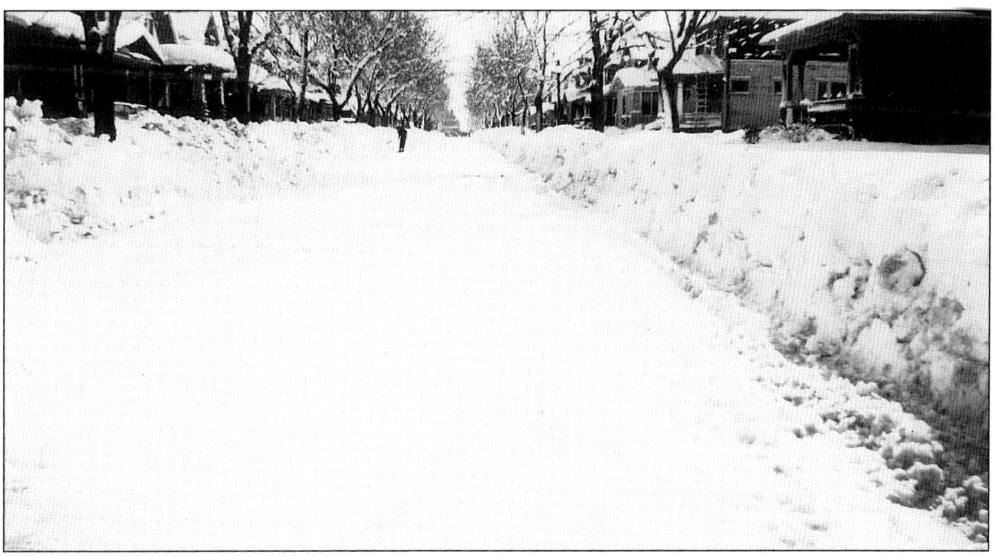

THE AFTERMATH OF A MAJOR SNOWFALL DURING THE WINTER OF 1935–36. While the Blizzard of 1977 may be the most widely remembered in recent years, it was hardly the only major snowstorm to affect Western New York's communities. Wabash Avenue is shown here near Eugene, looking east toward Delaware. The village plows have made the street passable, but all of those sidewalks and long driveways would need to be shoveled clean by hand.

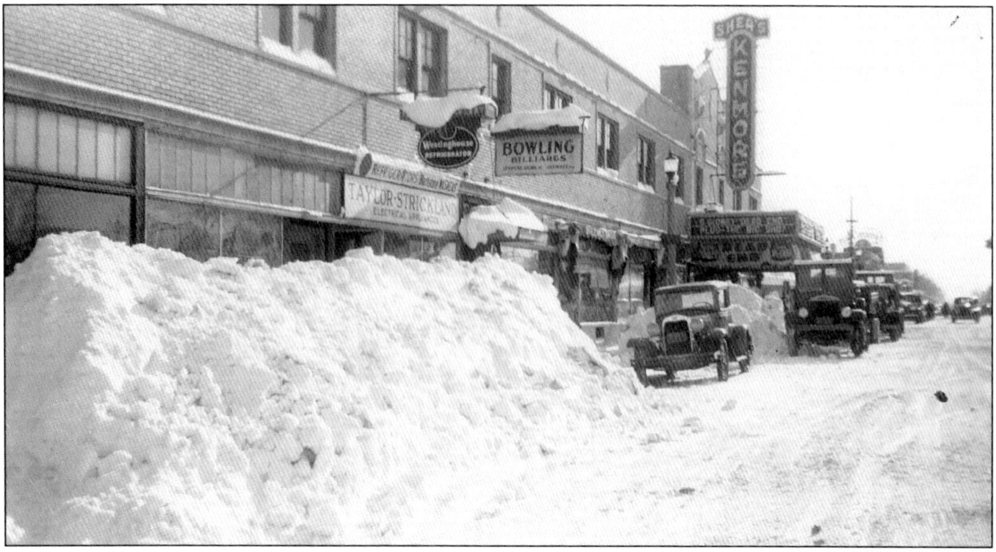

Snow piled high along Delaware Avenue in front of the Kenmore Theater block on March 27, 1936, ten days after the infamous St. Patrick's Day storm. Perhaps March was never more cruel to local residents than in 1936 when, just as the hint of spring was in the air, winter returned with a fury not seen for two decades, paralyzing the area with heavy, wet snow. Travel came to a halt and schoolchildren enjoyed an early "spring" vacation.

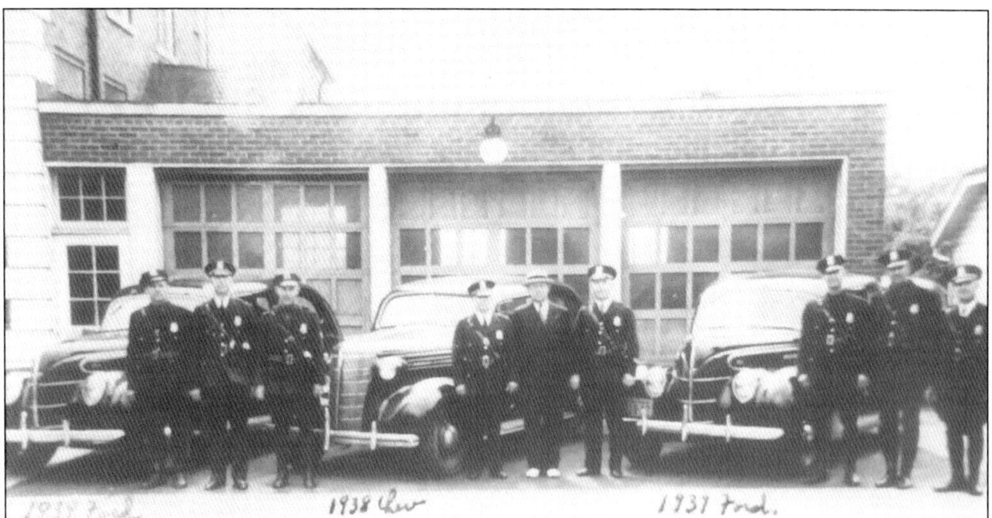

Two new 1939 Ford police cars flanking the chief's 1938 Chevrolet in front of the police garage on Nash Road. At center is Mayor Clifford Lane, who served from 1935 to 1948. To his left is venerable Kenmore Police Chief Clarence Youchum, who served on the force from 1919 to 1954. In that era the village alternated the purchase of police cars each year between two village auto dealers, Lou Awald Chevrolet and Kenmore Motors (Ford). The chief always used a year-old patrol car; the others were traded toward new patrol cars.

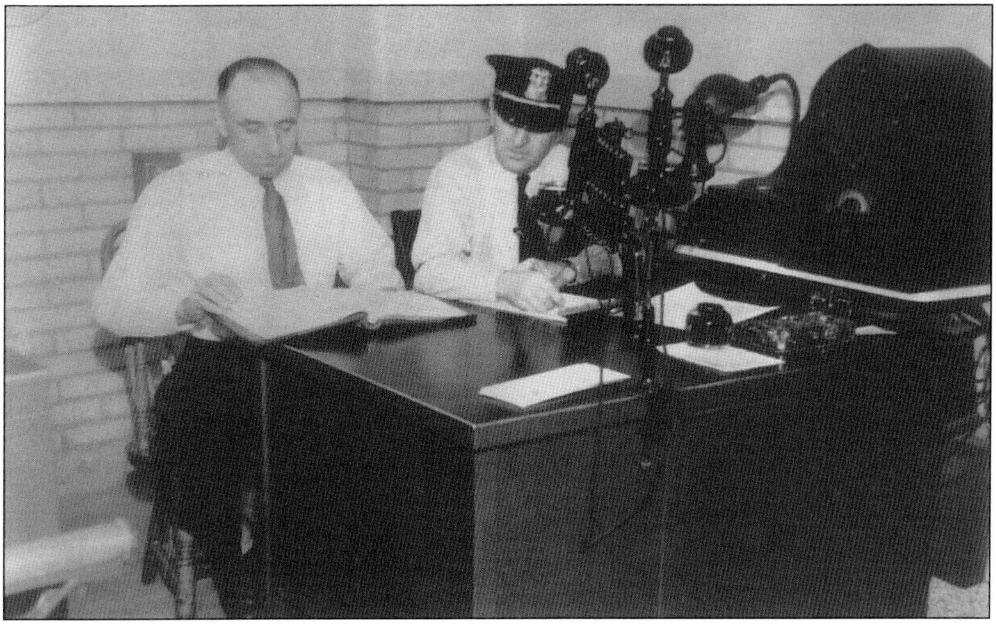

KENMORE'S NEW POLICE STATION, WHICH OPENED IN 1929 IN THE COMBINATION FIRE AND POLICE HALL ON NASH ROAD. This 1934 photo shows Desk Lieutenants E. Schultz and W.C. Thorpe (with hat) handling the modern radio equipment the village used in fighting crime. Police vehicles were kept in a garage at the rear of the building. The police department moved to Elmwood Avenue in 1951.

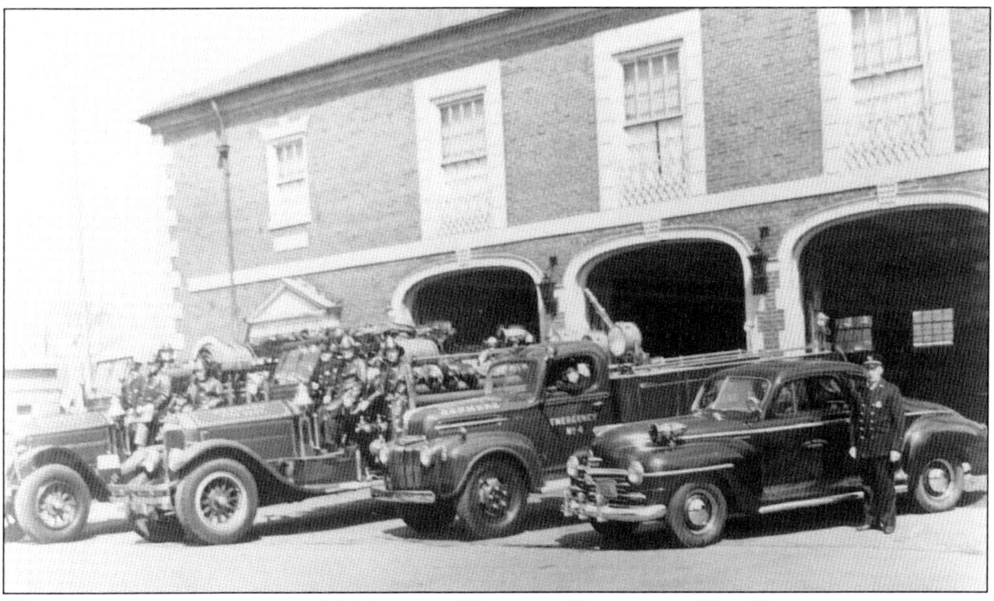

NEW EQUIPMENT ACQUIRED IN 1946 BY THE KENMORE VOLUNTEER FIRE DEPARTMENT PROUDLY DISPLAYED IN FRONT OF THE FIRE HALL. During World War II, automotive production was designated toward the war effort, and community fire-fighting units had to make do with whatever pre-war apparatus they had. In 1946, the Kenmore Volunteer Fire Department was able to acquire some new equipment, including a truck built on a Ford chassis. (KVFD collection.)

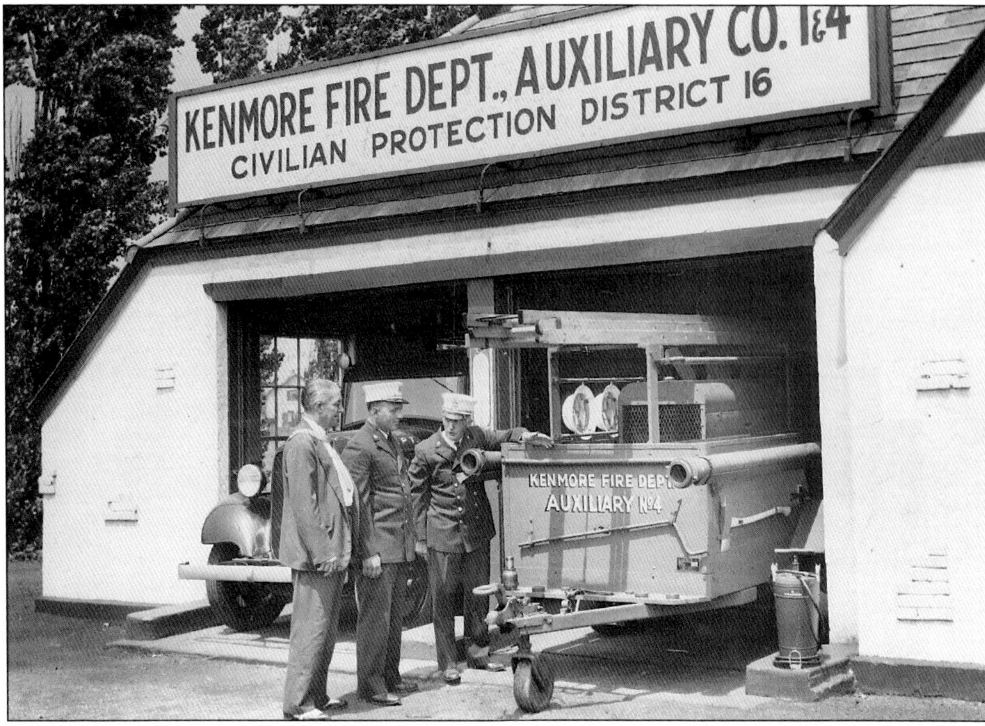

THE AUXILIARY FIRE STATION SET UP DURING WORLD WAR II AT THE CORNER OF KENTON ROAD AND DELAWARE AVENUE. Shown inspecting the equipment in this 1943 photograph are, from left to right, Civil Defense Director Guy Malden Sr., Kenmore Volunteer Fire Department Chief Charles Wolff, and Village of Kenmore Fire Marshall Raymond Kirsch. (KVFD collection.)

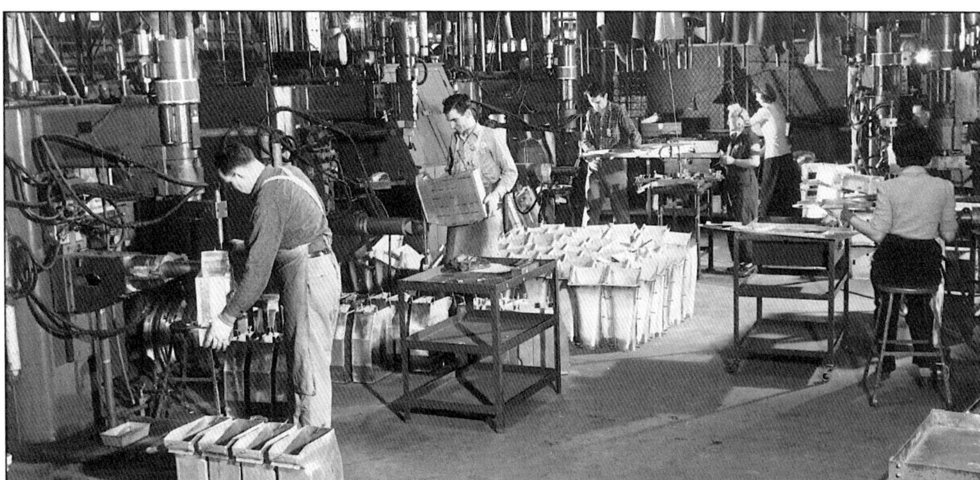

THE ORIGINAL BELL AIRCRAFT PLANT ON ELMWOOD AVENUE, JUST SOUTH OF THE VILLAGE LINE. Constructed for Curtiss during World War I, the plant later housed the Consolidated aircraft factory (whose first Catalina flying boat was built there). Many Kenmore residents worked on Bell's assembly lines during World War II, producing Airacobra and King Cobra fighters and a few pusher-propeller Airacudas, along with aerial machine gun mounts. Bell airplanes were used by air forces of both the United States and its wartime allies.

Five

The Mature Village

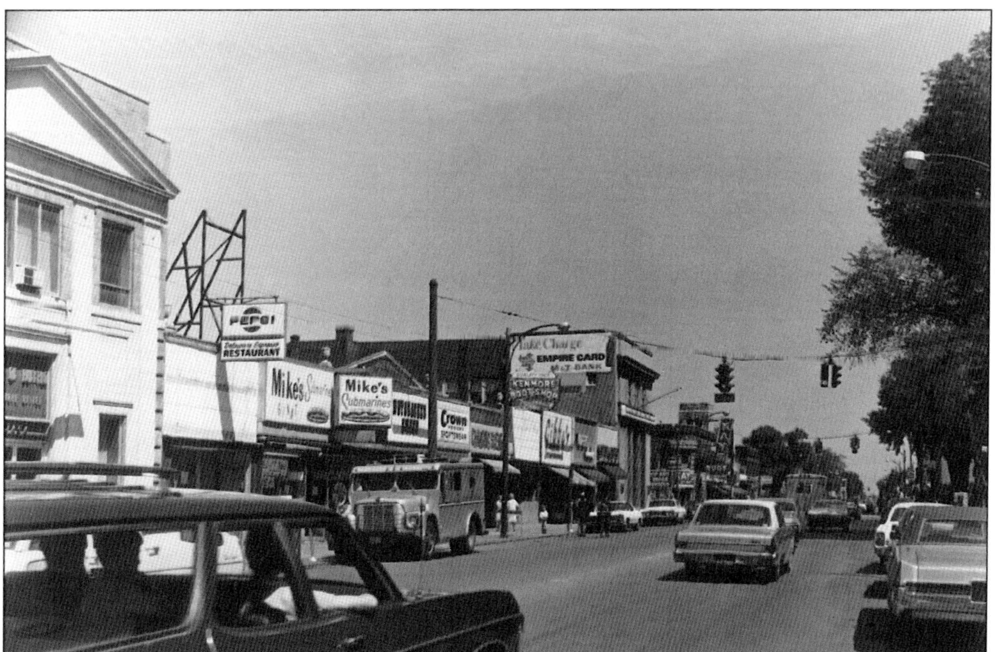

THE BANK OF BUFFALO (LATER THE BANK OF NEW YORK, NOW THE KEY BANK) AND THE M&T BANK FARTHER NORTH ON THE WEST SIDE OF DELAWARE AVENUE BETWEEN MANG AND LINCOLN IN 1971. Of the other businesses in the photograph, only two, Mike's Submarines and Hofert's Jewelers, both of them locally owned, survived into the late 1990s.

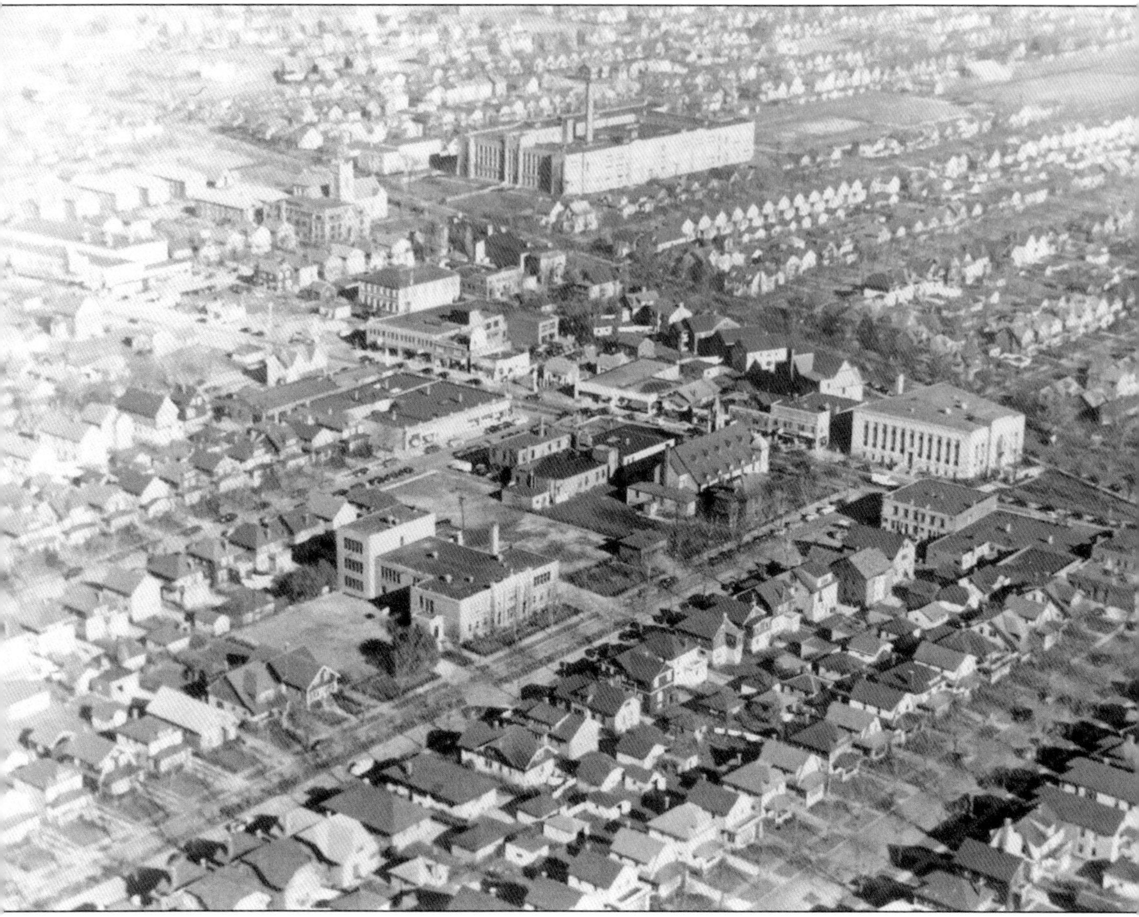

DOWNTOWN KENMORE LOOKING NORTHEAST, C. 1941. The municipal building is at right center, Kenmore Junior High School is at top center, and St. Paul's Church, rectory, and school are in the center of this photograph. St. Paul's parochial school was built in 1925 to replace an earlier wooden building. Children attended grades one through eight, then usually went on to Mount St. Mary Academy, Canisius High School, St. Joseph's Collegiate Institute, or Kenmore Senior High School.

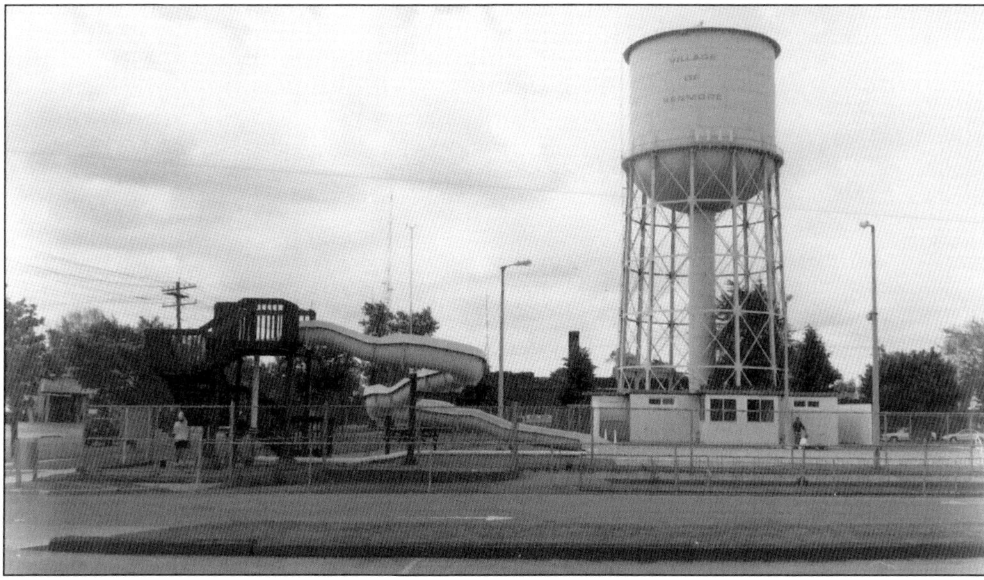

Two of the most visible landmarks in the western portion of Kenmore. The million-gallon water tower behind the public works building on Elmwood Avenue was erected in 1927 to provide reliable pressure throughout the village. The Mang pool, operated by the town parks and recreation department, dates from 1958; a wading pool was added to the site in 1973.

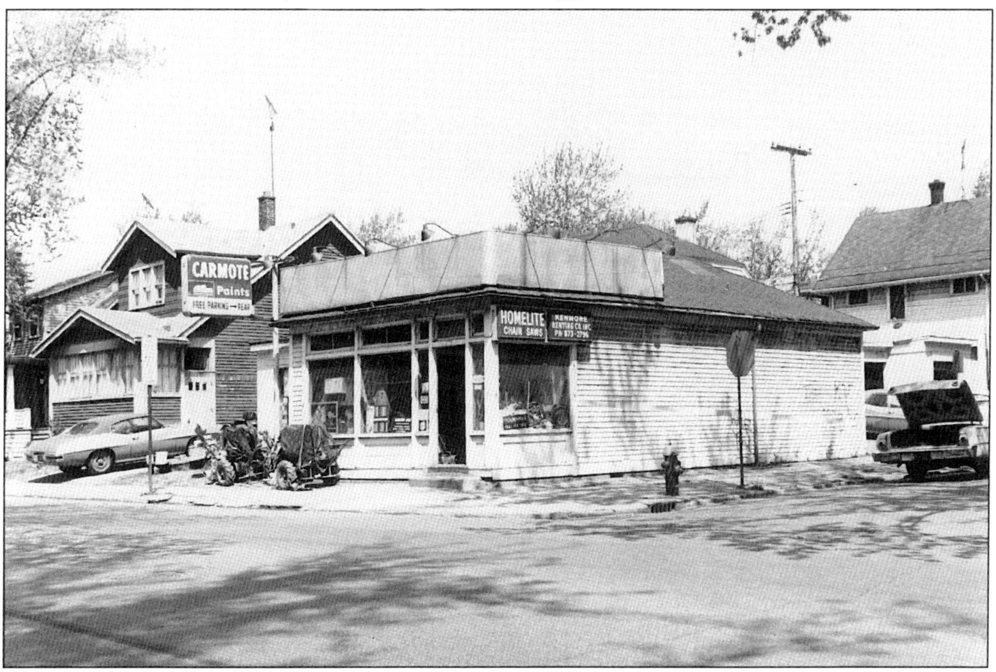

Kenmore Rental. For over half a century, Kenmore Rental, which replaced a general store at the corner of Kenmore and Myron Avenues, has supplied temporarily needed tools to residents of the village and adjacent areas in North Buffalo. What is less known is that a small stream, Cornelius Creek, once flowed roughly along the line of Myron, and at this location a bridge carried traffic over it. During heavy rainstorms, reminders of the watery past have been known to inconvenience area homeowners. (Larry H. Oskin photo, TKHS collection.)

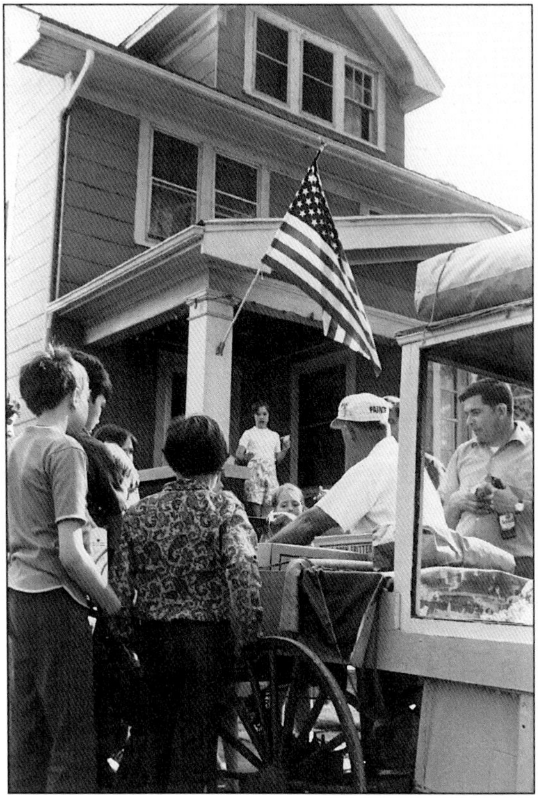

THE POPCORN MAN MAKING HIS ROUNDS ON EAST HAZELTINE IN JUNE 1971. At number 131 a confirmation party was in progress for Maureen Mullen. Given the opportunity to treat his guests and the neighbors, Mr. Mullen bought out the itinerant vendor's entire stock. No disappointment is evident on these faces. (Larry H. Oskin photo, TKHS collection.)

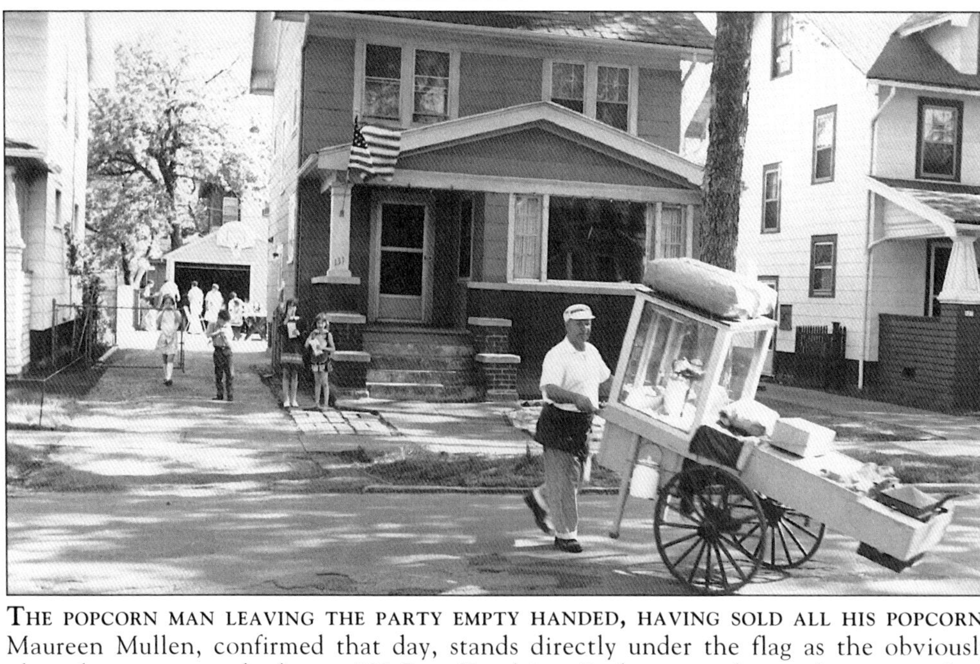

THE POPCORN MAN LEAVING THE PARTY EMPTY HANDED, HAVING SOLD ALL HIS POPCORN. Maureen Mullen, confirmed that day, stands directly under the flag as the obviously pleased popcorn vender leaves 131 East Hazeltine. Pushcart vendors and scenes such as these were common in suburban, as well as urban, areas until recently. (Larry H. Oskin photo, TKHS collection.)

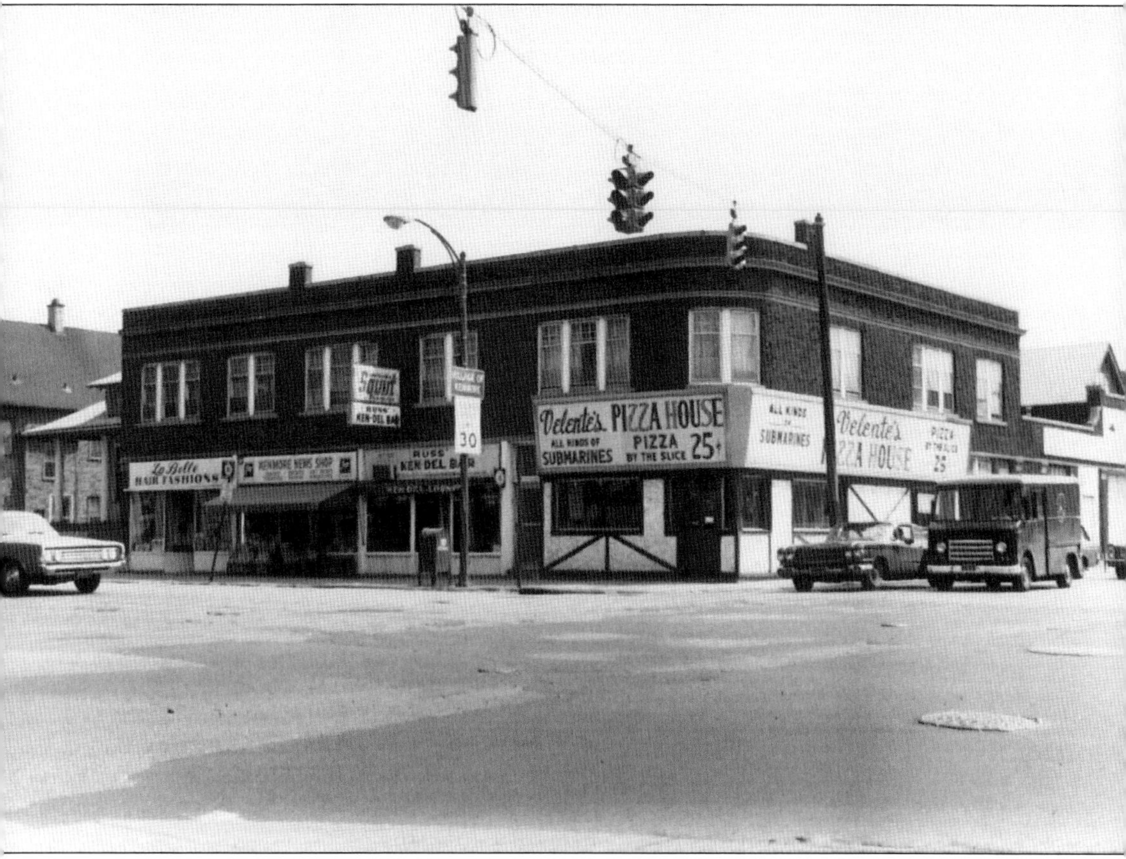

The corner of Delaware and Kenmore Avenues, May 1971. Valente's Pizza House began in business the previous year, having recently replaced the Deco, which in turn had replaced Love's Ice Cream on the corner. A tavern, a news shop, and a beauty parlor complete the set of stores along the avenue. The front porch of the old Eberhardt real estate office can be seen just to the right. The corner building is the one shown under construction on p. 47. (Larry H. Oskin photo, TKHS collection.)

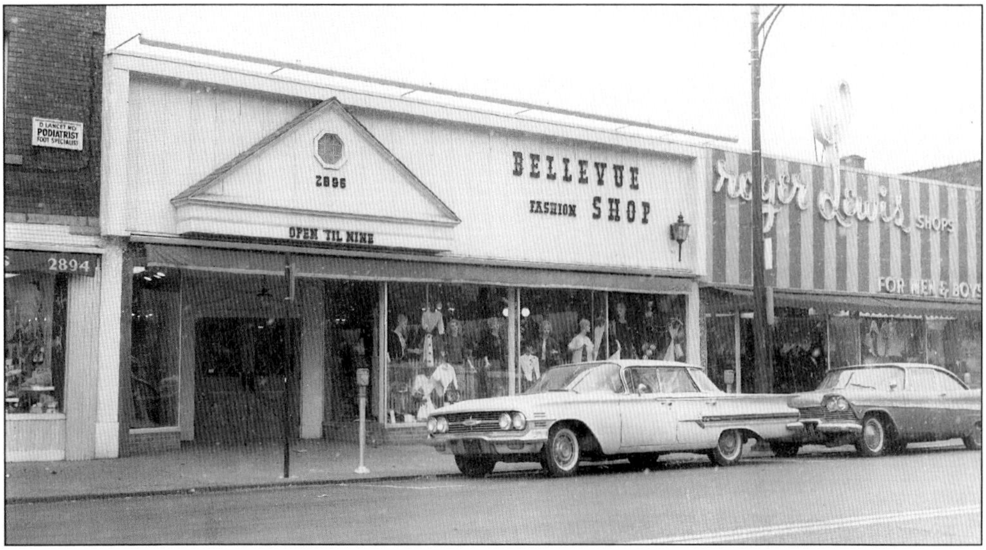

THE WEST SIDE OF DELAWARE BETWEEN LINCOLN AND VICTORIA IN 1961. To the left of the Bellevue Shop is a corner of Siefert's shoe store, which later moved a block south. A number of specialty stores have opened and closed in this block over the years. For many years previously, a W.T. Grant store occupied this location.

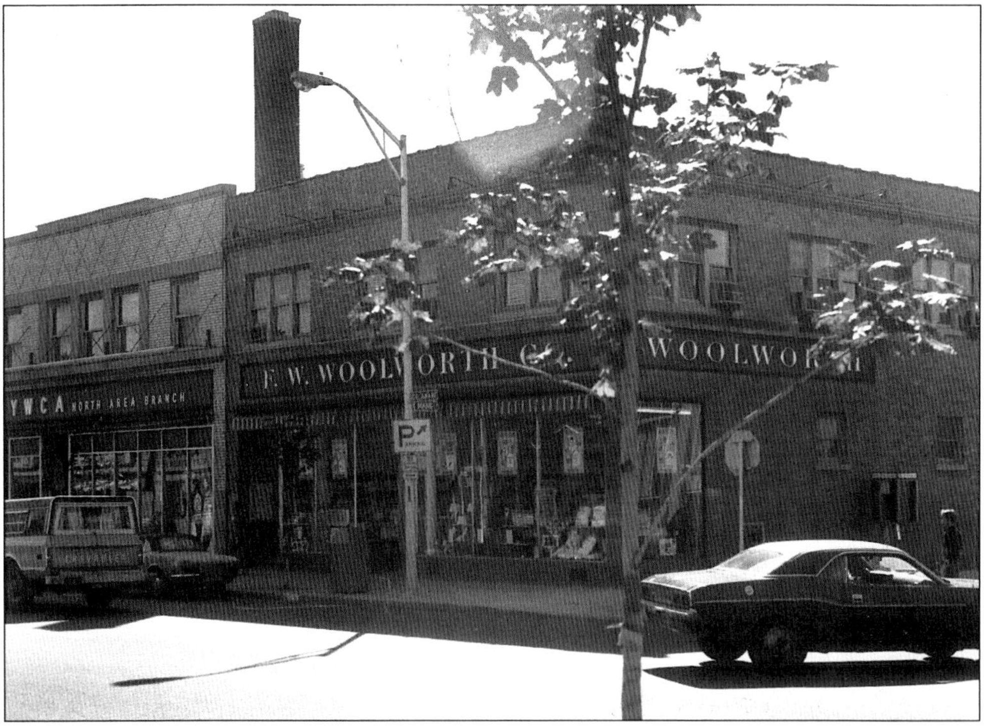

WOOLWORTH'S, LOCATED ON THE SOUTHWEST CORNER OF DELAWARE AND MANG AVENUES. This was the first and last chain "five and ten" store in the village's main shopping district. As happened throughout the country, it was replaced by the "big box" discount stores, and in the 1990s the entire Woolworth operation succumbed. This store briefly was a CVS drug store; it now houses The Fitness Factory.

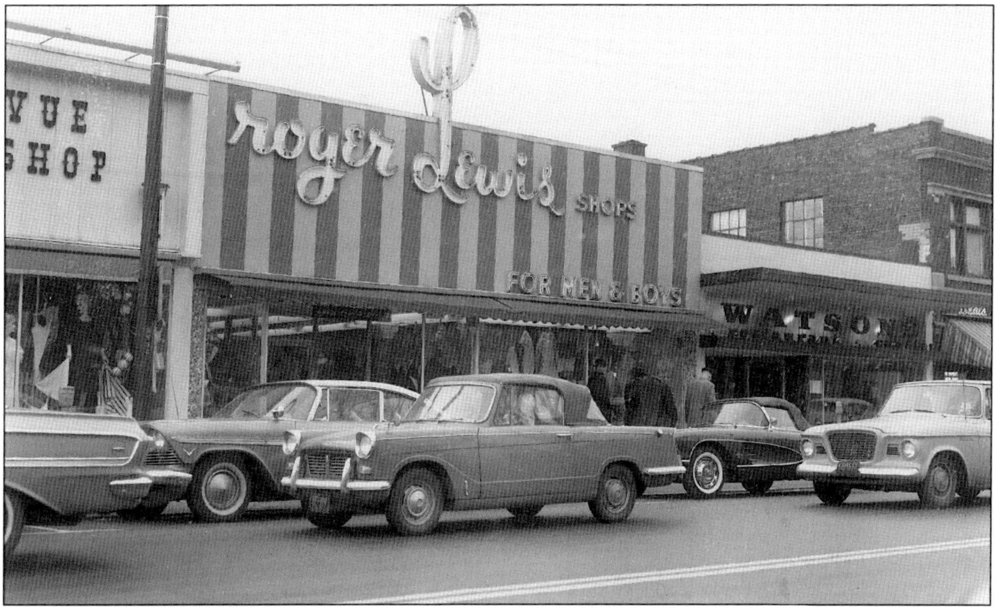

THREE OF KENMORE'S FORMER BUSINESSES IN 1961. The Bellevue Shop (left) became the Jacqueline Shop and moved away in the 1990s; a video rental store took its place. The Roger Lewis men's store is now a wallpaper outlet. Watson's, long a popular village eatery, was replaced by the Plaka, continuing the tradition of a full-service restaurant in the middle of the village.

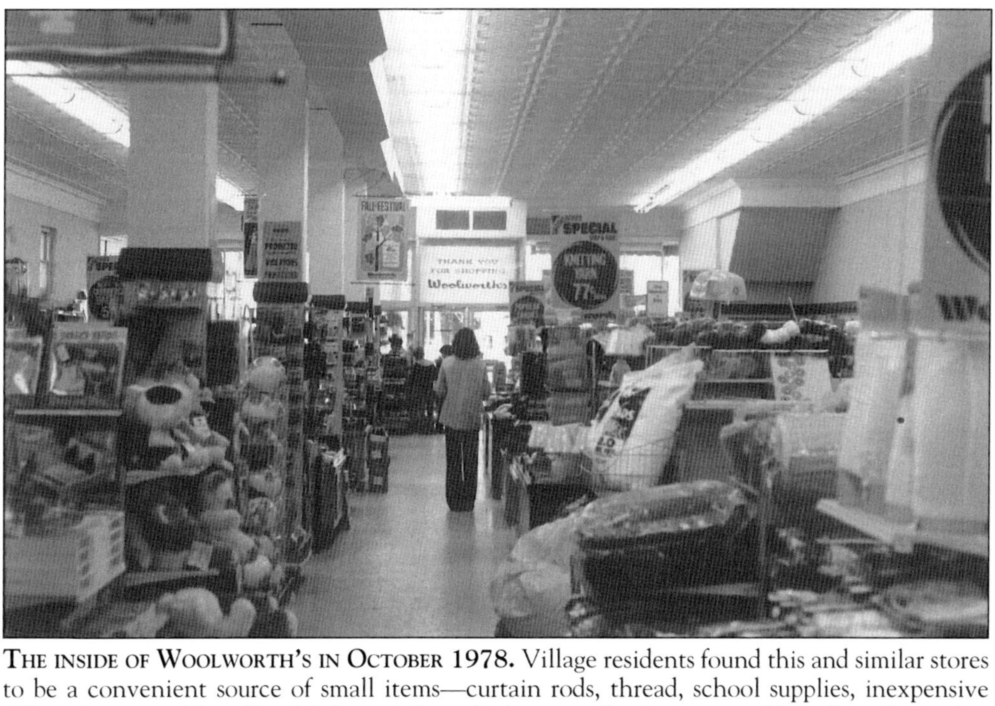

THE INSIDE OF WOOLWORTH'S IN OCTOBER 1978. Village residents found this and similar stores to be a convenient source of small items—curtain rods, thread, school supplies, inexpensive gifts, mittens and handkerchiefs, and those little cans of paint you could find nowhere else. When the store was closed, the announcement was made that, although it was not losing money, it was not making enough to satisfy the corporation.

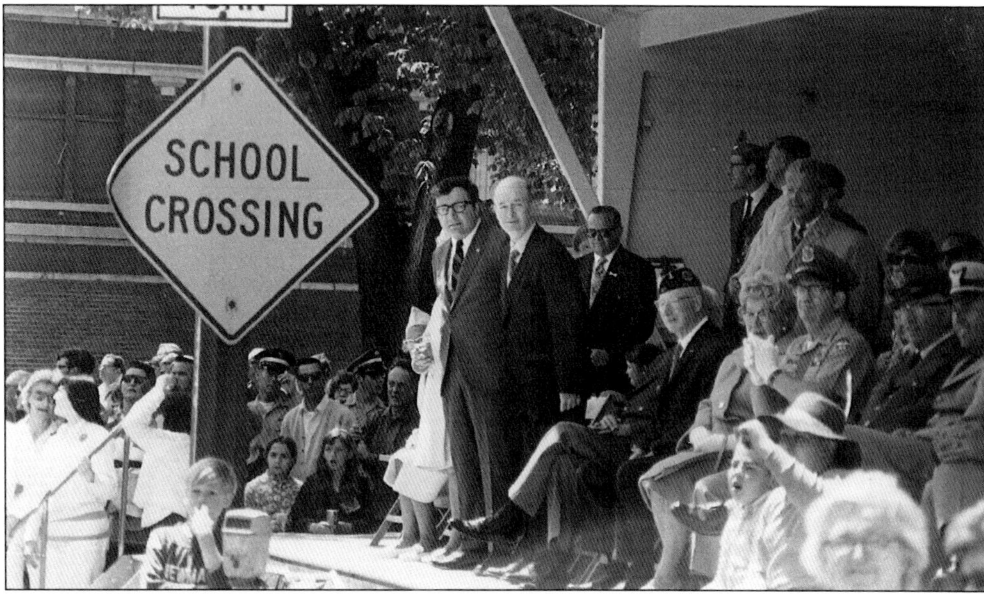

KENMORE'S ANNUAL MEMORIAL DAY PARADE, A TOWN AND VILLAGE TRADITION FOR YEARS. It attracts large numbers of spectators, and, not surprisingly, local political leaders. Standing together on the reviewing stand in 1971 were then State Senator (eventually long-term Congressman) John LaFalce and Mayor Robert Malloy, one of the few Democrats to hold village office in recent memory. (Larry H. Oskin photo, TKHS collection.)

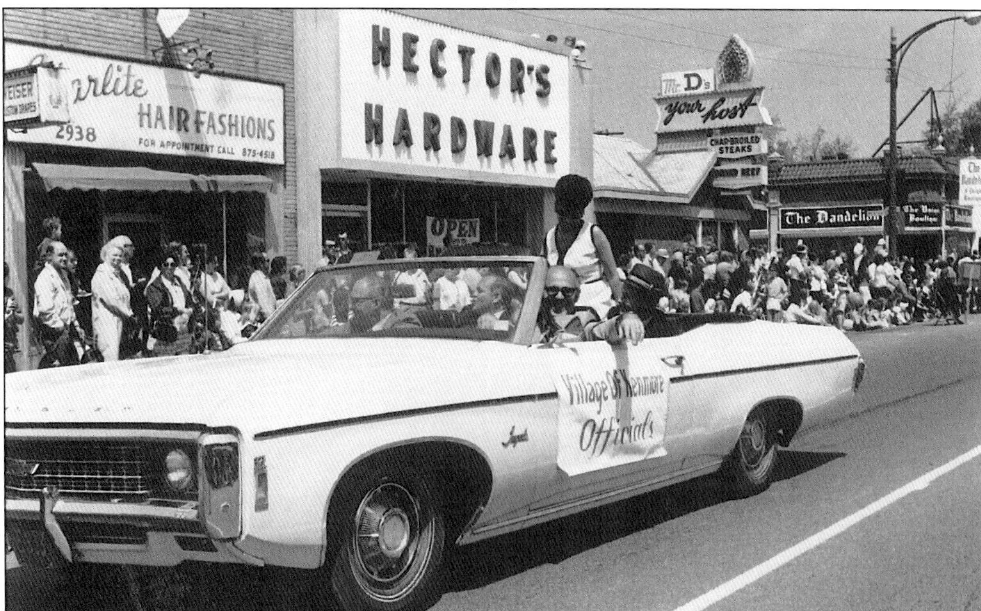

VILLAGE TRUSTEE GUST SERVIS DRIVING FELLOW VILLAGE BOARD MEMBERS ALONG DELAWARE AVENUE SOUTH OF WESTGATE IN THE 1971 MEMORIAL DAY PARADE. Of the stores in the background, only Starlite Hair Fashions remains on the avenue. Hector's Hardware no longer has a Kenmore outlet; Your Host, which absorbed the remnants of the Deco chain, has gone out of business; and the Dandelion Shop has been replaced by H&R Block. (Larry H. Oskin photo, TKHS collection.)

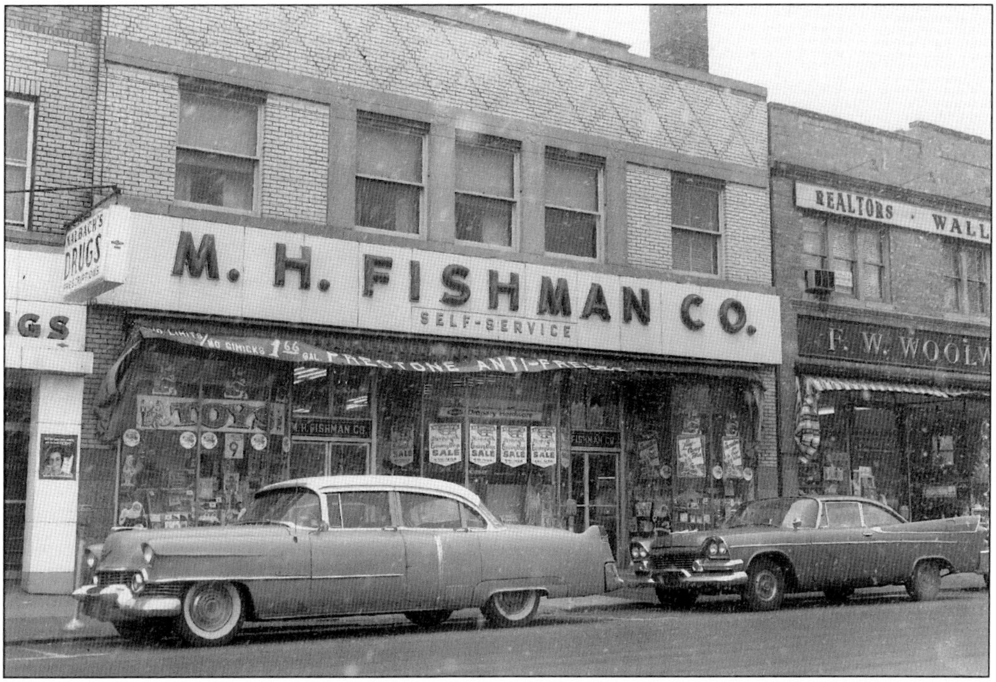

A 1961 view of the crowded display windows that were typical of "dime stores." In 1955 the Kresge's store in the building immediately south of Woolworth's was replaced by Fishman's. The falling snow, the sign advertising anti-freeze, and the Santa Claus visible above the hood of the Cadillac all testify to a November or December date. Nalbach's drug store was next door.

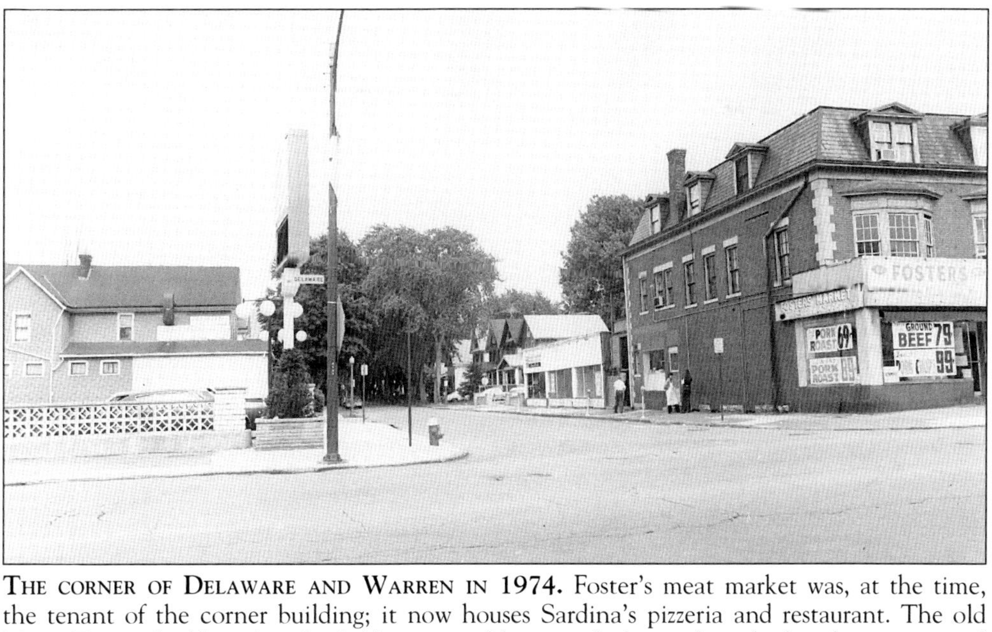

The corner of Delaware and Warren in 1974. Foster's meat market was, at the time, the tenant of the corner building; it now houses Sardina's pizzeria and restaurant. The old Mang Tavern building (on the left), occupied by an upholstery shop, had undergone several changes, including having the porch incorporated into the rest of the structure and the wooden clapboards replaced by siding.

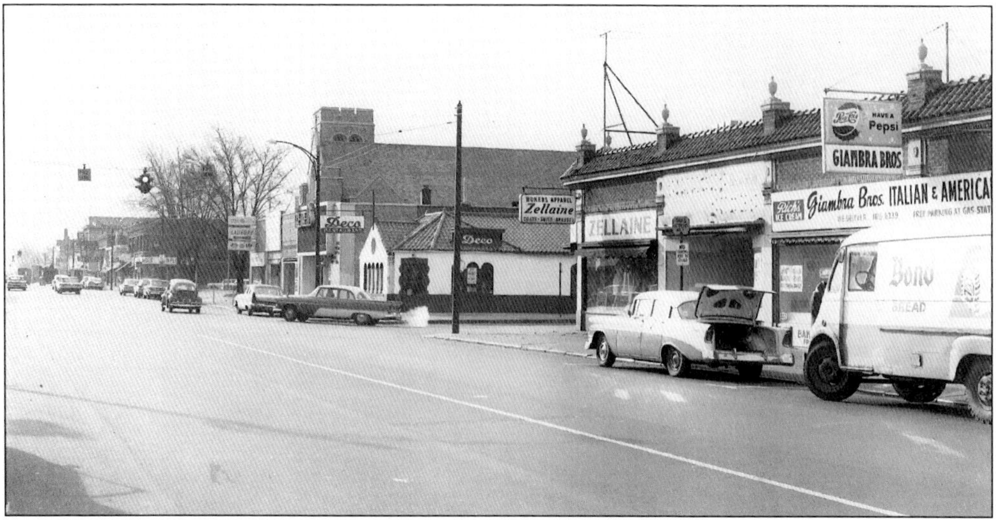

LOOKING SOUTH ALONG DELAWARE AVENUE IN 1961. Giambra Bros. Italian & American Foods occupied much of the block between Westgate and Wabash. Farther south, next to the vacant store, was Zellaine's women's clothing store, and across Westgate stood one of the numerous Deco restaurants that were familiar throughout Western New York. Henel's Dairy and the Coin-o-Matic Laundry shared the remainder of the next block with the new St. Paul's Church.

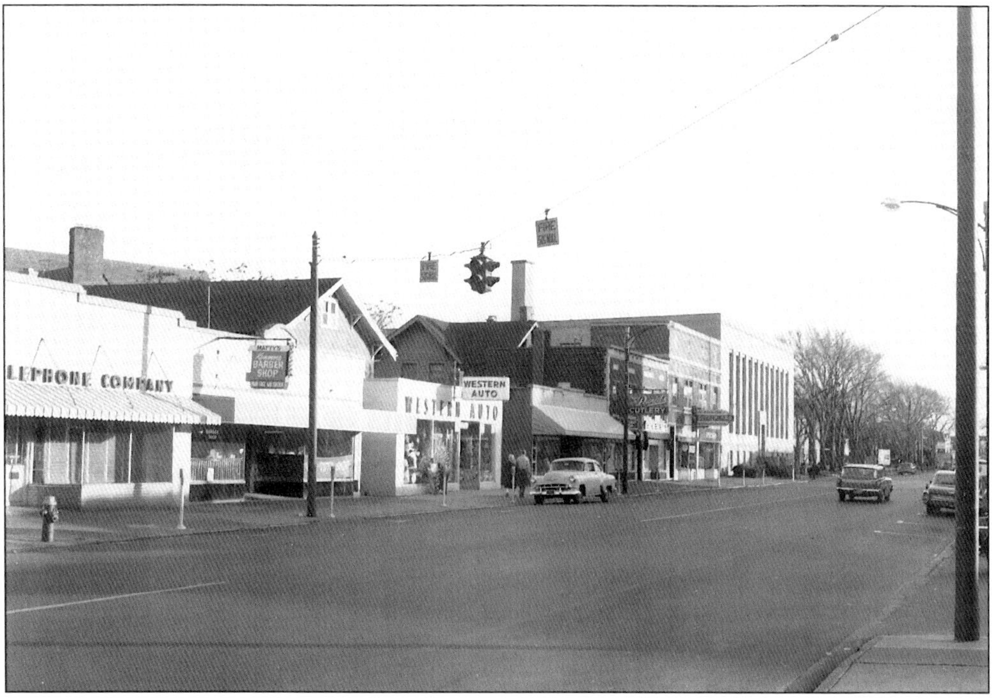

DELAWARE AVENUE LOOKING SOUTHEAST FROM WESTGATE AVENUE IN 1961. The stoplight was used to halt traffic when Kenmore Fire Department trucks needed to cross Delaware at Nash Road. The building adjacent to the Kenmore Municipal Building was the home of Gibson & Doty, opticians, and the Sutherland Stationery store. Matty's Kenmore Barber Shop was virtually a village institution.

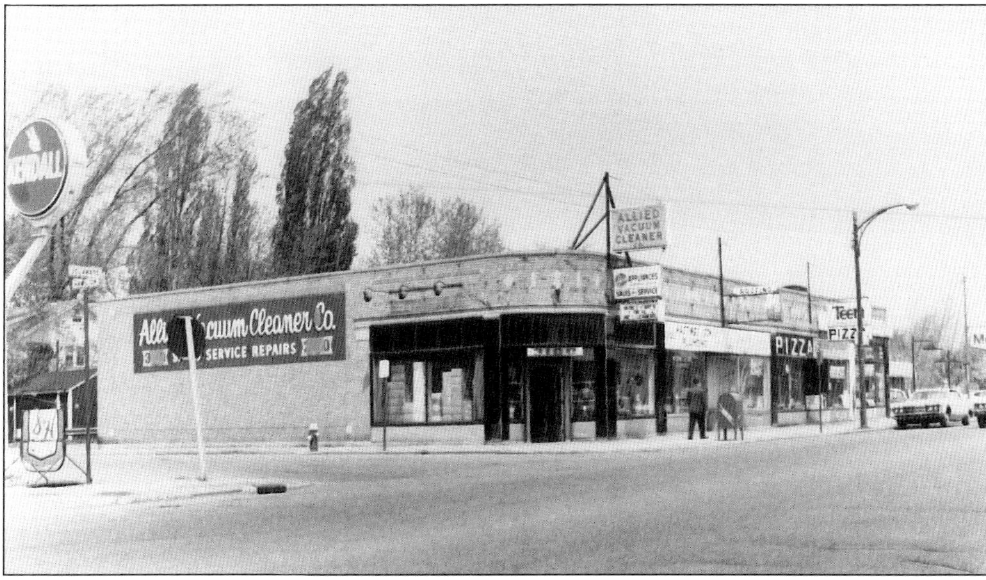

The building at the corner of Delaware Avenue and Hamilton in 1971. The two service stations shown here are now gone. Probably the most controversial business in the village has been an "adult" bookstore, which opened in this block a few years later. Despite protests by local residents and organized picketing by representatives of area churches, it remained in operation. (Larry H. Oskin photo, TKHS collection.)

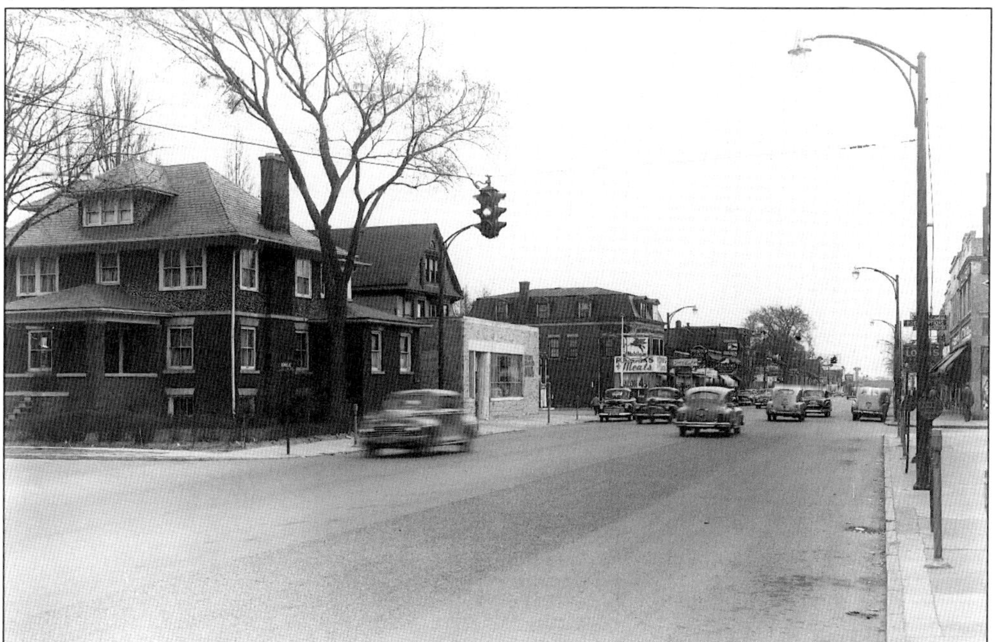

The corner of Delaware and Knowlton Avenues, looking south, in the late 1940s. Among the businesses whose signs appear on the east side of Delaware are the First Federal Savings and Loan, Striker's Mobil station, Putnam's Meats, the Your Host restaurant, the Western Auto store, Caruso's Shoe Repair, and the Red Lobster restaurant. The bridges carrying the Erie and DL&W tracks over Delaware can be seen in the far background.

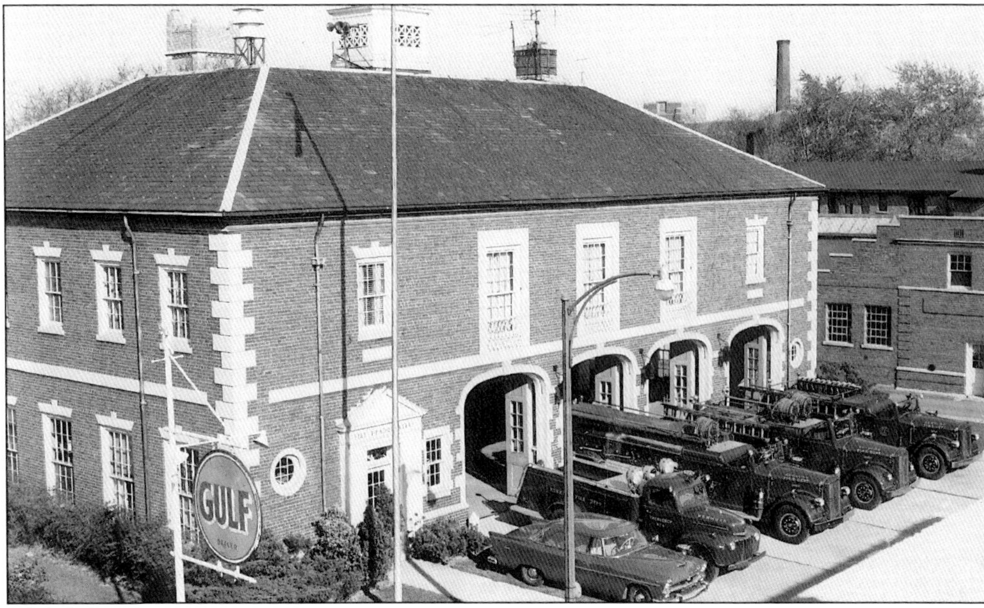

KENMORE FIRE HALL, C. 1956. The original 1929 building included the police department until 1951. The right-hand bay was installed where the old police headquarters had been. The building at right was the old post office building, closed in 1960 when the present Kenmore Post Office was opened. The Gulf filling station stood at Delaware Avenue and Nash Road for many years.

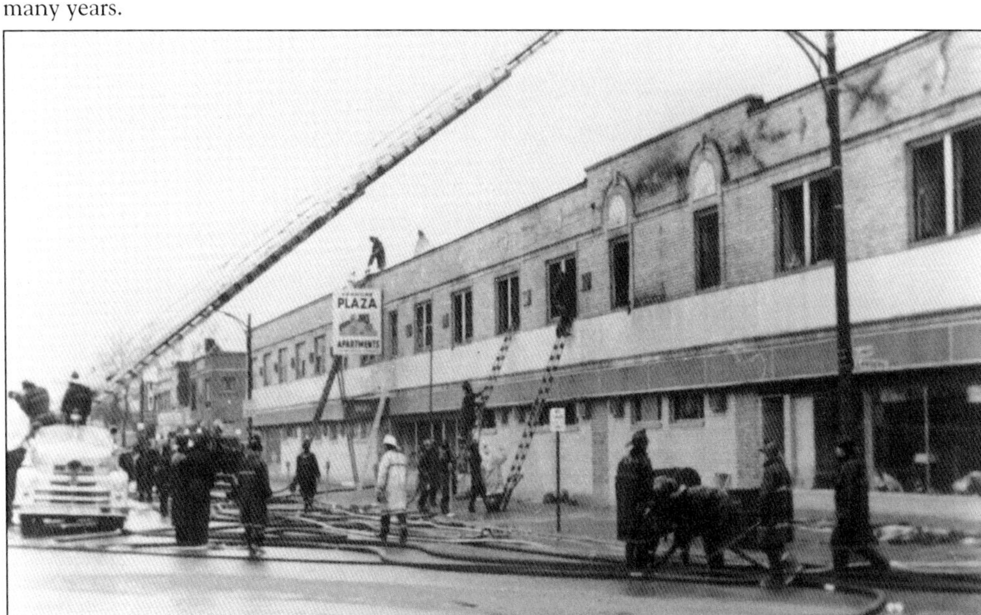

THE KENMORE THEATER BUILDING. This was the site of three major fires—the first in 1927, a second in 1947, and a third one in 1968, after its conversion into apartments. Two residents died as a result of the final fire; one elderly tenant escaped with her important personal papers intact only because every night she put them in her purse, which she then placed next to her bed. The building was subsequently demolished and replaced by the Kenmore Towers. (KVFD collection.)

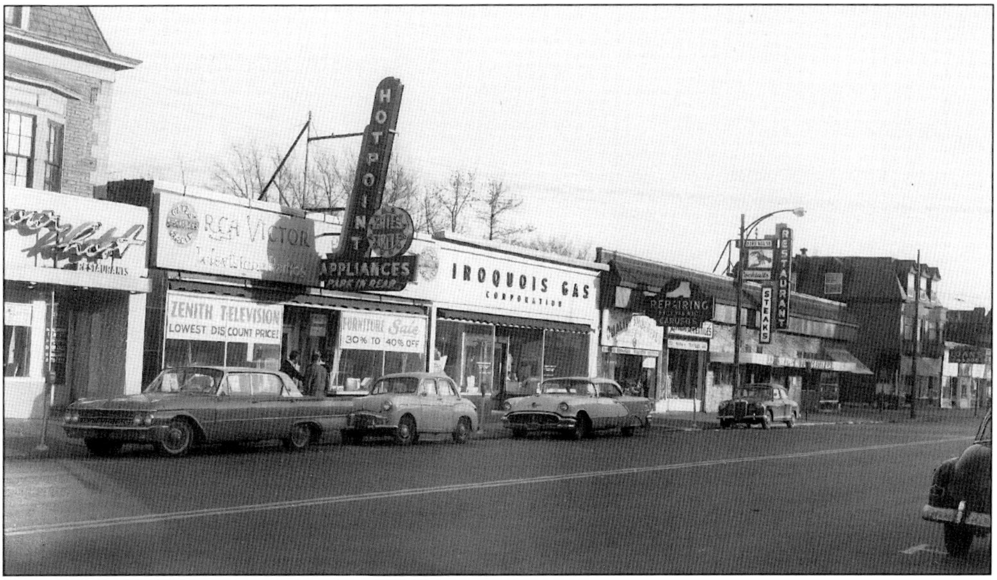

The block between Warren and Euclid Avenues as it appeared in 1961. Your Host occupied the southern portion of the corner building; its immediate neighbor was Gates Circle Appliances, which had moved to the village from Buffalo and would move again to north of the Municipal Building. Next door was Iroquois Gas. Remember when you could walk in and pay your gas bill whenever you were "downtown?" A 1965 fire would consume the next three businesses on the block.

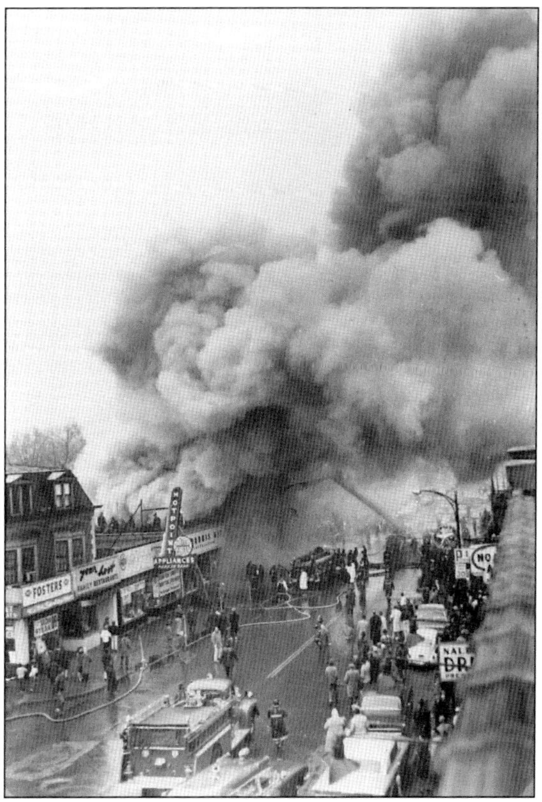

Fire fighters responding to one of the most extensive and spectacular conflagrations of 1965. Kenmore suffered three major fires that year, and fire damage in the village totalled almost $400,000. This blaze destroyed the Ebb Tide restaurant, Caruso's Shoe Repair, and Shaw's textile shop at the corner of Delaware and Euclid Avenues. (KVFD collection.)

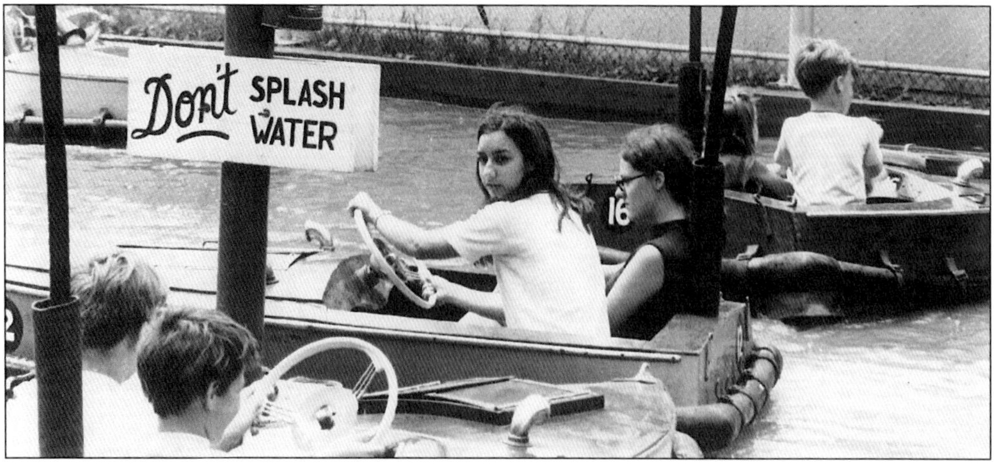

THE ANNUAL KENMORE DAY AT CRYSTAL BEACH, A HIGHLIGHT OF SUMMER IN THE COMMUNITY FOR MANY YEARS. Discount tickets were sold by the Kenmore Merchants Association, and picnickers could ride the steamer *Canadiana* across the lake to the Ontario amusement park. If that boat ride wasn't enough, there was the Water Scooter, which allowed you, for a few minutes, to be the captain of your own, if smaller, vessel. (Larry H. Oskin photo, TKHS collection.)

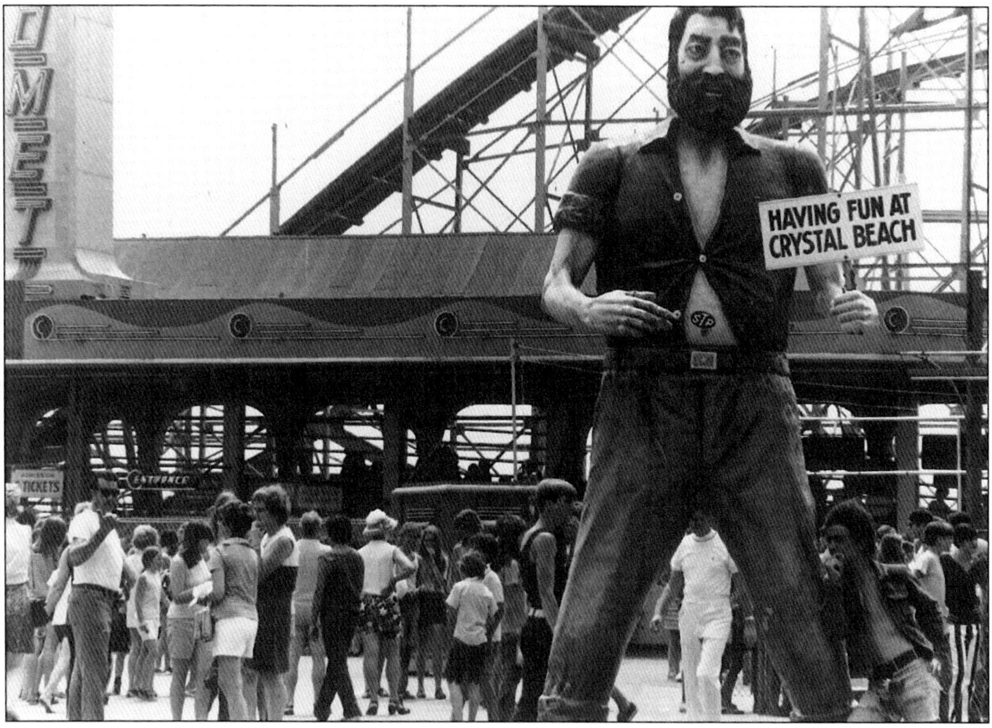

THE COMET ROLLER COASTER, THE HIGHLIGHT OF MANY YOUNGSTERS' DAYS AT CRYSTAL BEACH. Kenmore Days at the park were no longer possible after 1989, when the amusement park closed down. The Comet, long considered among the best of its type, was dismantled, moved, and rebuilt at Lake George, New York, where it now operates. "Paul Bunyan" was recruited to sell Christmas trees on Sheridan drive in the Town of Tonawanda. (Larry H. Oskin photo, TKHS collection.)

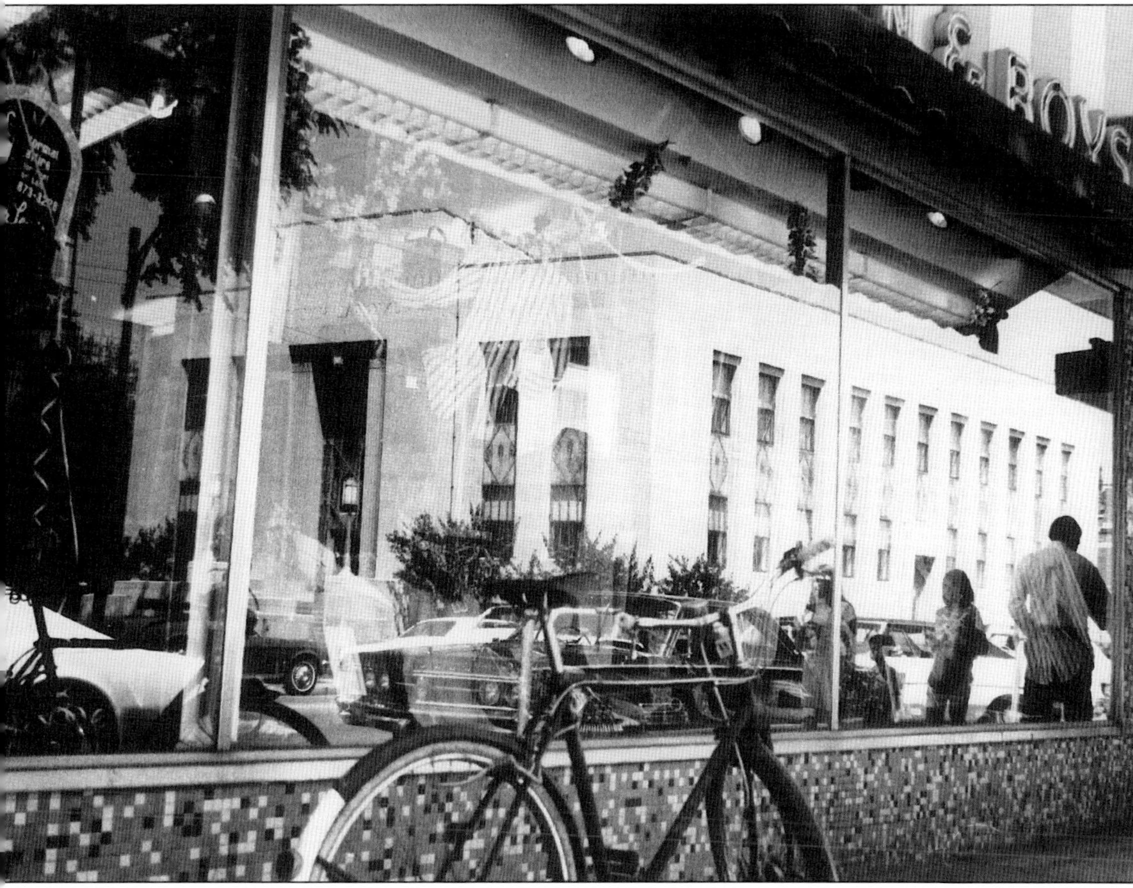

THE MUNICIPAL BUILDING REFLECTED IN THE WINDOW OF THE ROGER LEWIS STORE. In 1971, photographer Larry H. Oskin was commissioned to take pictures of important and interesting sites in Kenmore and the town. Several of those photos appear in this book. Here, he has caught a reflection of the Municipal Building in the window of the Roger Lewis men's store, a business eventually replaced by the Discount Wallpaper Outlet. (Larry H. Oskin photo, TKHS collection.)

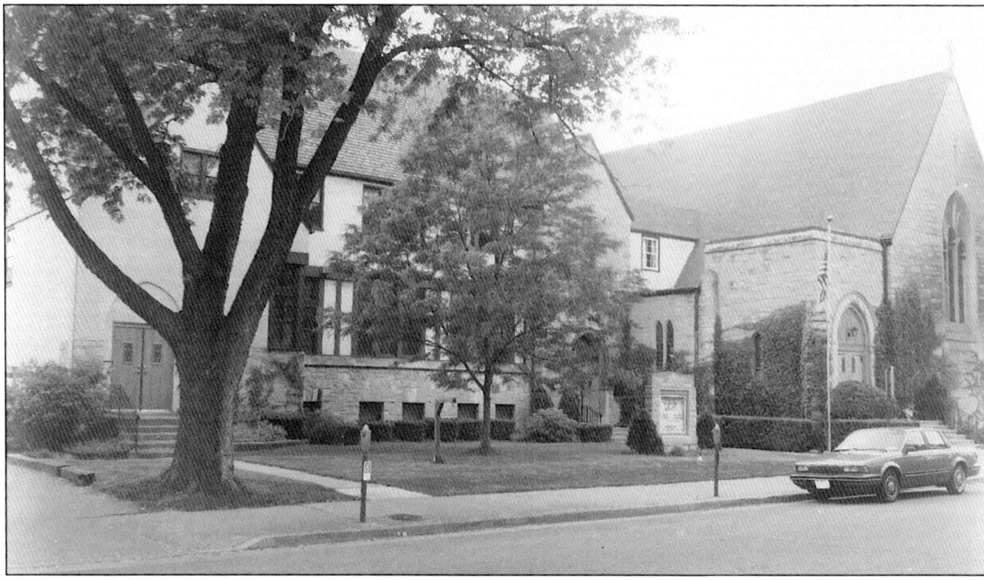

The Episcopal Church of the Advent. The church was founded in 1904 as a mission of the Church of the Good Shepherd. Members worshiped in parishioners' homes, then in the old village hall at Delaware near Warren, until building a small church at the northeast corner of Eugene and LaSalle Avenues in 1911. In 1923, the growing congregation moved into what is now the parish hall (on the left in the picture) at 54 Delaware Road, adjacent to the present municipal building. The present English-style church edifice was dedicated in 1952.

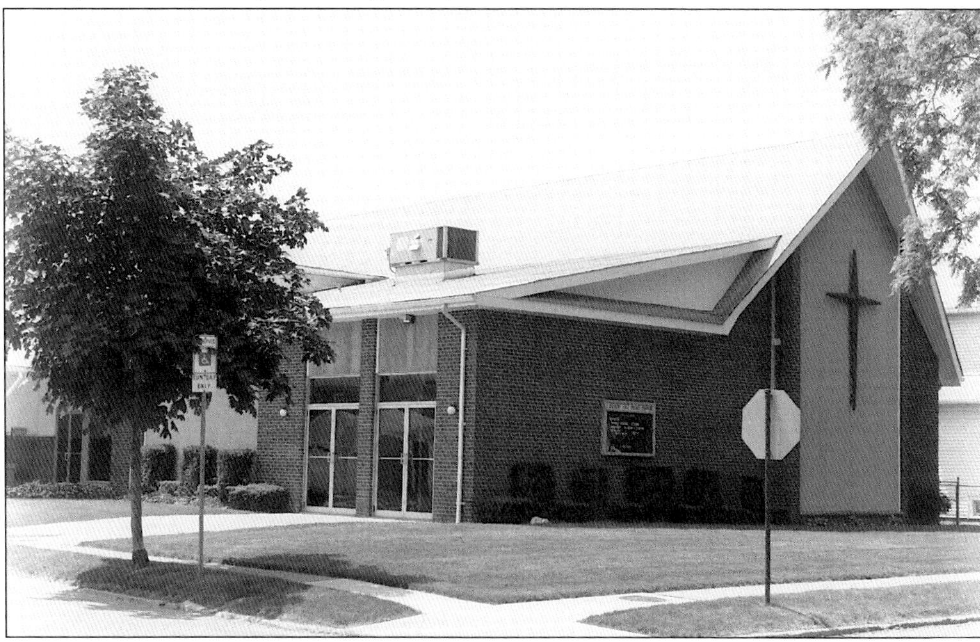

The Full Gospel Church at the corner of Somerton Avenue and Grammercy Place. This building has been home to three different congregations. St. Mark's Evangelical Lutheran Church used it until moving to Delaware Road in 1949. Subsequently, it was the Kenmore Alliance Church, until that congregation relocated in 1977. The present congregation has worshiped there since.

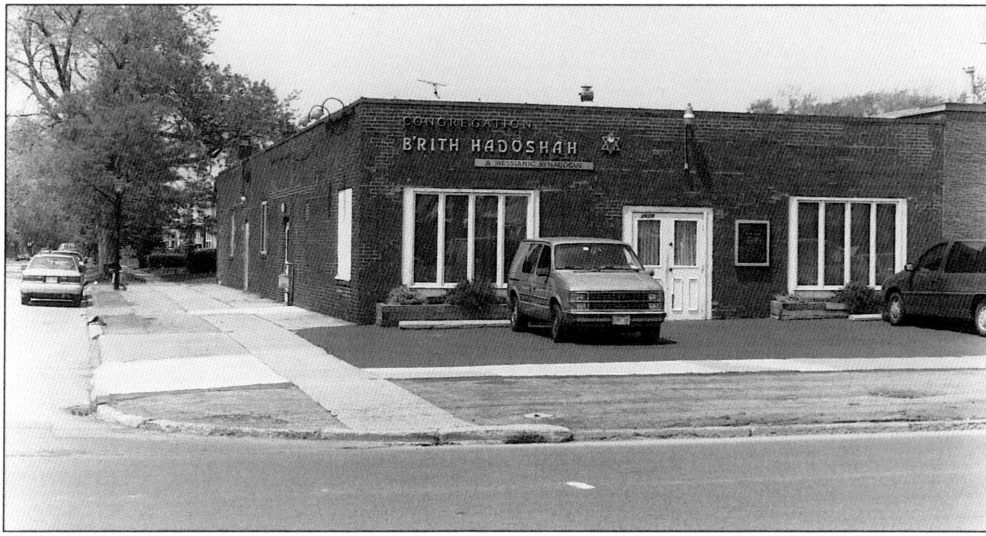

CONGREGATION BRITH HADOSHAH. Founded within the New Covenant Tabernacle in the town of Tonawanda, this Messianic Jewish congregation serves, in the words of its rabbi/pastor, "Jewish and non-Jewish people who believe Jesus is the Messiah." It became independent in July 1987, and has occupied this building at Elmwood and Hamilton Avenues since 1990. "Brith Hadoshah" is Hebrew for "New Covenant."

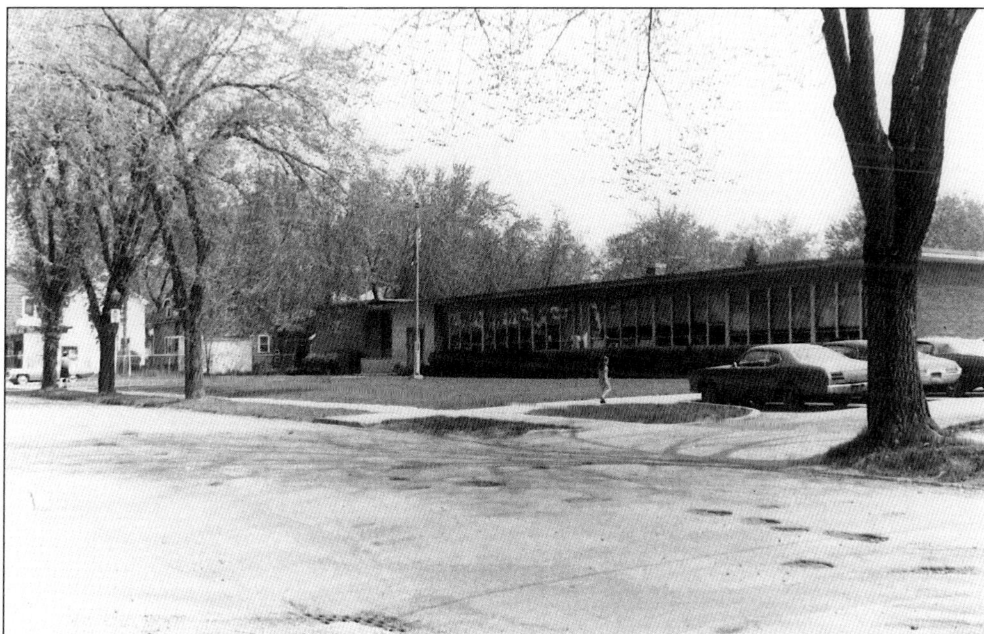

THE HENRY W. LONGFELLOW SCHOOL, LOCATED ON MYRON AVENUE, DIRECTLY BEHIND WHAT WAS THEN THE JUNIOR HIGH SCHOOL. This was one of several "neighborhood schools," serving children in kindergarten through third grade, that were built by the school district during the baby boomer years. All of its pupils lived within easy walking distance (some did not even have to cross a street). It shared a principal with the nearby George Washington Elementary School. Opened in 1956, Longfellow was closed in June 1981, and was converted into a school district maintenance facility.

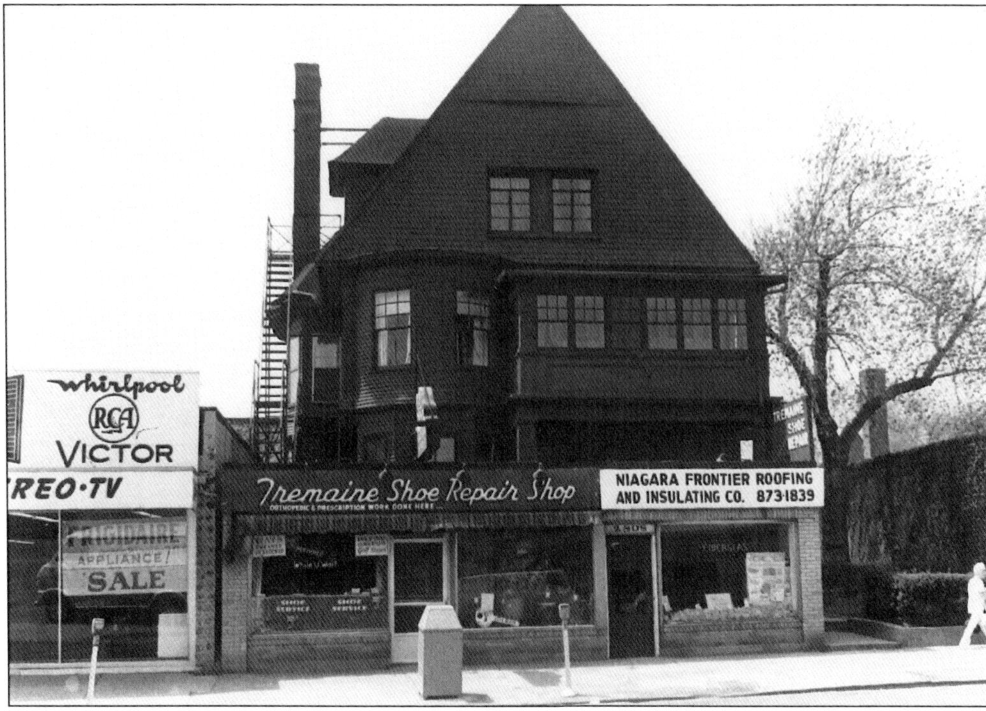

A 1971 VIEW OF HERBERT ZIMMERMAN'S HOUSE ON DELAWARE AVENUE. When James Byron Zimmerman built this house in the early days of the village, it cost him $8,000. As happened to many of the old homes on Delaware Avenue, it was eventually converted for business use, with apartments in the rear and on the upper floors. At the time this photograph was taken, a shoe repair and a contractor occupied the store portion in front. By the late 1990s, it housed a taco and sandwich shop. (Larry H. Oskin photo, TKHS collection.)

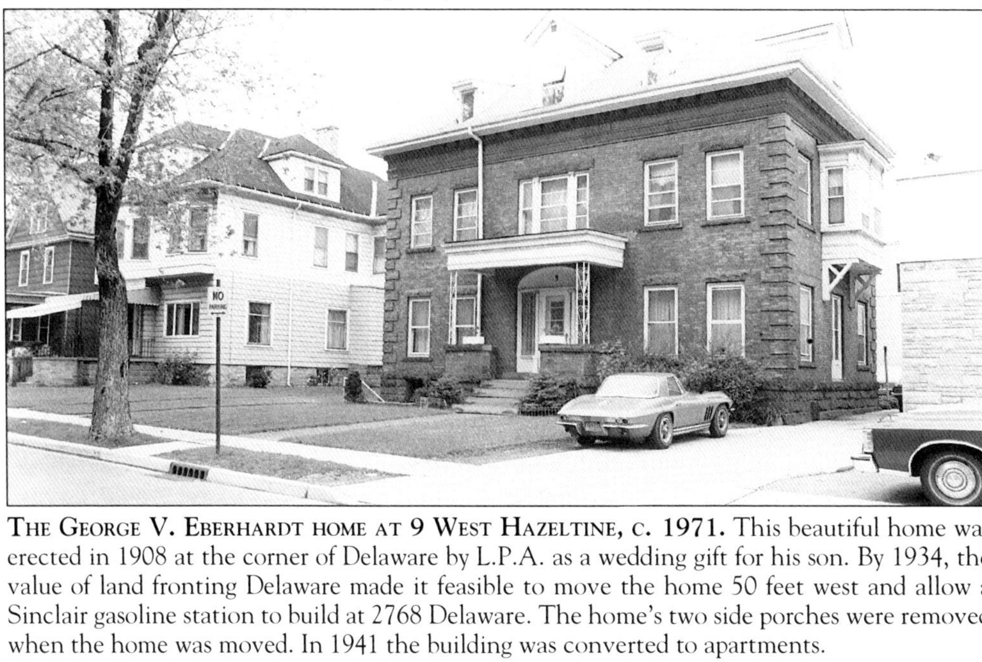

THE GEORGE V. EBERHARDT HOME AT 9 WEST HAZELTINE, C. 1971. This beautiful home was erected in 1908 at the corner of Delaware by L.P.A. as a wedding gift for his son. By 1934, the value of land fronting Delaware made it feasible to move the home 50 feet west and allow a Sinclair gasoline station to build at 2768 Delaware. The home's two side porches were removed when the home was moved. In 1941 the building was converted to apartments.

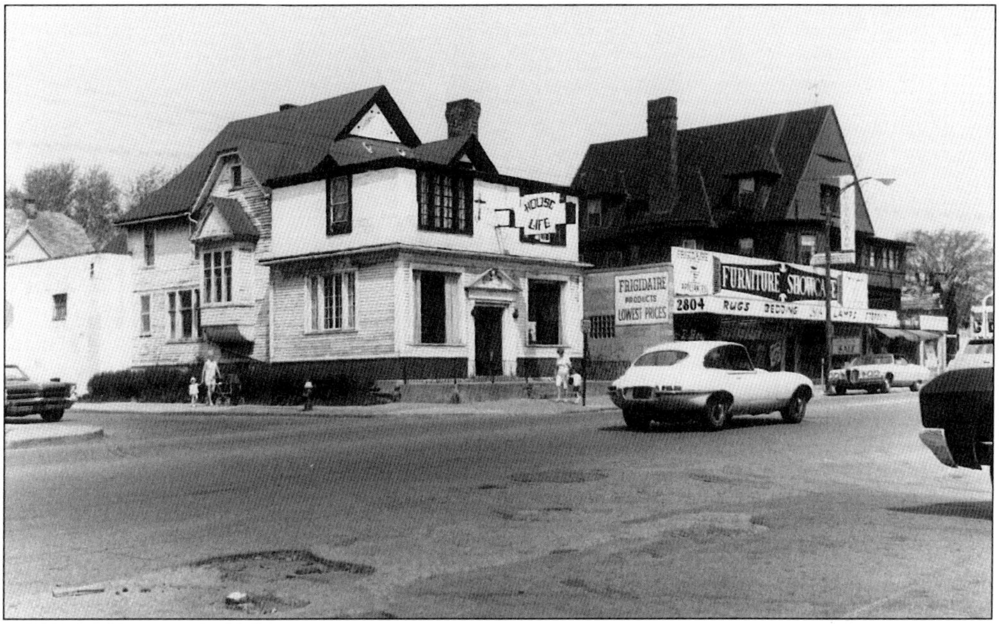

Myron Phelps' home in its last years. By the 1970s, this building, one of the oldest in Kenmore, had been renovated almost beyond recognition. A number of businesses used the structure, and for a time the New Testament Christian Community occupied it under the name House of Life. When that closed, another business followed until the structure was demolished. (Larry H. Oskin photo, TKHS collection.)

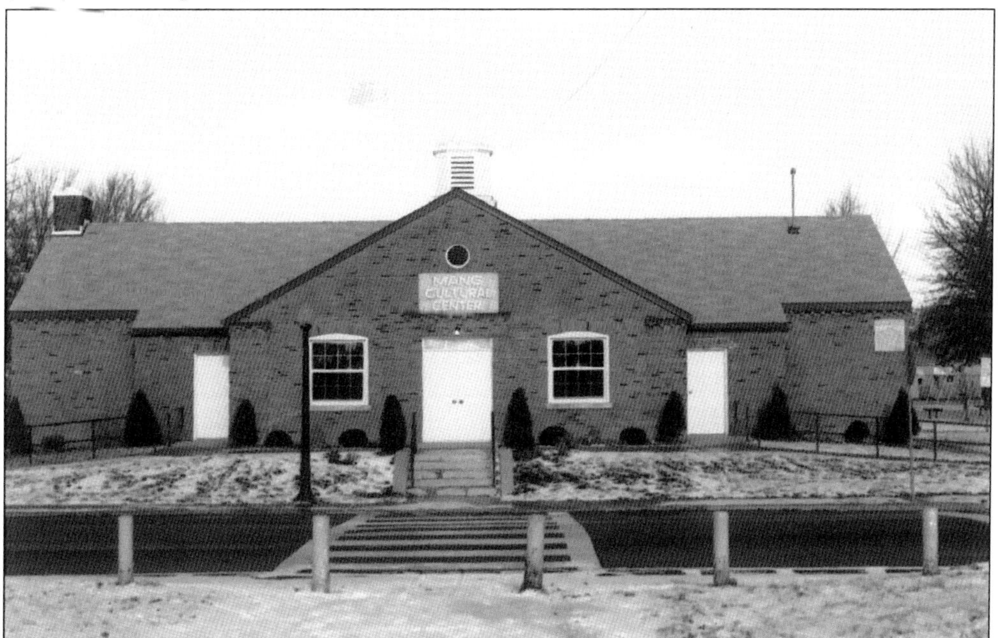

The Mang Cultural Center in 1986. This building, erected as a shelter house for the Mang wading pool in 1939, provided changing rooms for waders in summer and ice skaters in winter when the shallow pool was frozen. It was extensively remodeled for the town's sesquicentennial in 1986 and now provides gathering space for many village events.

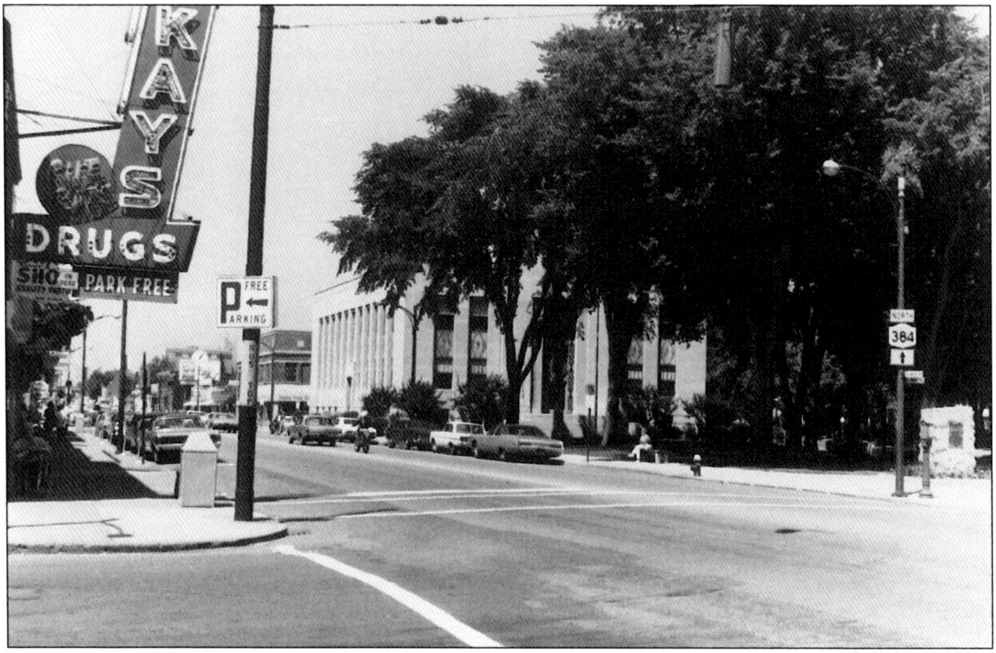

THE CORNER OF DELAWARE AVENUE AND LINCOLN BOULEVARD IN 1971. To provide convenient parking for shoppers, the village purchased and demolished a number of homes immediately behind the businesses on the west side of Delaware Avenue. The result is a free parking lot that extends from LaSalle Avenue to Victoria Boulevard. Similar facilities exist east of Delaware. (Larry H. Oskin photo, TKHS collection.)

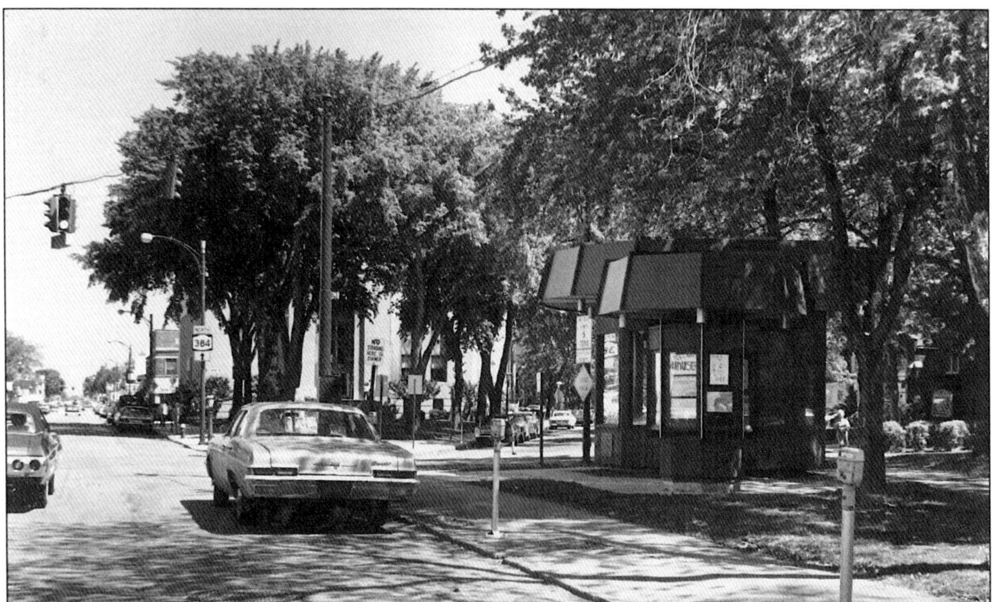

THE TWO KIOSKS IN FRONT OF WASHINGTON SCHOOL, ACROSS FROM THE MUNICIPAL BUILDING. Kiosks were fashionable additions to downtowns in 1971, when these two were built. Three decades later, they remain in place, providing advertising and display place for community organizations and activities. (Larry H. Oskin photo, TKHS collection.)

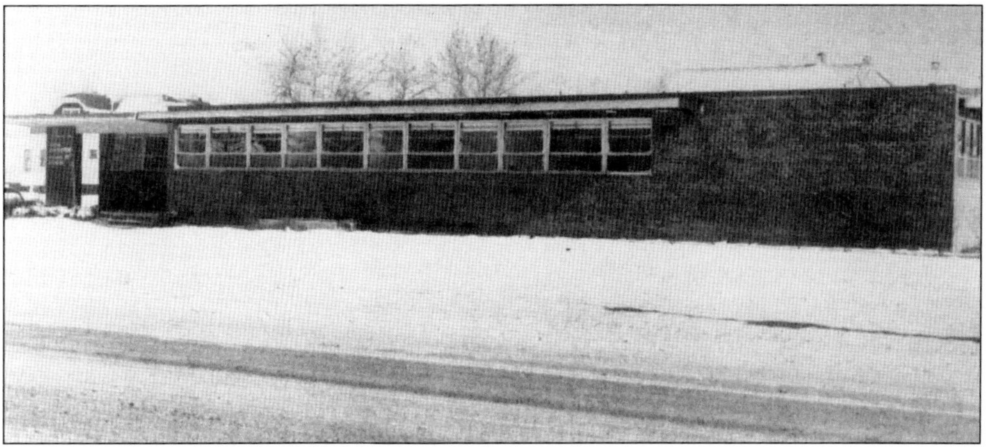

The present police station at the corner of Elmwood Avenue and Lincoln Boulevard. From 1929 to 1951, the Kenmore Police Department shared space with the Kenmore Fire Department, but by the 1960s, both departments had so expanded that it was necessary to construct a new police station and allow the firefighters to occupy the entire Nash Road building.

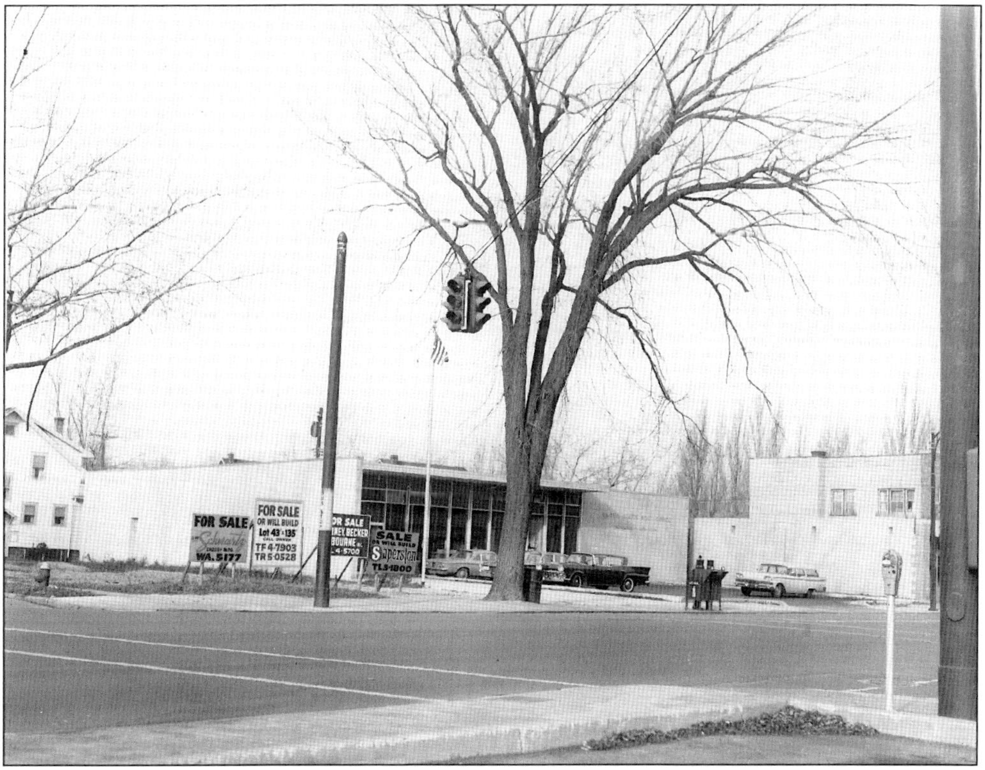

A 1961 photograph of the present Kenmore Post Office at Delaware Avenue and Tremont. This post office opened in 1960, replacing the older building on Nash Road, which had become outdated and lacked convenient parking. Even with its own small lot, there was still not enough room for patrons' vehicles, and eventually the corner lot with the "for sale" signs was purchased and paved over for a parking area serving the post office and nearby businesses.

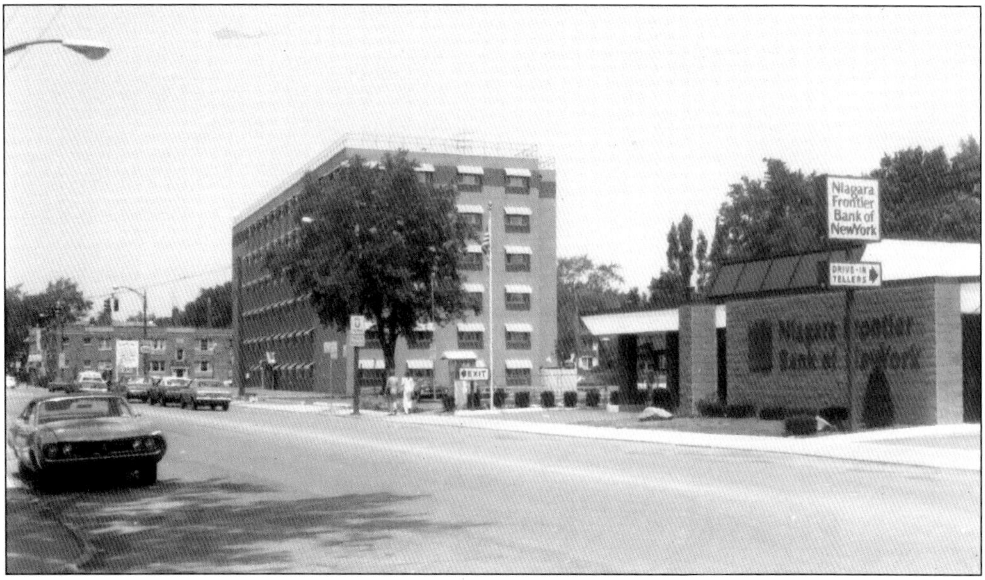

KENMORE TOWERS, THE VILLAGE'S FIRST HIGH-RISE APARTMENT BUILDING. Kenmore Towers opened in 1970 on the site of the old Kenmore Theater. Controversy over its massive appearance, along with the loss of a village parking lot across Chapel Road, may have contributed to the voters rejecting incumbent candidates and electing a Democratic mayor and trustees majority in the subsequent village election.

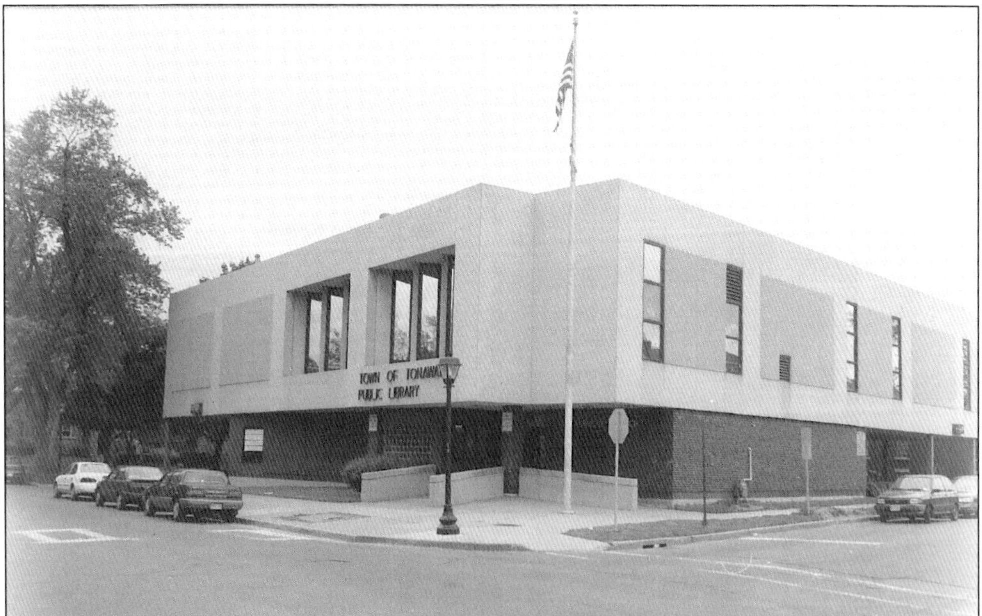

THE KENMORE BRANCH LIBRARY. When the village library outgrew its 1929 structure at Delaware and Chapel Roads, this new library building was built on the same site and opened in 1977. During its construction, the library temporarily utilized the old post office on Nash Road. The handicapped-accessible building is fully equipped as a modern library, and includes a computerized catalog, meeting rooms for public functions, and a parking area underneath the rear portion.

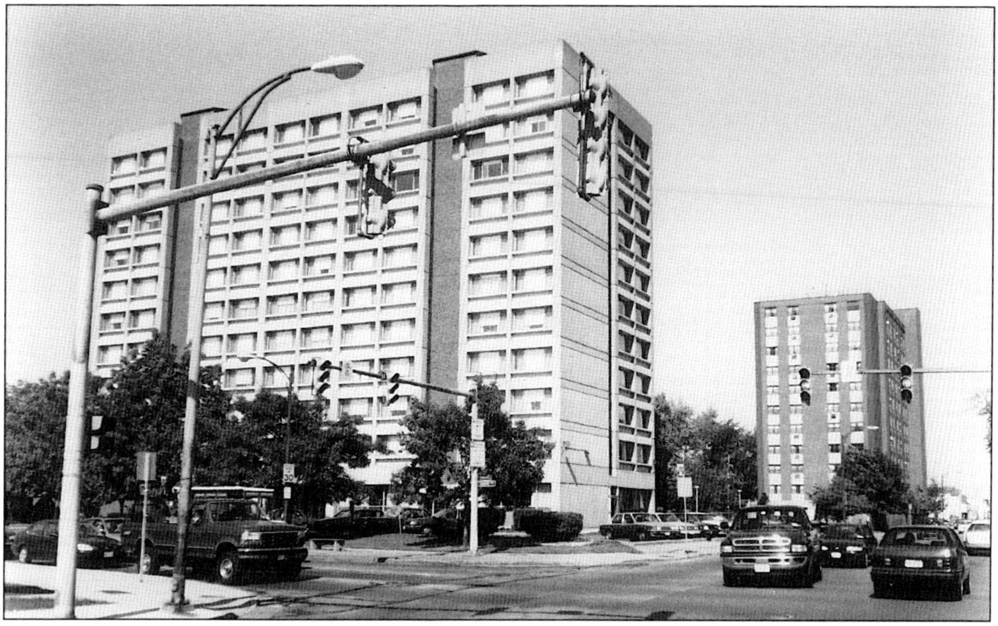

TEN-STORY SENIOR CITIZENS' APARTMENT BUILDINGS, BUILT IN THE 1970S AND 1980S BY THE KENMORE HOUSING AUTHORITY (WITH THE ASSISTANCE OF FEDERAL FUNDING). Village residents with limited incomes were given preference in rentals. The first of these, at the corner of Kenmore and Colvin (in the foreground), was quickly filled with residents; as a result, the second, on the site of the former Colvin Theater, was constructed to provide additional space.

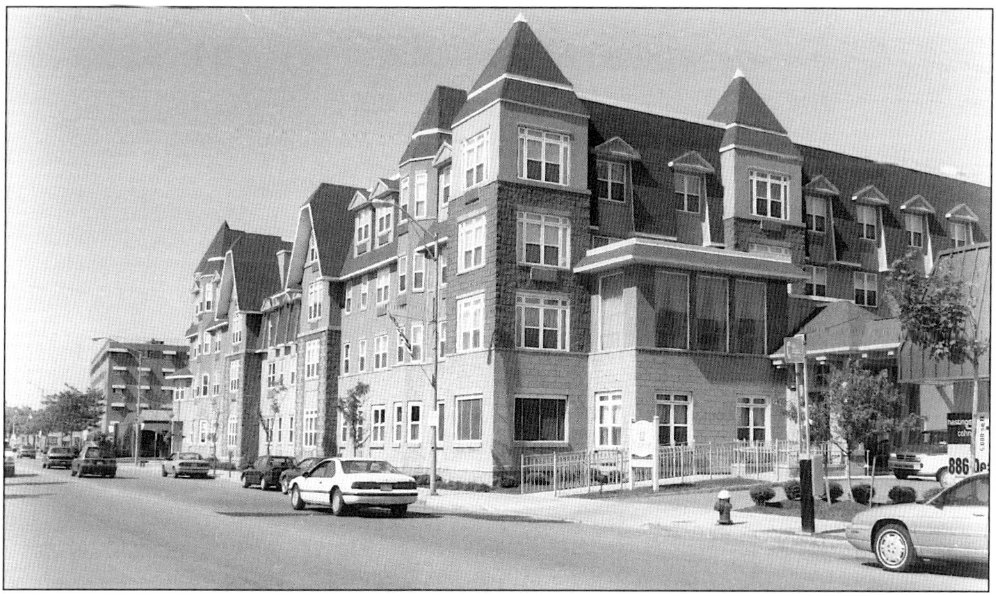

THE WYNWOOD COMMONS AT KENMORE, LOCATED AT THE CORNER OF DELAWARE AVENUE AND NASH ROAD. In 1994 the Pioneer Development Company broke ground for what later was named the Wynwood Commons at Kenmore. The site had been the location of, at various times, Premier Liquor, two auto dealerships, and several other businesses. A newspaper article of the time indicated hopes that its 113 units would attract senior citizens from the village, thus making their homes available to young families.

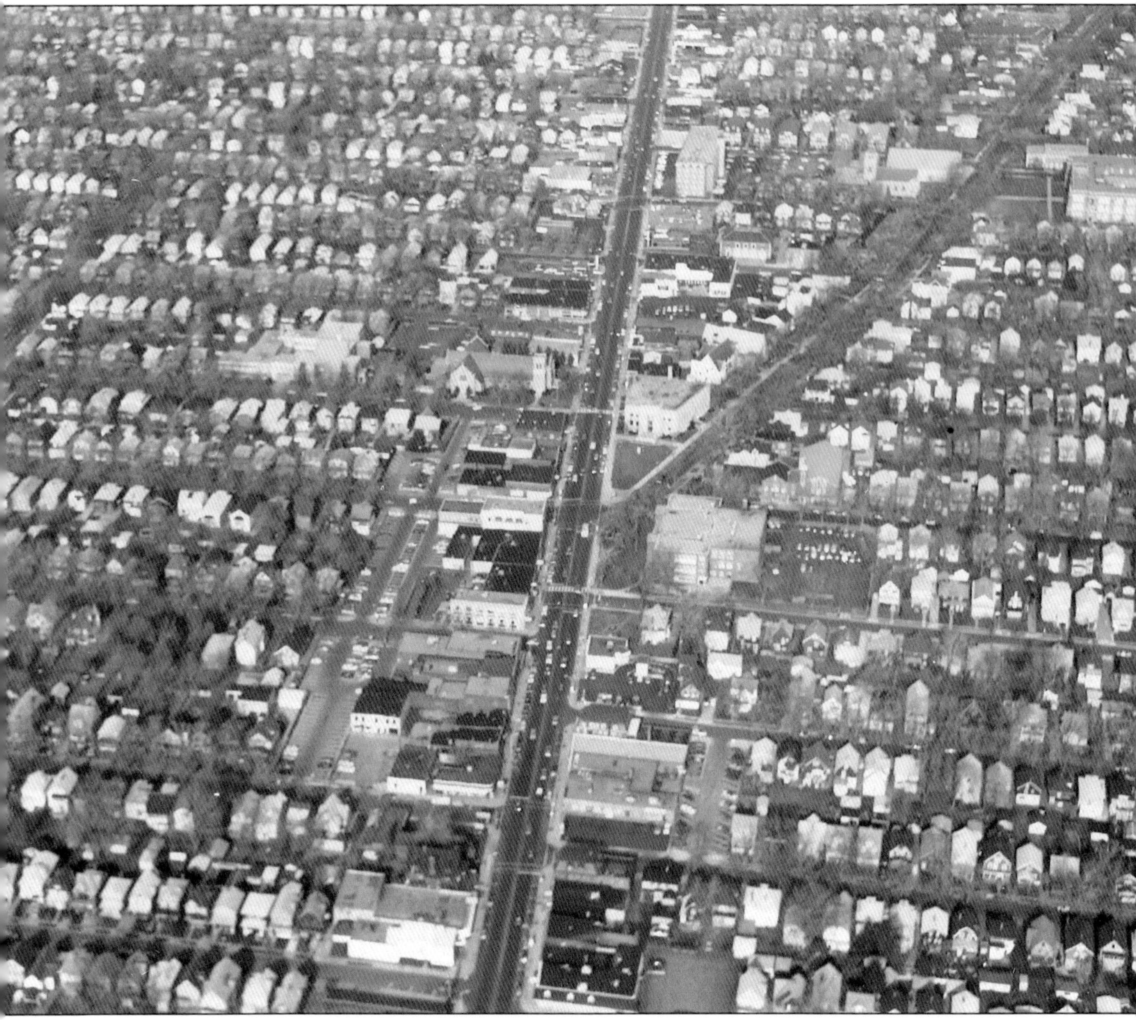

DOWNTOWN KENMORE, LOOKING NORTH, C. 1985. Delaware Avenue divides the village into "east side-west side" and Delaware Road follows the original Native-American trail north through the town. Two of Kenmore's former high schools are in this photograph, as are five churches, the Municipal Building, the fire hall, Kenmore Towers, St. Paul's School, the Masonic Temple, dozens of Kenmore's businesses, and hundreds of well-kept homes. Many homes were removed in the mid-1900s to provide off-street parking behind the downtown business blocks. The old buildings on the current site of the Wynwood Commons at Kenmore can be seen here, and the 1954 St. Paul's Church is clearly visible in the center of the photograph.

Six

VANISHED KENMORE

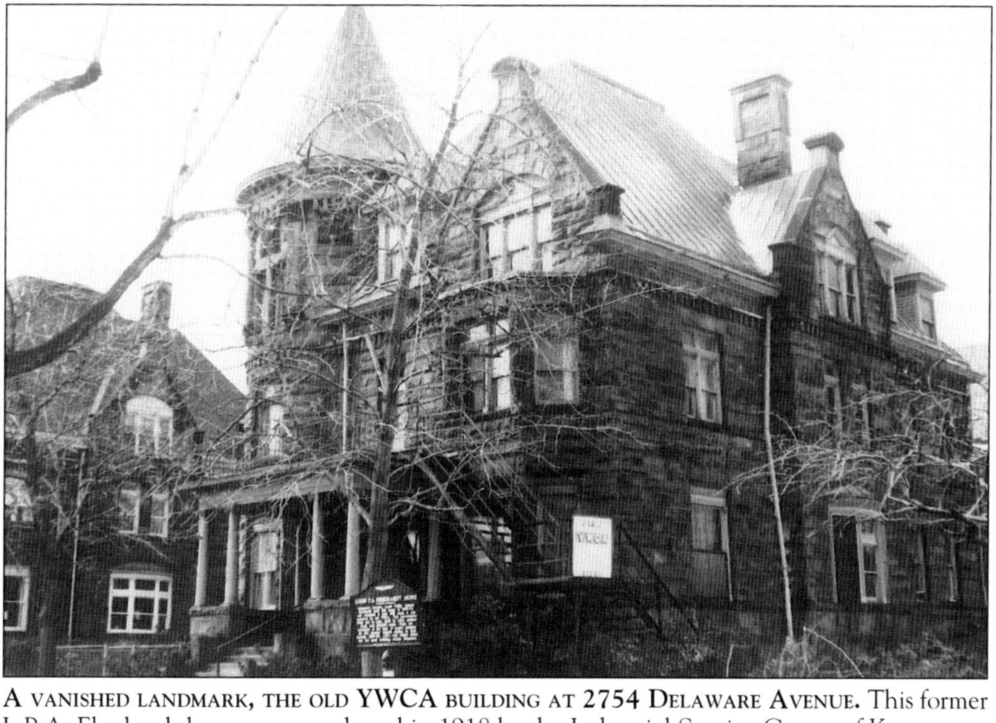

A VANISHED LANDMARK, THE OLD YWCA BUILDING AT 2754 DELAWARE AVENUE. This former L.P.A. Eberhardt home was purchased in 1918 by the Industrial Service Center of Kenmore, a predecessor of the Kenmore Young Women's Christian Association. It was established to aid young women who came to the area seeking employment during the Great World War. The ISC provided rooms and meals in a secure Christian atmosphere. The building also provided space for the Kenmore Free Library from 1918 to 1920. The YWCA operated a popular cafeteria in their annex behind the house for many years, before it was purchased by the next-door Wheel Chair Home in 1976. In spite of strong opposition from the community, including the YWCA board and the Tonawanda-Kenmore Historical Society, the building was demolished the first week of 1978.

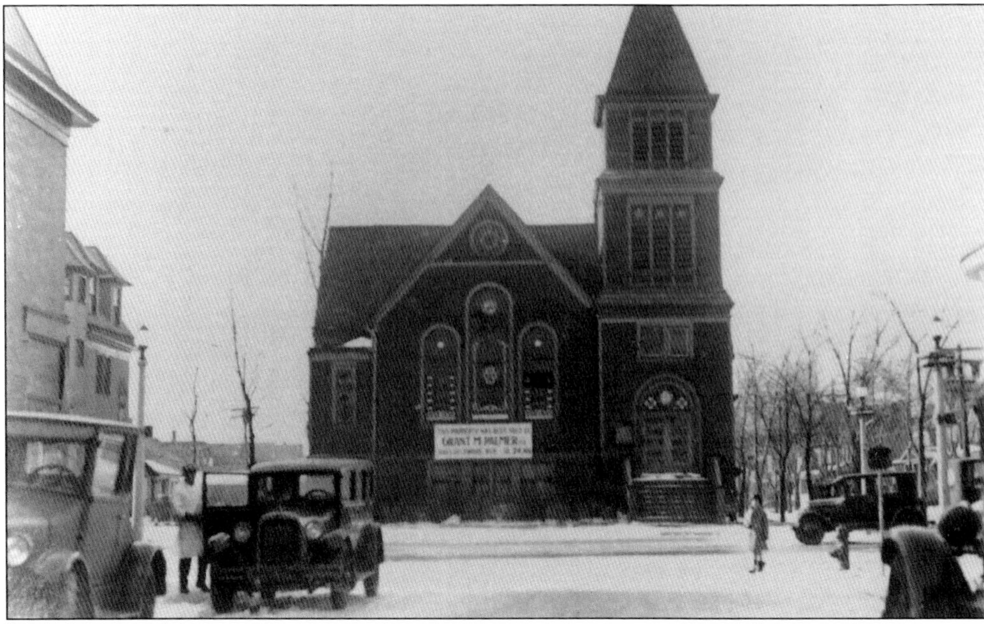

THE KENMORE METHODIST-EPISCOPAL CHURCH BUILDING UP FOR SALE, AS VIEWED FROM EUCLID AVENUE DURING THE WINTER OF 1928–29. This building, the first church erected in Kenmore, served its congregation from 1893 to 1928. The congregation, which at the time consisted of 625 people, had outgrown its original building. The property was put up for sale when the new stone church building at Landers and Delaware Road was occupied in June 1928. Grant M. Palmer was the realtor who sold the property. The church edifice was dismantled and a B.F. Goodrich tire dealer and service station operated there for the next half-century. Today the site at LaSalle and Delaware is occupied by the Broad-Elm Tire Co.

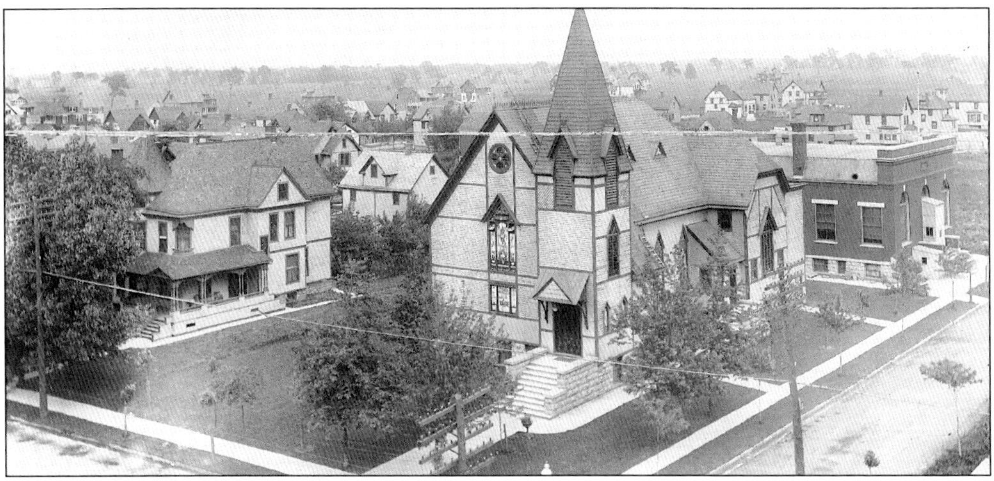

A VIEW LOOKING NORTHEAST FROM THE TOP FLOOR OF THE L.P.A. EBERHARDT HOME, C. 1908. Kenmore Presbyterian Church stands at the corner of Delaware Avenue and East Hazeltine Avenue at right. Next to the church is a home occupied for many years by the William Gudgel family. Behind the church is the Elite Theater, erected in 1907 for the church and community by L.P.A. Eberhardt. Note that Parkwood and Euclid are well developed halfway to Myron Avenue. Little was built north of Euclid in 1908. Most of Kenmore's east side was open fields with scattered trees.

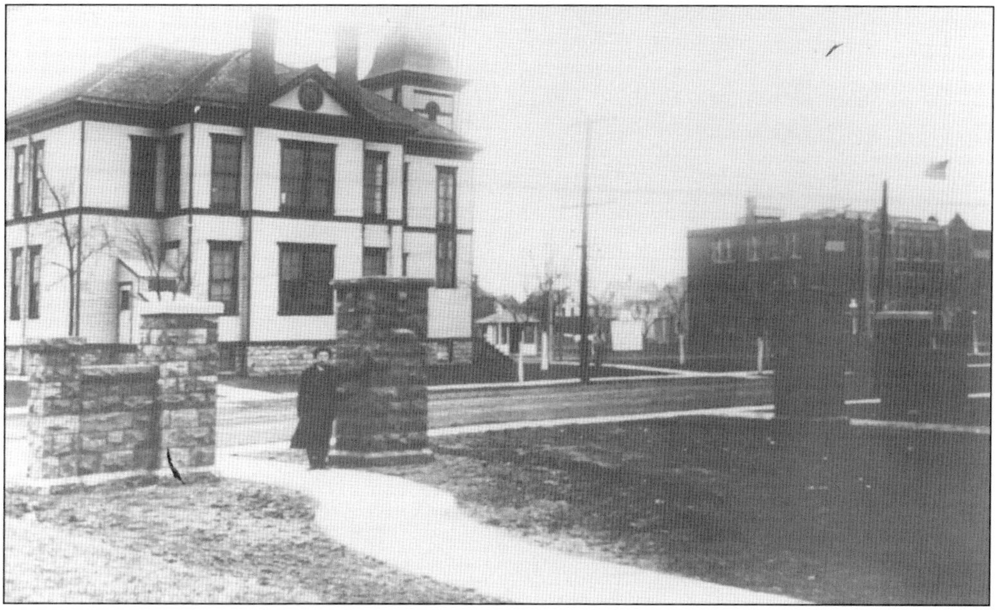

A VIEW OF THE WEST SIDE OF THE OLD VILLAGE HALL FROM VICTORIA AVENUE, C. 1912. The original Kenmore High School, later Washington School, can be seen at right. Several Kenmore streets had pillars facing Delaware Avenue, such as these at Victoria. They were later removed as traffic hazards as the automobile age reached Kenmore. Victoria also had a center boulevard until mid-20th century.

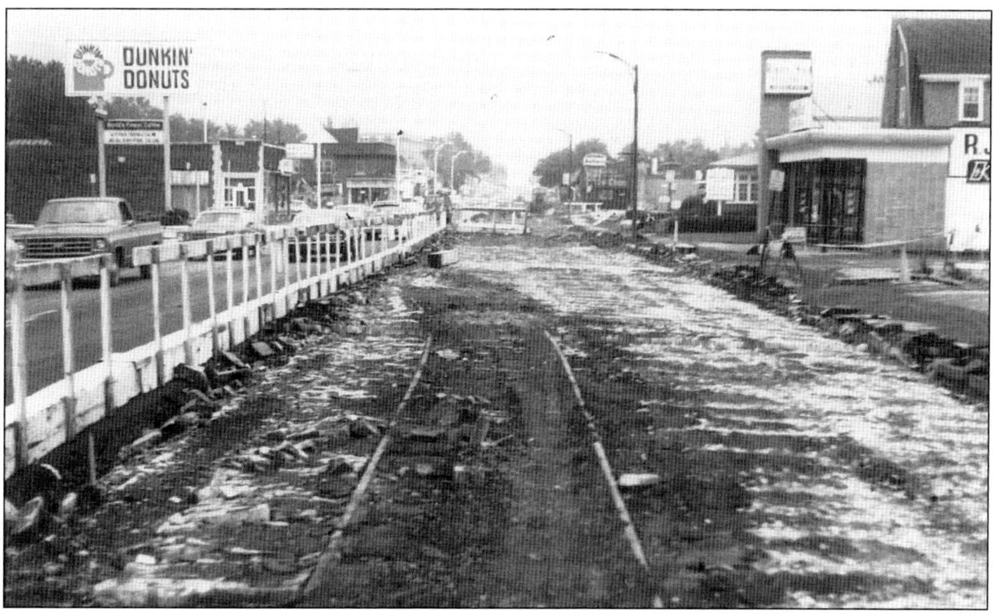

DELAWARE AVENUE, LOOKING SOUTH FROM GIRARD, JULY 8, 1977. Major reconstruction of the state highway through Kenmore required the removal of all the previous pavements down to the earthen base. The oldest pavement uncovered was the 1893–94 brick pavement with the Kenmore & Tonawanda Electric Railway tracks still in place. The streetcar line had been abandoned in 1926. The R.J. Koch building (at right) was built for the Nixon Camera Shop, which operated there for many years.

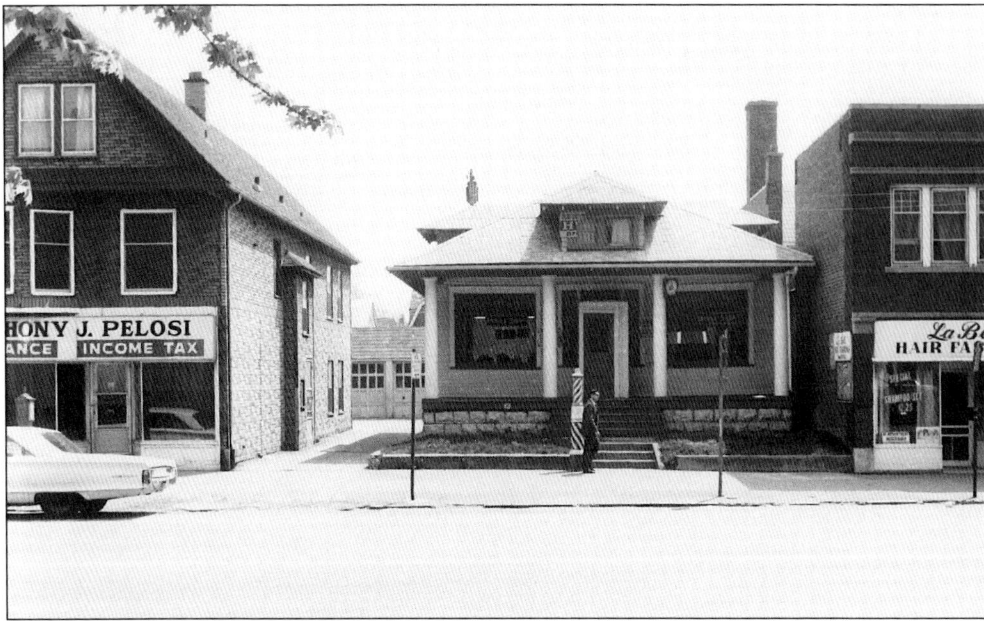

A 1971 PHOTOGRAPH OF THE REAL ESTATE OFFICE BUILT ON THE SITE OF L.P.A. EBERHARDT'S FIRST HOME ON DELAWARE AVENUE. When L.P.A. Eberhardt's first home burned down in 1894, he moved to a new home across the street, and eventually replaced the old house with this real estate office, from which he conducted his sales of property to potential Kenmore residents. It was a barber shop at the time this photograph was taken; seven years later it was demolished for a parking lot. (Larry H. Oskin photo, TKHS collection.)

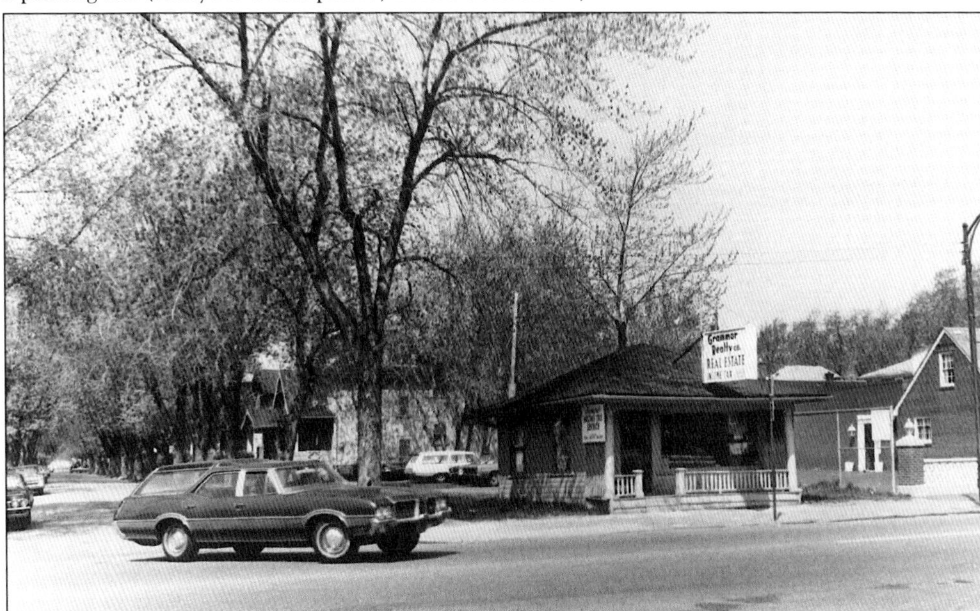

A SMALL BUILDING AT DELAWARE AND WABASH THAT HOUSED SEVERAL BUSINESSES OVER THE YEARS. During the 1930s, George Eberhardt (son of L.P.A.) and George Tolsma operated a real estate business out of this building. By the 1970s, it had become the office of Grammar Realty. The structure was eventually demolished and replaced by a professional office building.

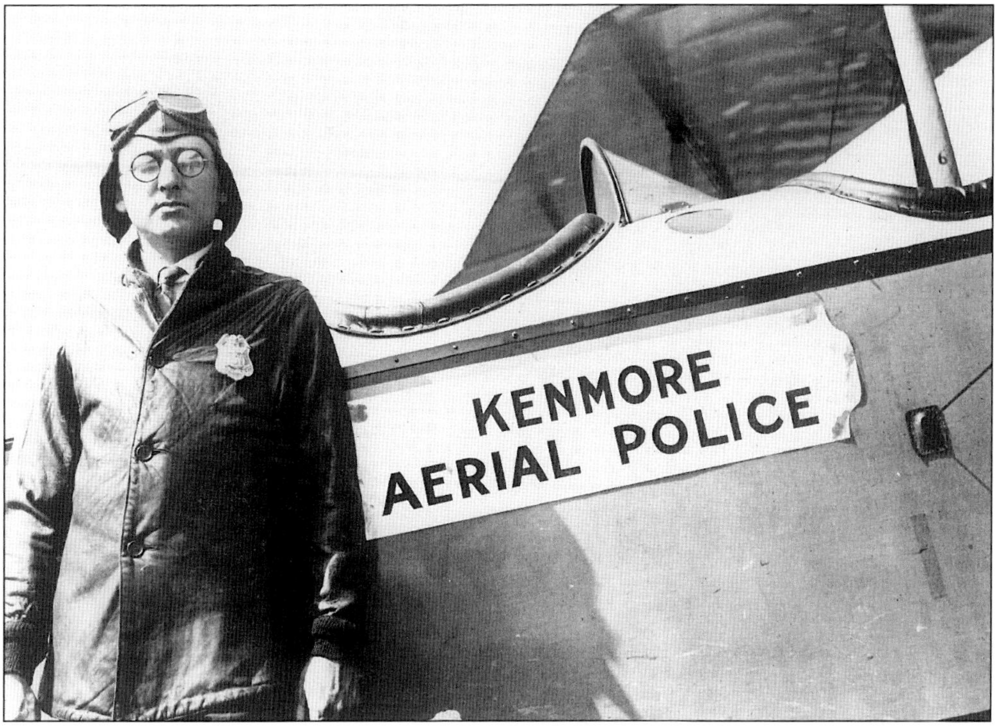

LESLIE L. IRVIN, INVENTOR OF THE MODERN PARACHUTE. Les Irvin and Mayor Roy Brockett "policed" the village and town using this Curtiss JN-4 "Jenny" during the 1920s. Irvin lived on Landers Road and headed the international Irving Airchute Company with factories in the U.S., Canada, and England. The letter "g" was inadvertently added to the company name when it incorporated.

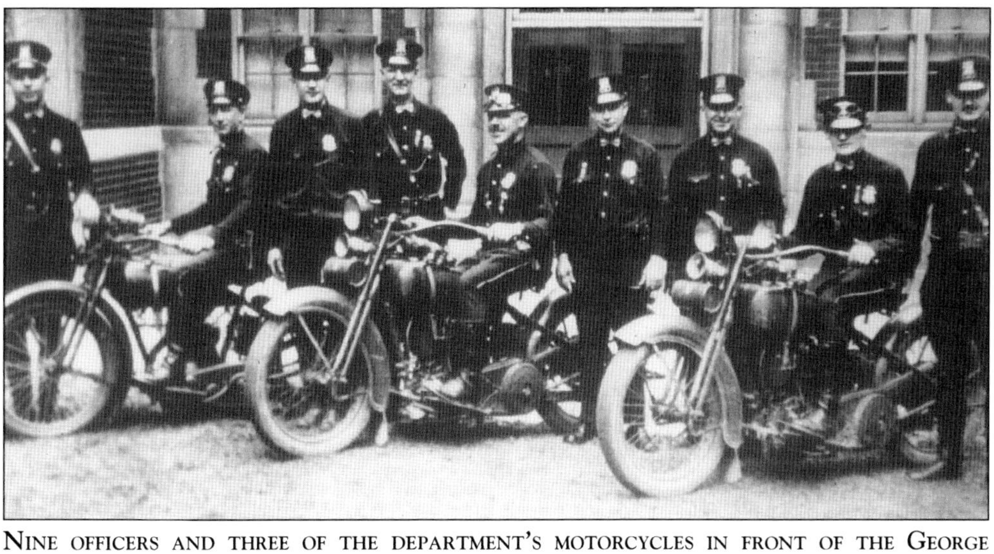

NINE OFFICERS AND THREE OF THE DEPARTMENT'S MOTORCYCLES IN FRONT OF THE GEORGE WASHINGTON SCHOOL IN THE CENTER OF THE VILLAGE. Kenmore was once known for its low speed limit, rigorously enforced by the village police. Motorists who believed that speed limits applied to someone else probably thought twice when they saw these guardians of the village's traffic ordinances ready to greet them.

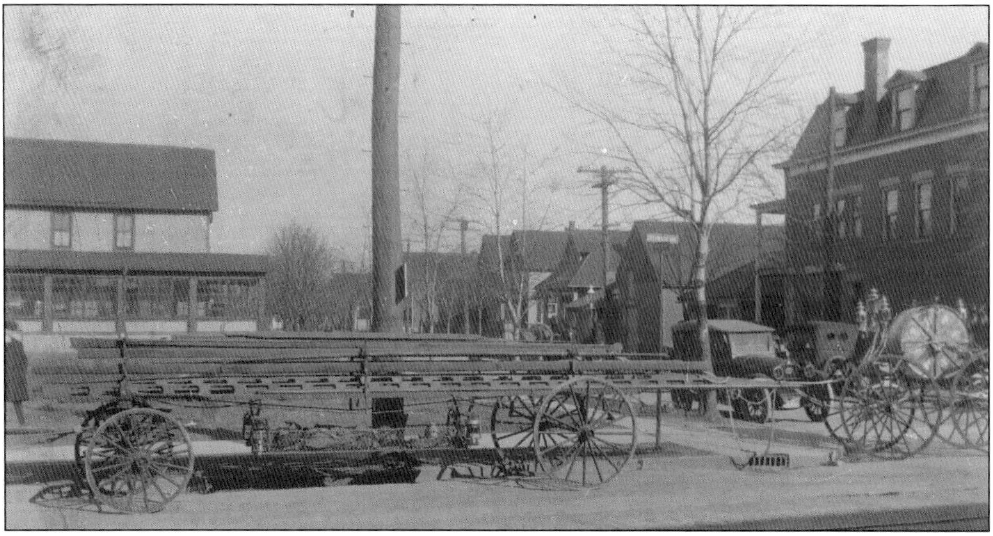

KENMORE'S FIRST HOOK AND LADDER, BOUGHT USED FROM THE VILLAGE (NOW CITY) OF TONAWANDA, ALONG WITH AN ORNATE HOSE REEL OF THE TYPE USED IN PARADES. The Warren Avenue portion of the former Mang Tavern appears on the left, its porch now enclosed. The buildings immediately behind the commercial block at Warren and Delaware have since been replaced by a new business structure and a municipal parking lot. (KVFD collection.)

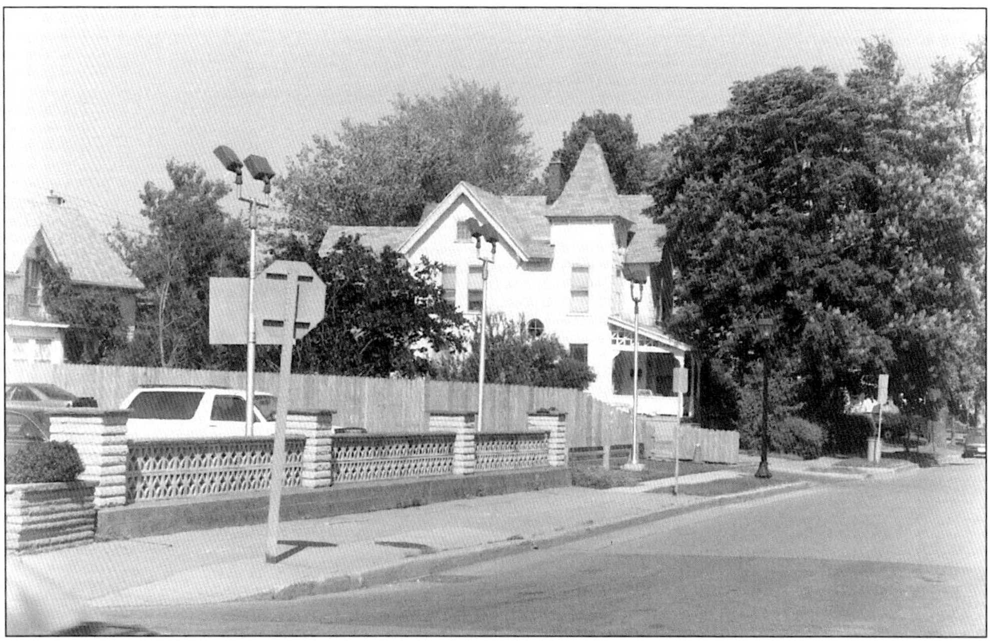

THE FORMER SITE OF THE MANG TAVERN AT 12 WARREN AVENUE, NOW A PARKING LOT OF THE MARINE MIDLAND BANK BRANCH ON DELAWARE AVENUE. By 1998 the portion of the former Mang Tavern at 12 Warren Avenue was gone. Having deteriorated over its last years, it was purchased and demolished to enlarge the parking lot of the Marine Midland Bank branch. If there was any historic gain, it was that the interesting dwellings at 16 Warren and the rear of the adjacent lot became more visible.

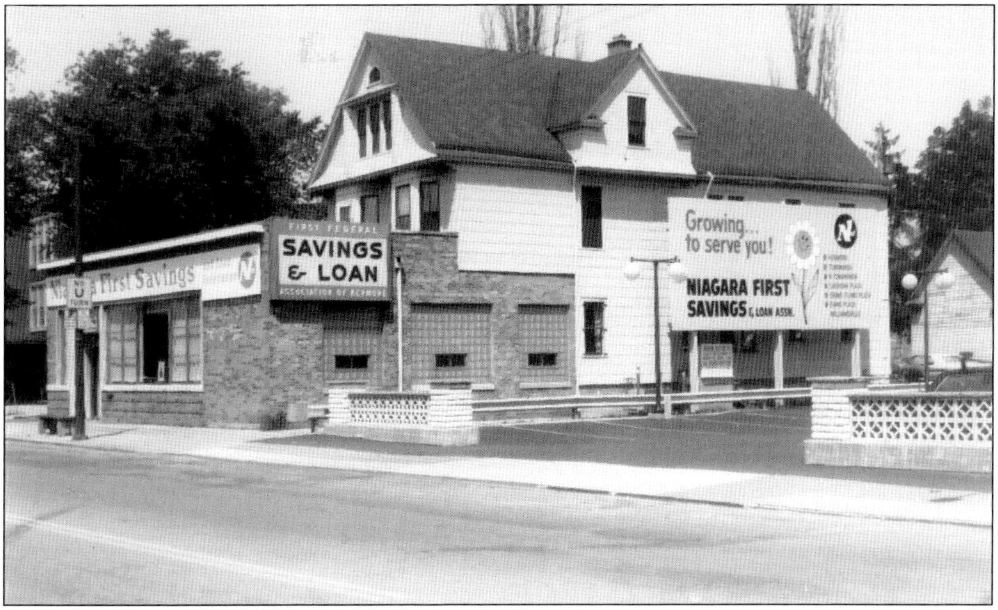

The First Federal Savings and Loan Association of Kenmore. L.P.A. Eberhardt was one of the founders of the First Federal Savings and Loan Association of Kenmore—a smart move for a real estate dealer to have a local source of mortgage credit available. By the 1970s, it was located on Delaware Avenue, between Warren and Knowlton, and had been merged into Niagara First Savings and Loan. With the house portion now demolished, the site is occupied by a branch of the Marine Midland Bank.

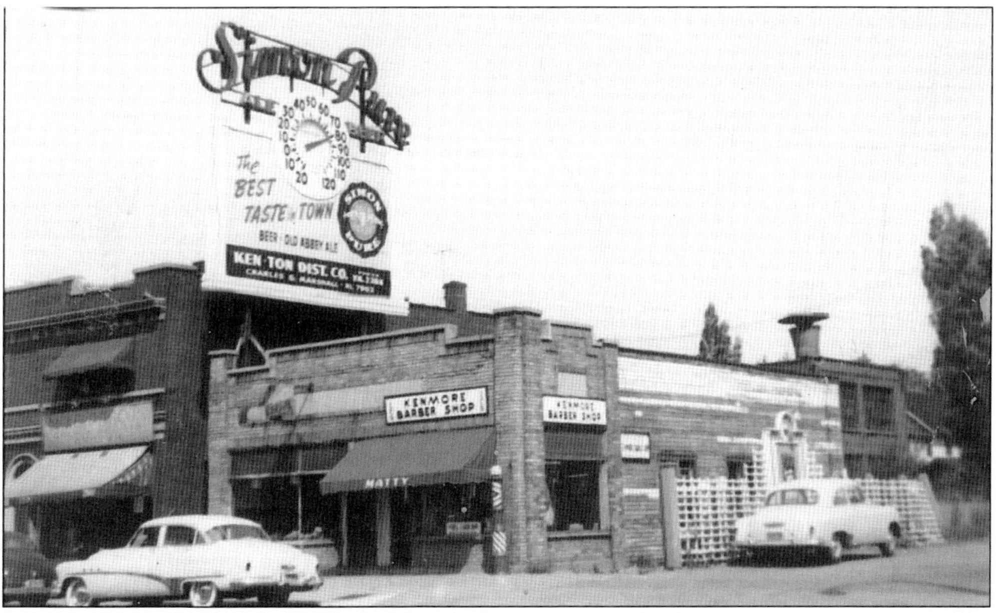

A 1952 photograph of the Kenmore barber shop at 2959 Delaware Avenue, operated by Matty Aronica. The vacant store next door had been a shoe repair business; next to that was Mike Parco's Golf and Sports Center and Reuter's Liquors. All of these buildings are now covered by the site of the Wynwood Commons at Kenmore. Simon Pure beer was made by Buffalo's last full-scale brewery, which ceased production in 1972.

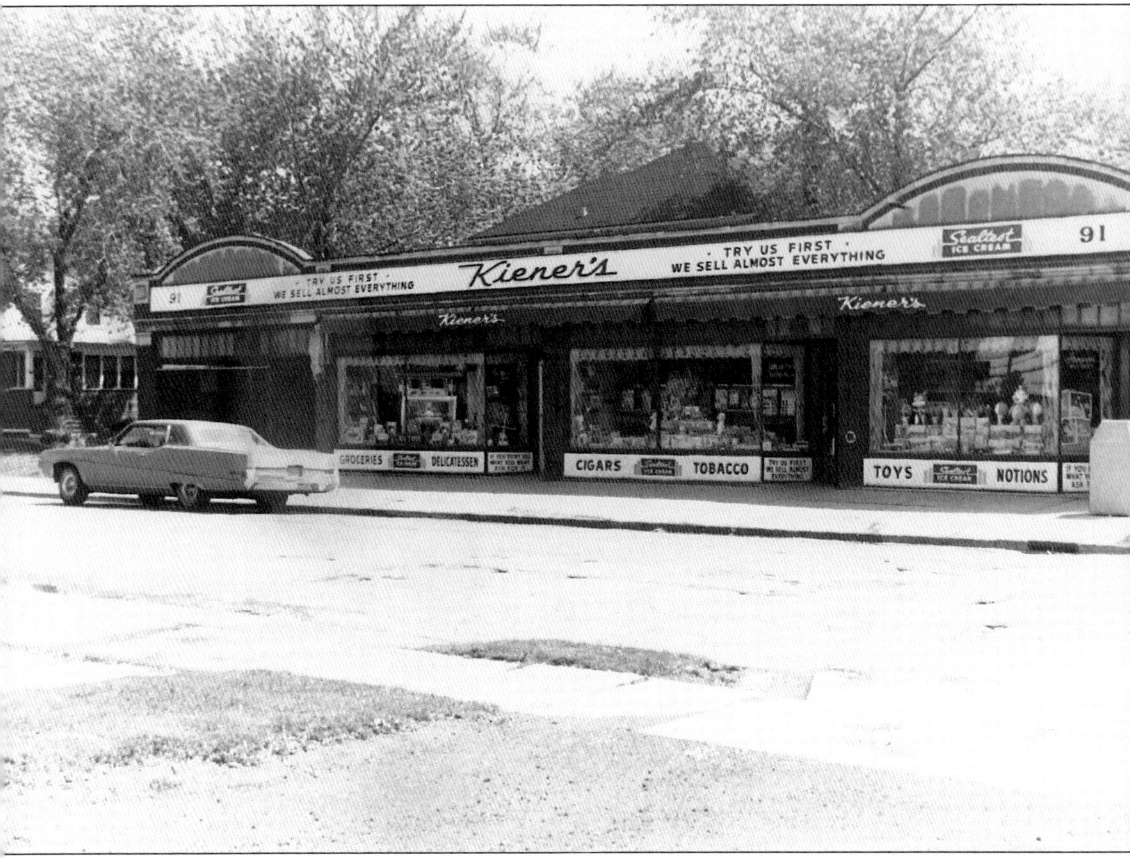

KIENER'S GENERAL STORE, WHICH ONCE OCCUPIED MOST OF THE BLOCK OF ROWLEY AVENUE BETWEEN WARREN AND EUCLID. Originally established at 1137 Kenmore Avenue by Max Kiener, the Rowley Avenue store was run by the Kiener sisters for nearly a half-century. This is where neighborhood kids could get a 5¢ bottle of pop and a 10¢ comic while mom or dad bought a fresh loaf of bread and a quart of milk. If you needed thread or a button, shoe polish or film, Kiener's had it. Later owners tried to carry on its tradition but shopping habits changed and the store finally closed in the 1990s. Caner's Bicycle Shop once occupied the left-hand quarter of the building. (Larry H. Askin photo, TKHS collection.)

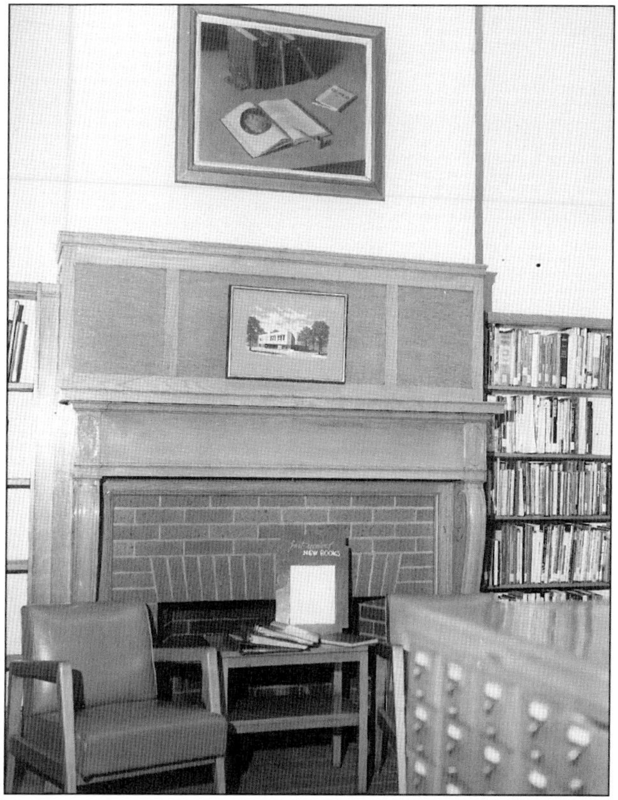

The interior of the old Delaware Road library. This was a familiar sight to village residents during the almost half-century that the building was in use. Although small, and often crammed with users, the library had a coziness about it, as seen in this reading area next to the fireplace and adjacent to the card catalog. The fact that this photograph was taken during the building's last years is evident by the picture of its replacement on the mantle shelf.

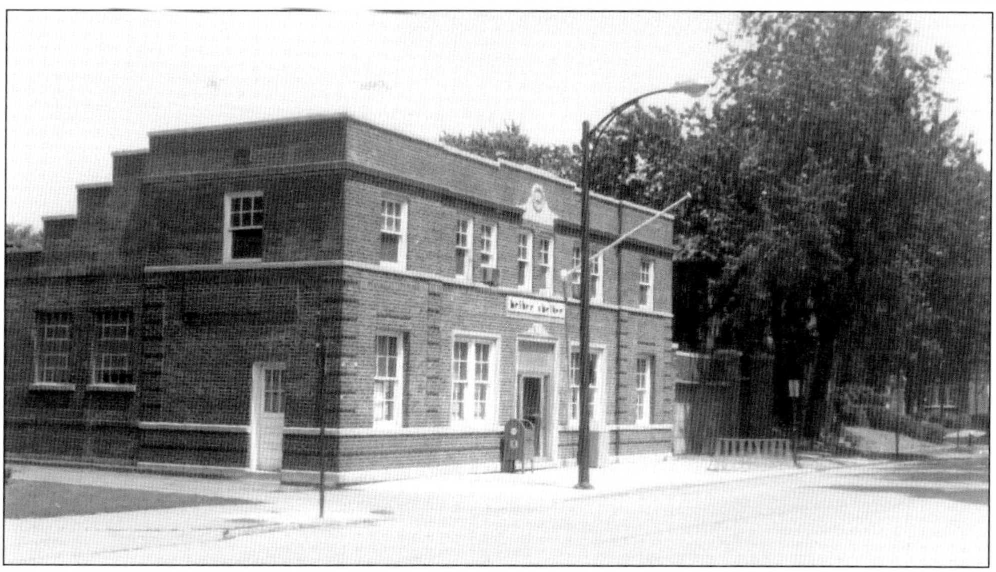

Kenmore's post office on Nash Road, erected in 1929. A home was moved from this site to Landers Road to allow construction to begin. After the present post office building was opened in 1960, the Nash Road building served the town of Tonawanda in a variety of ways, including as the water department, historical society storage, a youth center, and as the temporary Kenmore Library while the present library was under construction. The old building was demolished in the 1980s.

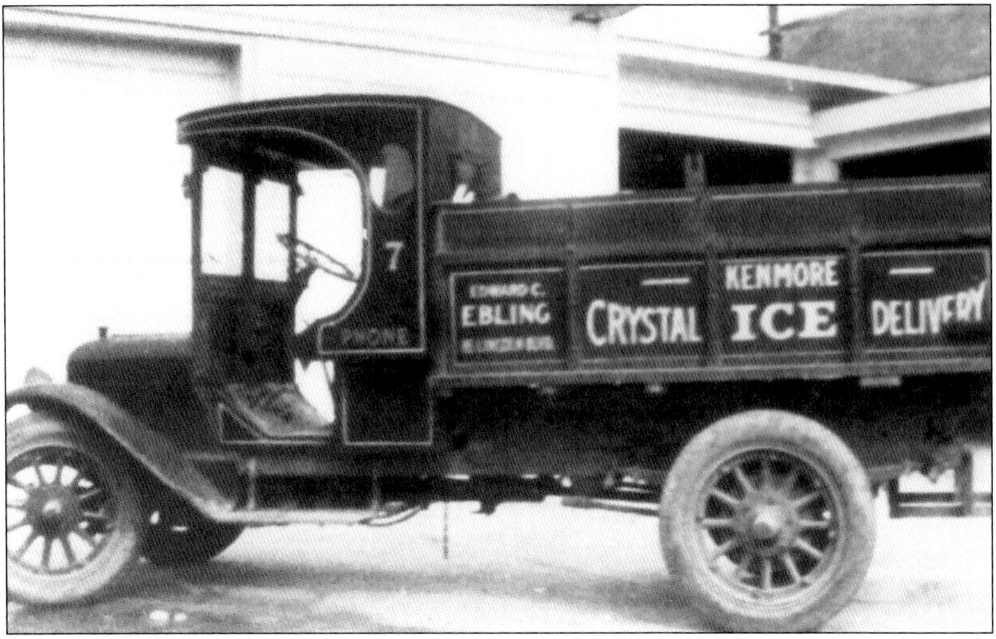

A KENMORE COAL & ICE COMPANY DELIVERY TRUCK, C. 1920. The company had its office and ice house at 16 Lincoln Boulevard. It was one of several area companies that provided home delivery of fuel for coal furnaces and ice for refrigeration. Edward C. Ebling's trucks also provided carting and storage service. By 1930 the company was owned by Edward Daigler, while Ebling concentrated on hardware and plumbing at 2840 Delaware Avenue.

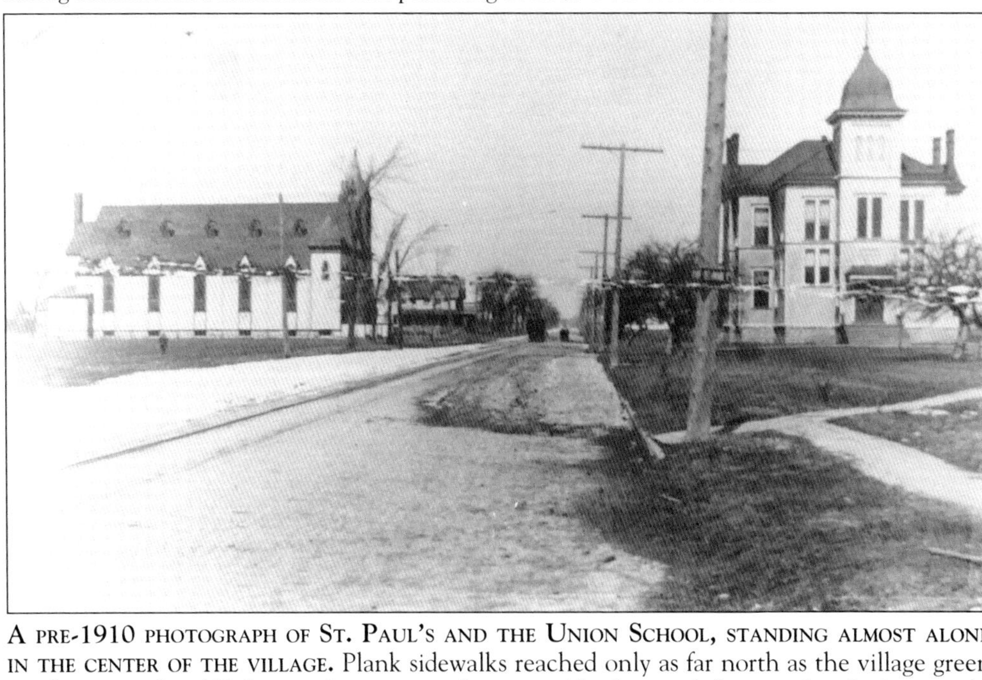

A PRE-1910 PHOTOGRAPH OF ST. PAUL'S AND THE UNION SCHOOL, STANDING ALMOST ALONE IN THE CENTER OF THE VILLAGE. Plank sidewalks reached only as far north as the village green on the east side of Delaware Avenue; on the west side they ended somewhat farther south. In the background, a trolley makes its way to or from Tonawanda—the single track served both directions.

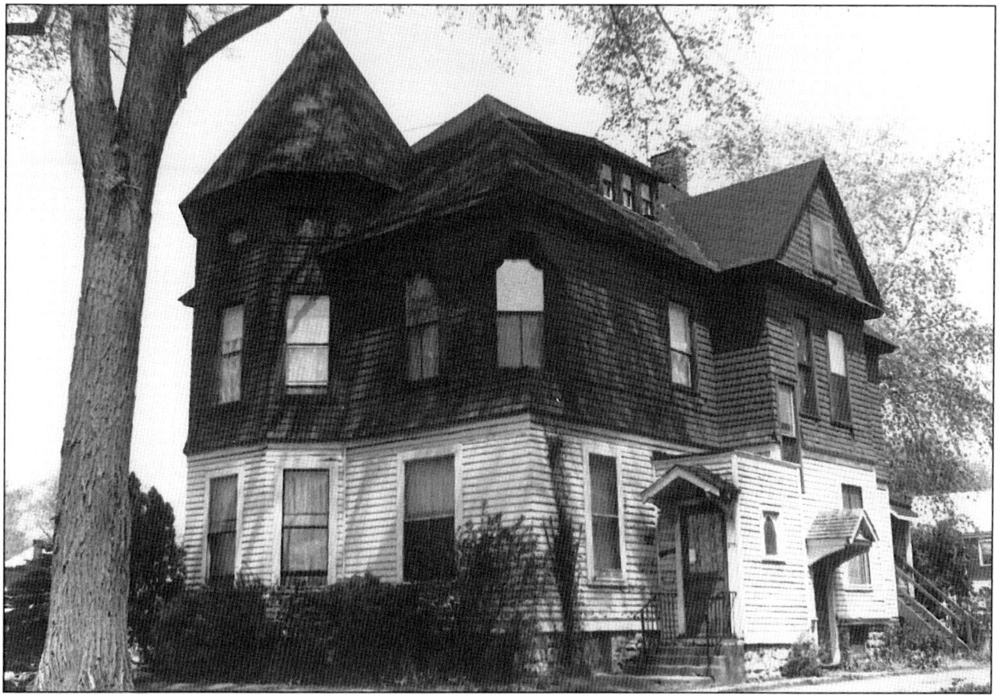

A HOME ON DELAWARE AVENUE, BETWEEN THE PRESBYTERIAN CHURCH AND PARKWOOD. When the church expanded its parking lot, the owners declined to sell, so the lot was built around it. It is shown here in 1971. A few years later the church acquired the property, had the home demolished, and covered the area with parking spaces. (Larry H. Oskin photo, TKHS collection.)

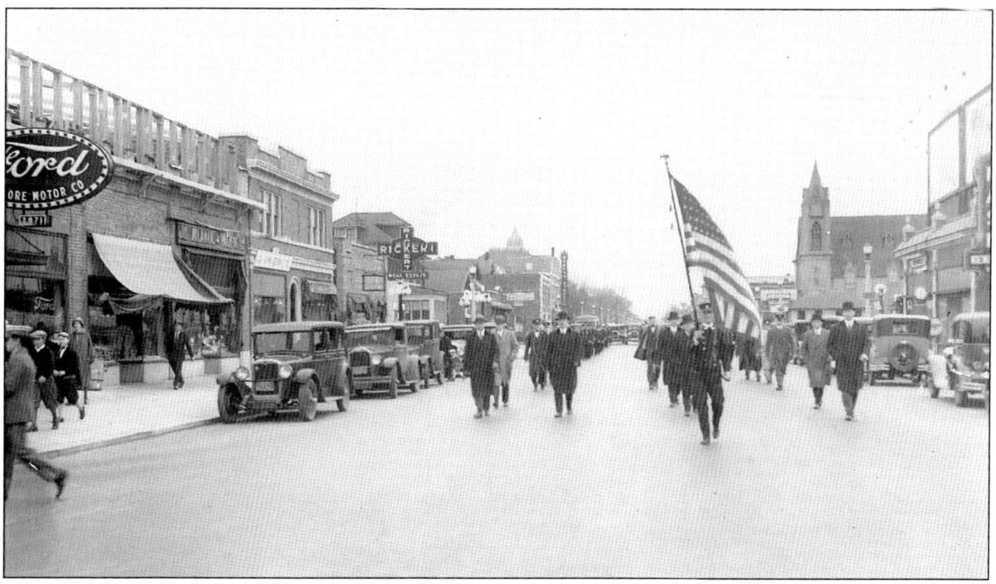

A PARADE PASSING "AUTO ROW," C. 1929. The Kenmore Motor Co. was the Ford dealer on the left; J. Fred Moore's Nash-Kenmore Co. is on the right. The local Chevrolet dealer was located farther south. Automobiles continue to be sold at three agencies on Delaware Avenue, near the north and south ends of the village.

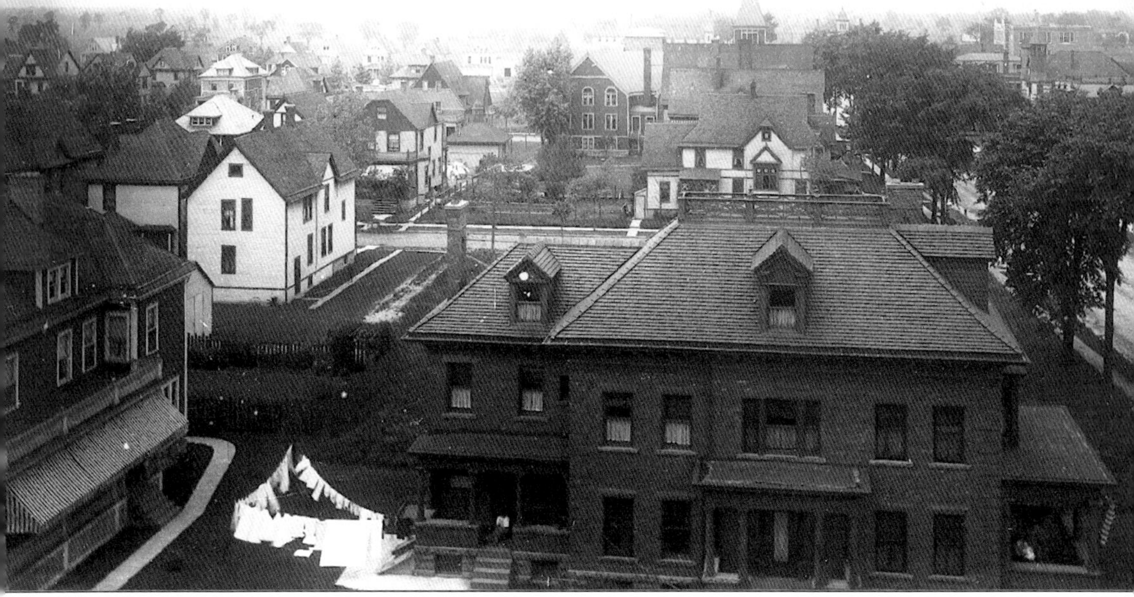

A VIEW TAKEN FROM THE TOWER OF L.P.A. EBERHARDT'S HOME, A FEW YEARS AFTER 1908, WHEN EBERHARDT HAD THE BRICK-AND-SANDSTONE HOUSE BUILT AT 2768 DELAWARE AVENUE AS A WEDDING PRESENT FOR HIS SON GEORGE. This view shows the house as it was before the front porch and rear wing were removed, and the structure moved 50 feet west to become number 9 West Hazeltine. A commercial building now faces Delaware, the decorative rail on the roof has been removed and dormers added, and the home has been divided into apartments. The house next door, at 17 West Hazeltine, has also been altered; most noticeably the wrap-around porch is gone. Almost all of the homes shown on the side streets west of Delaware still stand, though have also been altered. Looking along Delaware, one can see on the west side the home of Myron Phelps and the old Methodist-Episcopal church, both now demolished, and the old St. Paul's, since replaced. On the east side, a close look will reveal the roofs of the Hitchcock Block at Delaware and Euclid, the commercial building at Delaware and Warren, and between them, the old village and fire hall. The then-new Kenmore High School appears in the background to the right of the flagpole, and just to the left of that is the tower of the former Union School, which had become the village hall.